STAR TREK

VOLUME 6

AFTER DARKNESS

STAR TREK®

VOLUME 6

AFTER DARKNESS

Collection Cover by Tim Bradstreet, Colors by Grant Goleash
Collection Edits by Justin Eisinger and Alonzo Simon
Collection Design by Gilberto Lazcano

Star Trek created by Gene Roddenberry.
Special thanks to Risa Kessler and John Van Citters of CBS Consumer Products for their invaluable assistance.

IDW founded by Ted Adams, Alex Garner, Kris Oprisko, and Robbie Robbins

ISBN: 978-1-61377-796-1

16 15 14 13 1 2 3 4

IDW®

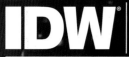

Ted Adams, CEO & Publisher
Greg Goldstein, President & COO
Robbie Robbins, EVP/Sr. Graphic Artist
Chris Ryall, Chief Creative Officer/Editor-in-Chief
Matthew Ruzicka, CPA, Chief Financial Officer
Alan Payne, VP of Sales
Dirk Wood, VP of Marketing
Lorelei Bunjes, VP of Digital Services

Become our fan on Facebook **facebook.com/idwpublishing**
Follow us on Twitter **@idwpublishing**
Check us out on YouTube **youtube.com/idwpublishing**
www.IDWPUBLISHING.com

Originally published as STAR TREK Issues #21–24.

Written by
MIKE JOHNSON

Art by
ERFAN FAJAR and
CLAUDIA BALBONI Issue 24

Additional Art by
AGRI KARUNIAWAN Issue 23

Inks by
MARINA CASTELVETRO Issue 24

Colors by
SAKTI YUWONO, IFANSYAH NOOR of Stellar Labs
and **ARIANNA FLOREAN** Issue 24

Colors Assist by
AZZURRA FLOREAN
and **VALENTINA CUOMO** Issue 24

Letters by
NEIL UYETAKE and **CHRIS MOWRY**

Creative Consultant
ROBERTO ORCI

Series Edits by
SCOTT DUNBIER

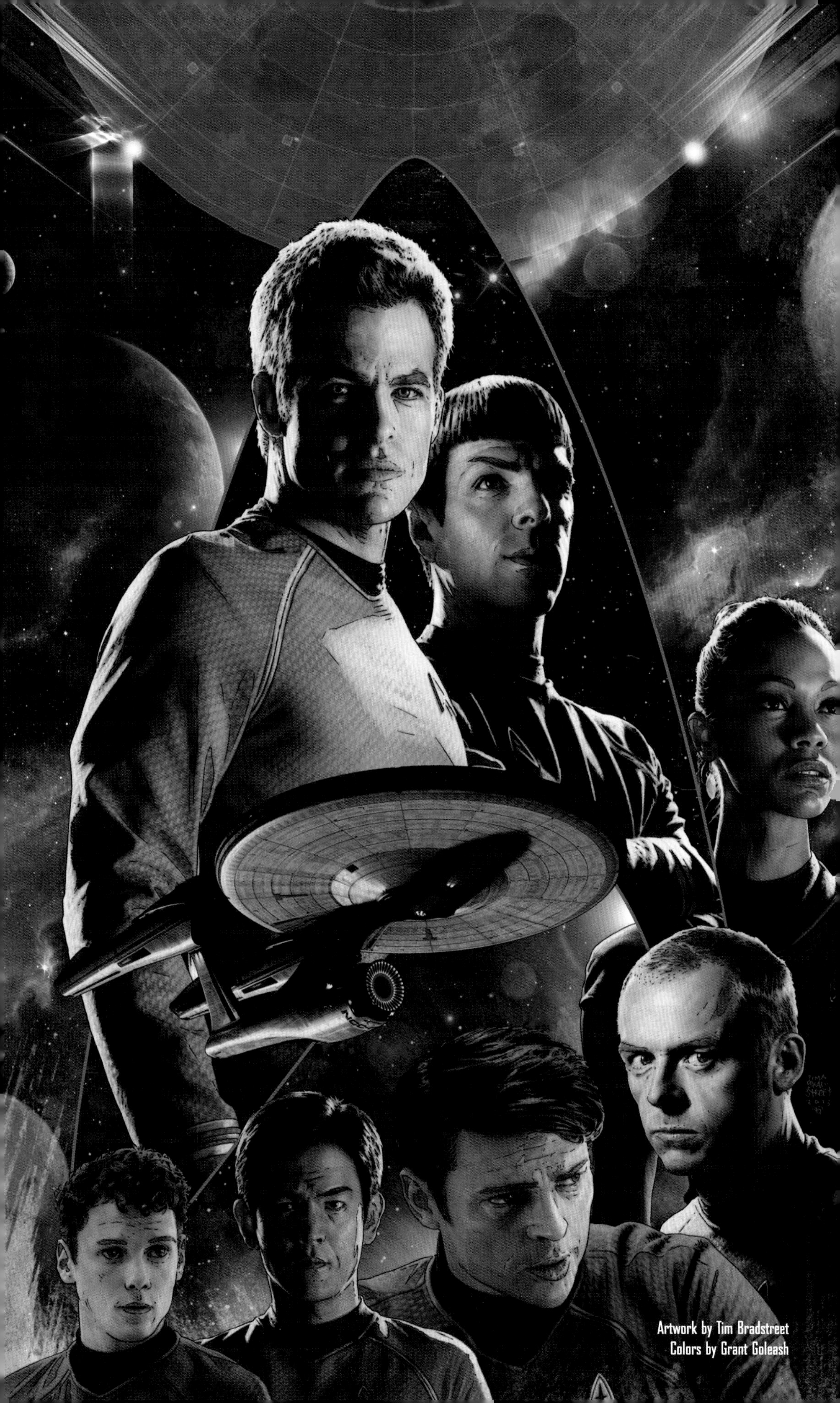

Artwork by Tim Bradstreet
Colors by Grant Goleash

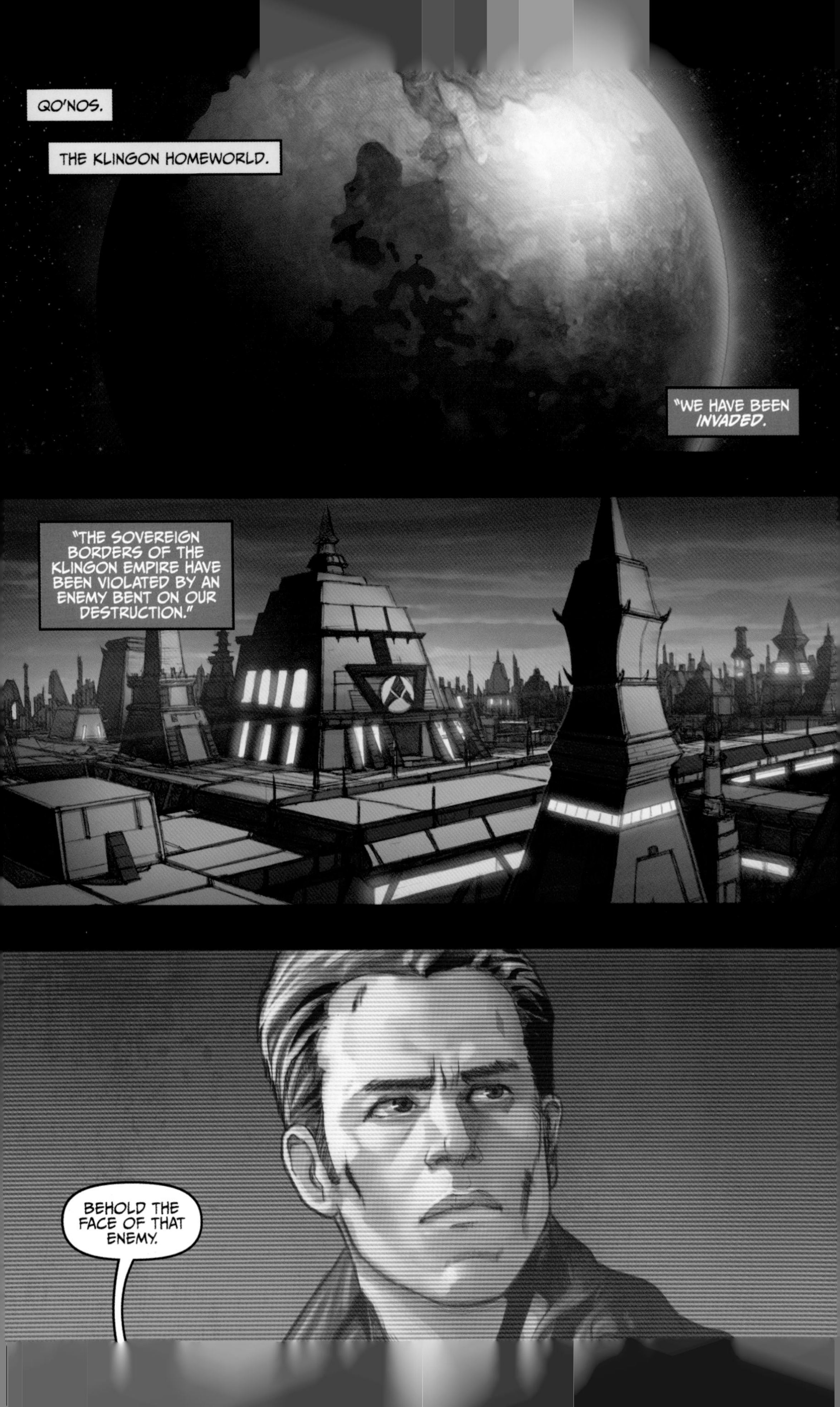
QO'NOS.
THE KLINGON HOMEWORLD.
"WE HAVE BEEN *INVADED*.
"THE SOVEREIGN BORDERS OF THE KLINGON EMPIRE HAVE BEEN VIOLATED BY AN ENEMY BENT ON OUR DESTRUCTION."
BEHOLD THE FACE OF THAT ENEMY.

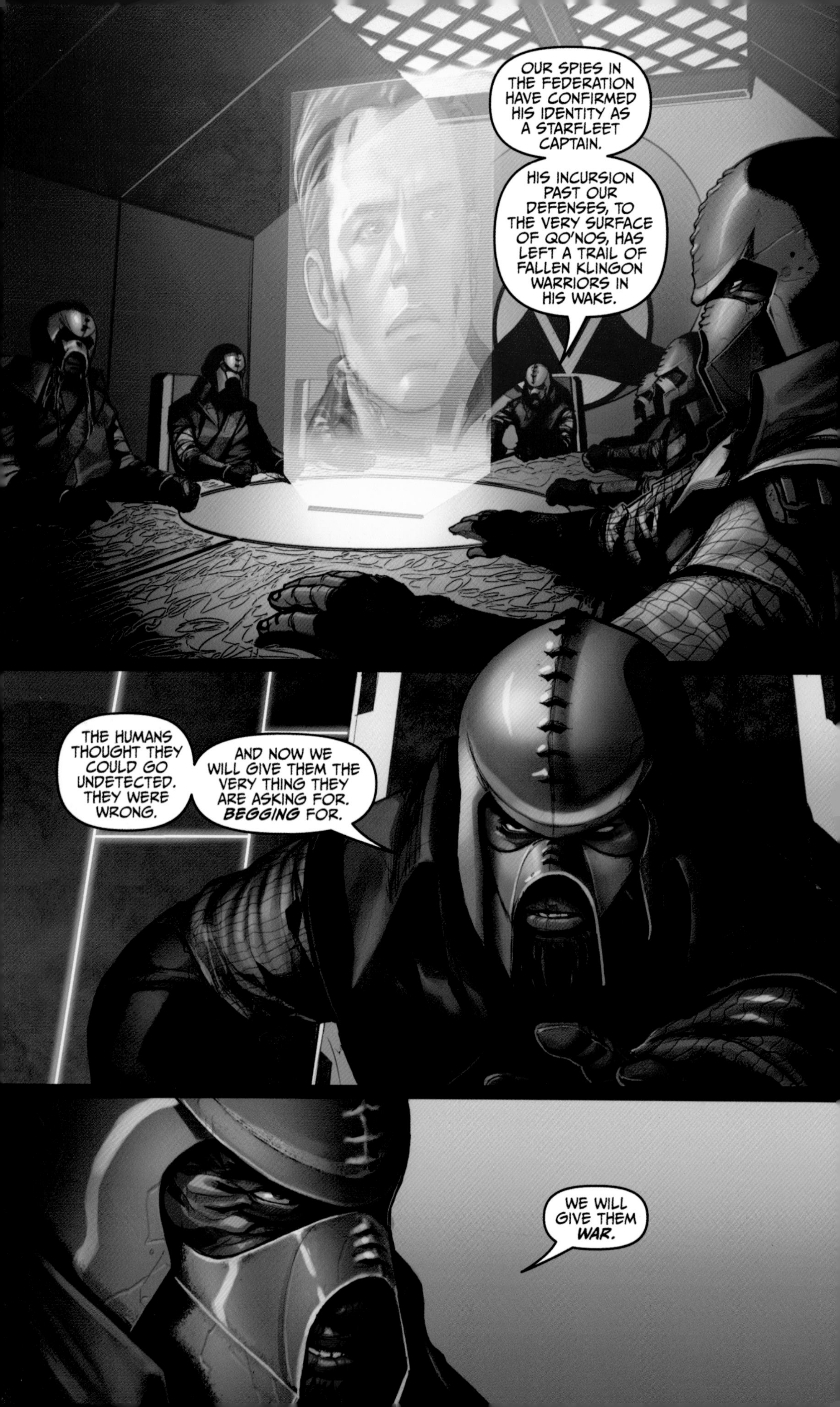
OUR SPIES IN THE FEDERATION HAVE CONFIRMED HIS IDENTITY AS A STARFLEET CAPTAIN.
HIS INCURSION PAST OUR DEFENSES, TO THE VERY SURFACE OF QO'NOS, HAS LEFT A TRAIL OF FALLEN KLINGON WARRIORS IN HIS WAKE.
THE HUMANS THOUGHT THEY COULD GO UNDETECTED. THEY WERE WRONG.
AND NOW WE WILL GIVE THEM THE VERY THING THEY ARE ASKING FOR. *BEGGING* FOR.
WE WILL GIVE THEM *WAR.*

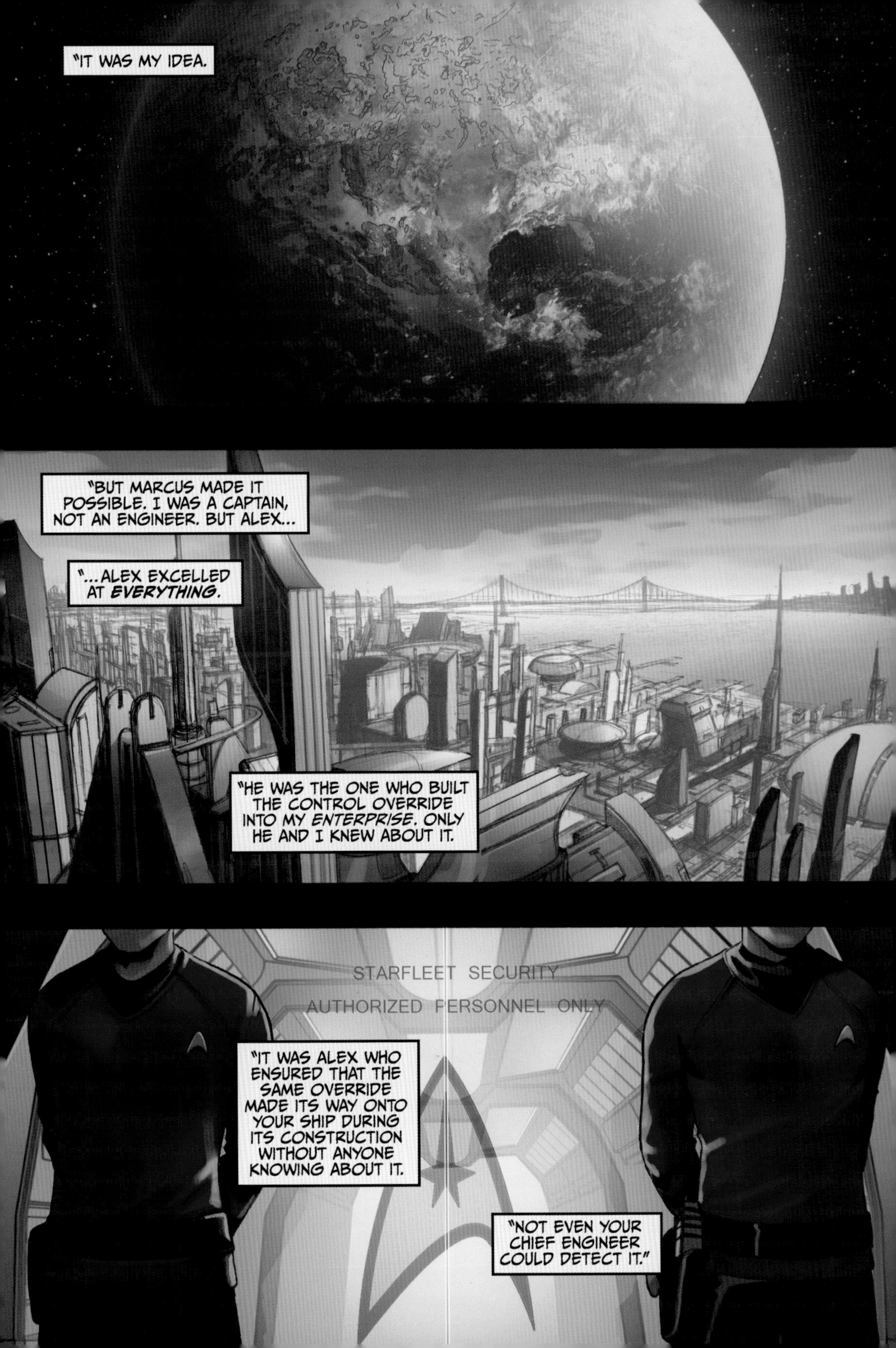
"IT WAS MY IDEA.
"BUT MARCUS MADE IT POSSIBLE. I WAS A CAPTAIN, NOT AN ENGINEER. BUT ALEX...
"...ALEX EXCELLED AT *EVERYTHING*.
"HE WAS THE ONE WHO BUILT THE CONTROL OVERRIDE INTO MY *ENTERPRISE*. ONLY HE AND I KNEW ABOUT IT.
STARFLEET SECURITY
AUTHORIZED PERSONNEL ONLY
"IT WAS ALEX WHO ENSURED THAT THE SAME OVERRIDE MADE ITS WAY ONTO YOUR SHIP DURING ITS CONSTRUCTION WITHOUT ANYONE KNOWING ABOUT IT.
"NOT EVEN YOUR CHIEF ENGINEER COULD DETECT IT."

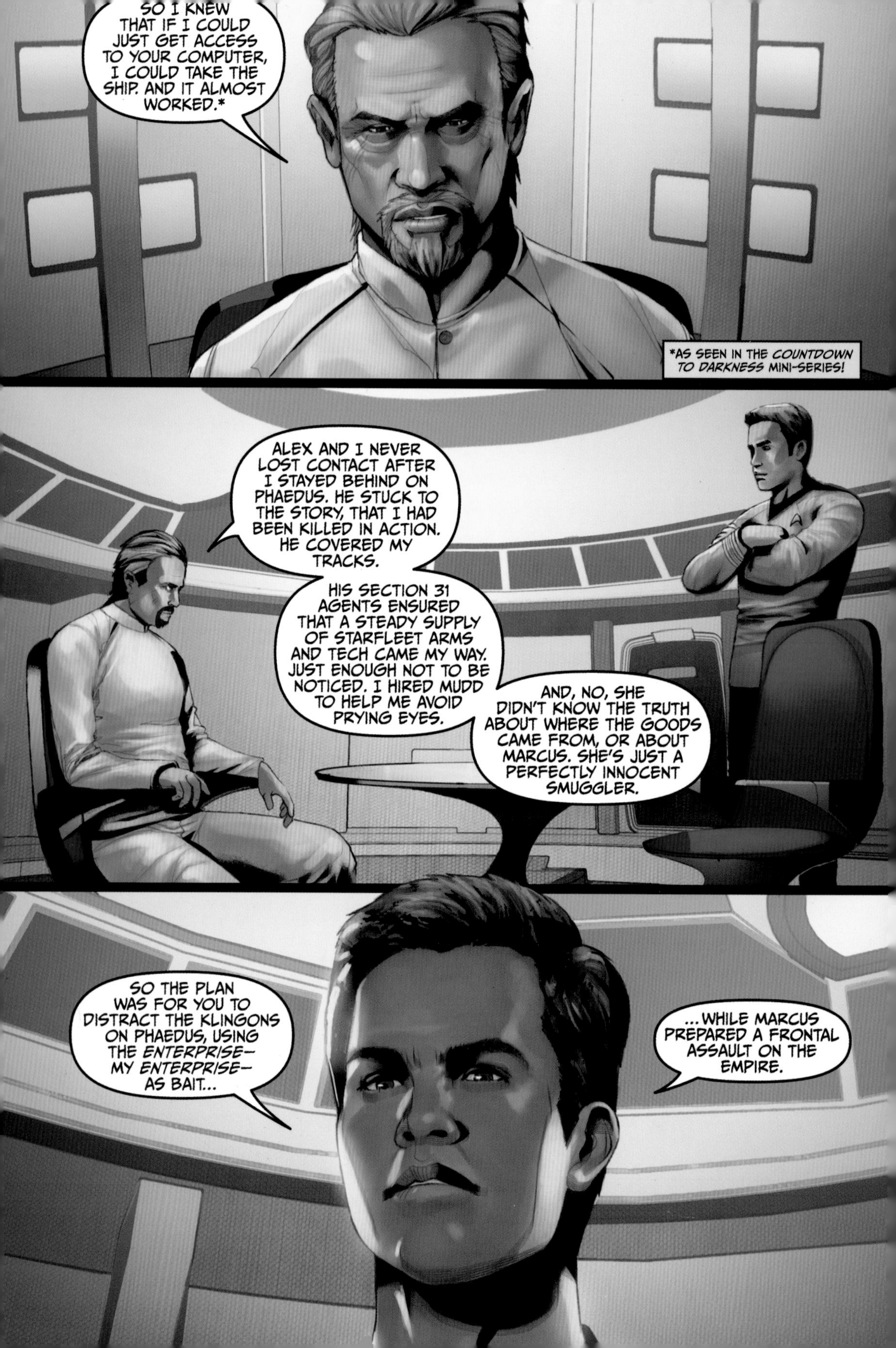
SO I KNEW THAT IF I COULD JUST GET ACCESS TO YOUR COMPUTER, I COULD TAKE THE SHIP. AND IT ALMOST WORKED.*
*AS SEEN IN THE *COUNTDOWN TO DARKNESS* MINI-SERIES!
ALEX AND I NEVER LOST CONTACT AFTER I STAYED BEHIND ON PHAEDUS. HE STUCK TO THE STORY, THAT I HAD BEEN KILLED IN ACTION. HE COVERED MY TRACKS.
HIS SECTION 31 AGENTS ENSURED THAT A STEADY SUPPLY OF STARFLEET ARMS AND TECH CAME MY WAY. JUST ENOUGH NOT TO BE NOTICED. I HIRED MUDD TO HELP ME AVOID PRYING EYES.
AND, NO, SHE DIDN'T KNOW THE TRUTH ABOUT WHERE THE GOODS CAME FROM, OR ABOUT MARCUS. SHE'S JUST A PERFECTLY INNOCENT SMUGGLER.
SO THE PLAN WAS FOR YOU TO DISTRACT THE KLINGONS ON PHAEDUS, USING THE *ENTERPRISE*— MY *ENTERPRISE*— AS BAIT...
...WHILE MARCUS PREPARED A FRONTAL ASSAULT ON THE EMPIRE.

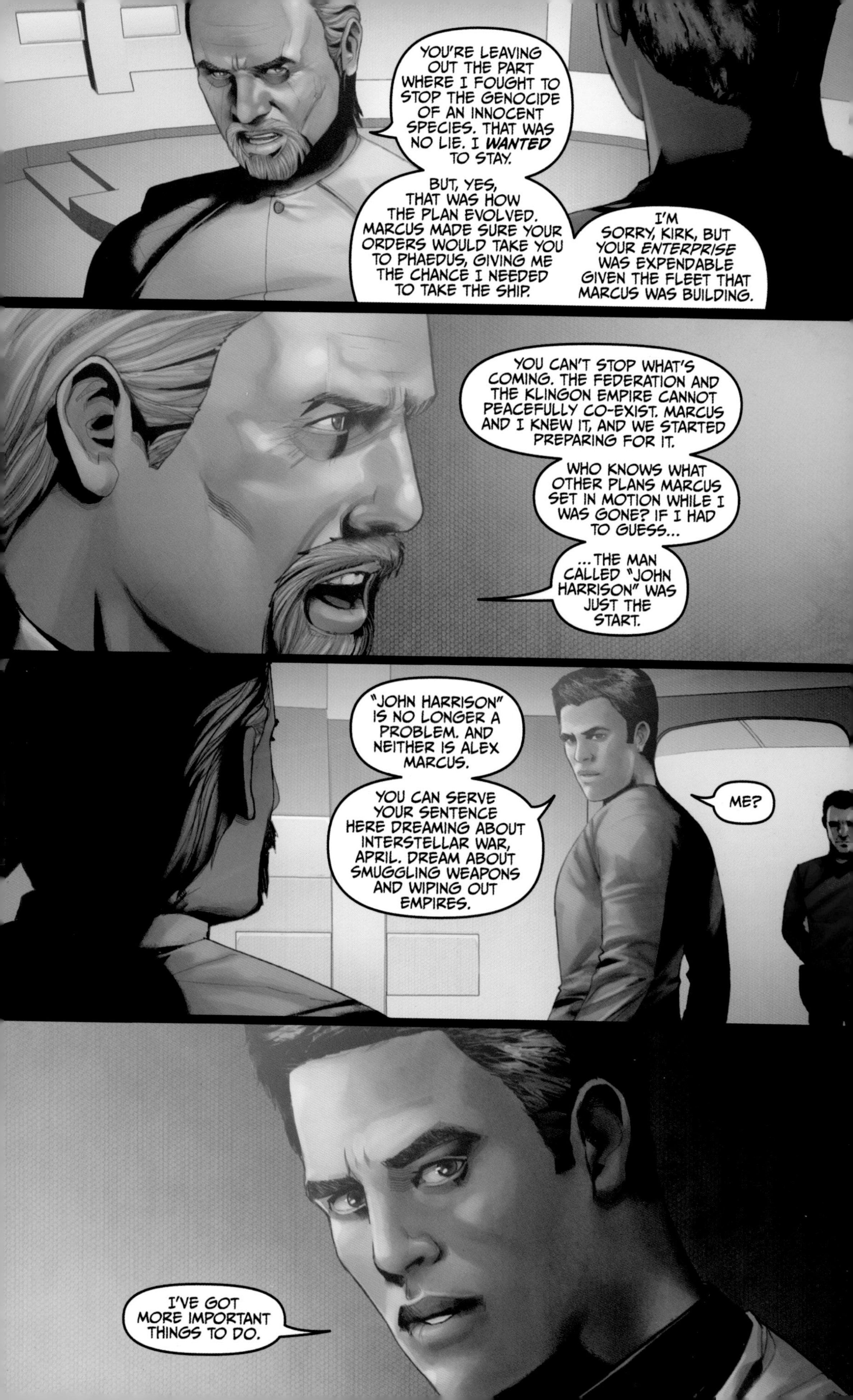
YOU'RE LEAVING OUT THE PART WHERE I FOUGHT TO STOP THE GENOCIDE OF AN INNOCENT SPECIES. THAT WAS NO LIE. I *WANTED* TO STAY.
BUT, YES, THAT WAS HOW THE PLAN EVOLVED. MARCUS MADE SURE YOUR ORDERS WOULD TAKE YOU TO PHAEDUS, GIVING ME THE CHANCE I NEEDED TO TAKE THE SHIP.
I'M SORRY, KIRK, BUT YOUR *ENTERPRISE* WAS EXPENDABLE GIVEN THE FLEET THAT MARCUS WAS BUILDING.
YOU CAN'T STOP WHAT'S COMING. THE FEDERATION AND THE KLINGON EMPIRE CANNOT PEACEFULLY CO-EXIST. MARCUS AND I KNEW IT, AND WE STARTED PREPARING FOR IT.
WHO KNOWS WHAT OTHER PLANS MARCUS SET IN MOTION WHILE I WAS GONE? IF I HAD TO GUESS...
...THE MAN CALLED "JOHN HARRISON" WAS JUST THE START.
"JOHN HARRISON" IS NO LONGER A PROBLEM. AND NEITHER IS ALEX MARCUS.
YOU CAN SERVE YOUR SENTENCE HERE DREAMING ABOUT INTERSTELLAR WAR, APRIL. DREAM ABOUT SMUGGLING WEAPONS AND WIPING OUT EMPIRES.
ME?
I'VE GOT MORE IMPORTANT THINGS TO DO.

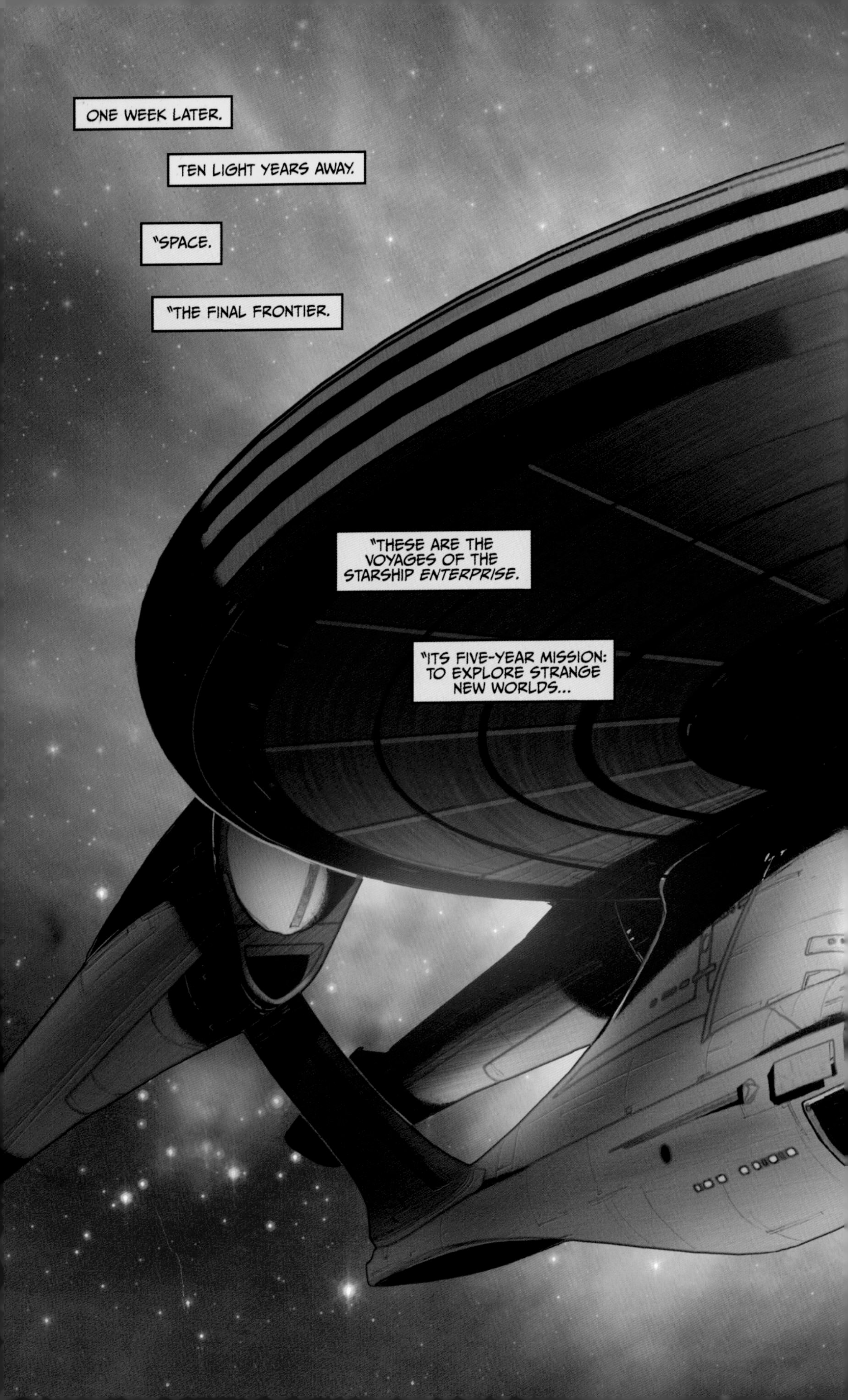
ONE WEEK LATER.
TEN LIGHT YEARS AWAY.
"SPACE.
"THE FINAL FRONTIER.
"THESE ARE THE VOYAGES OF THE STARSHIP *ENTERPRISE*.
"ITS FIVE-YEAR MISSION: TO EXPLORE STRANGE NEW WORLDS...

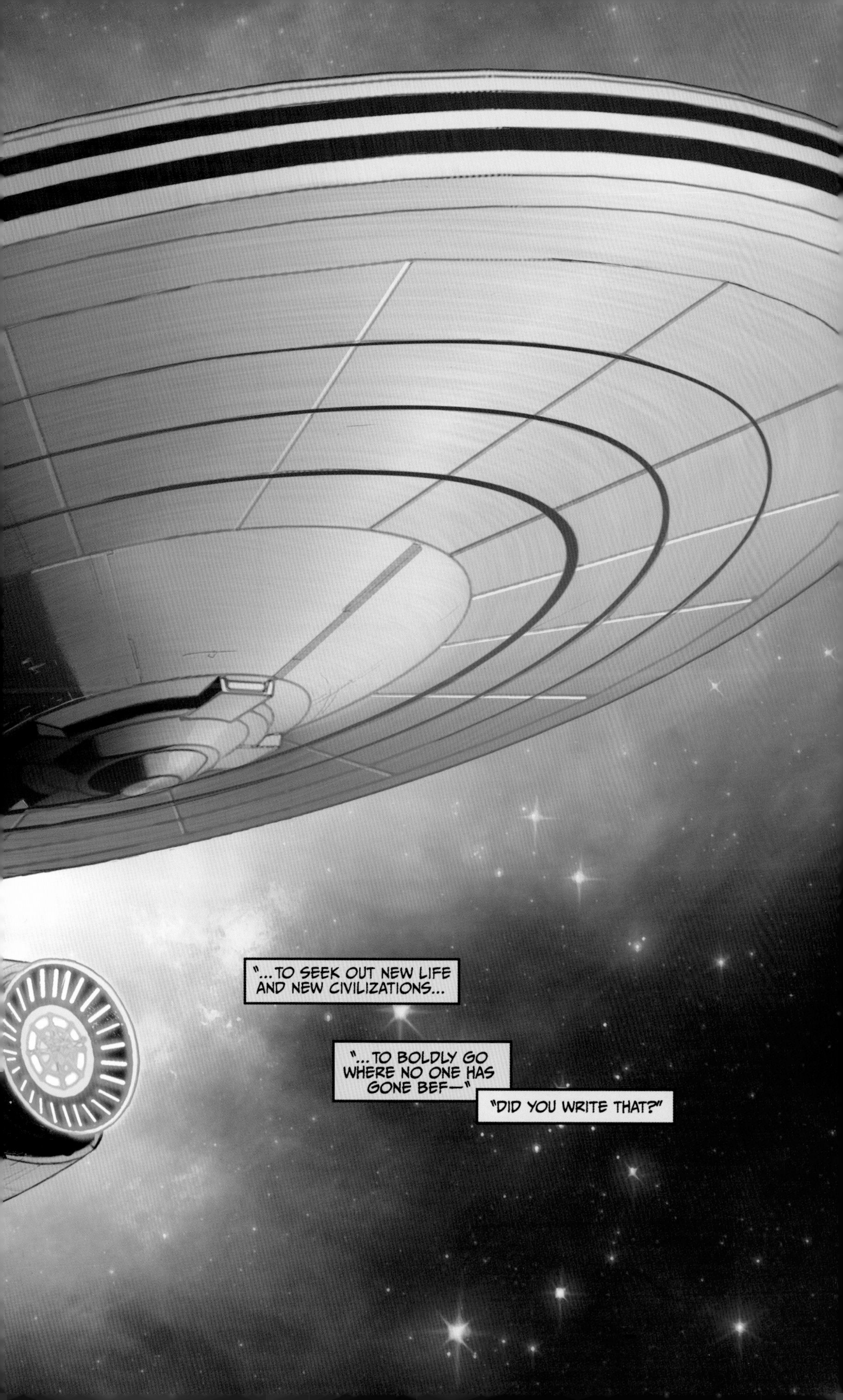
"...TO SEEK OUT NEW LIFE AND NEW CIVILIZATIONS...
"...TO BOLDLY GO WHERE NO ONE HAS GONE BEF—"
"DID YOU WRITE THAT?"

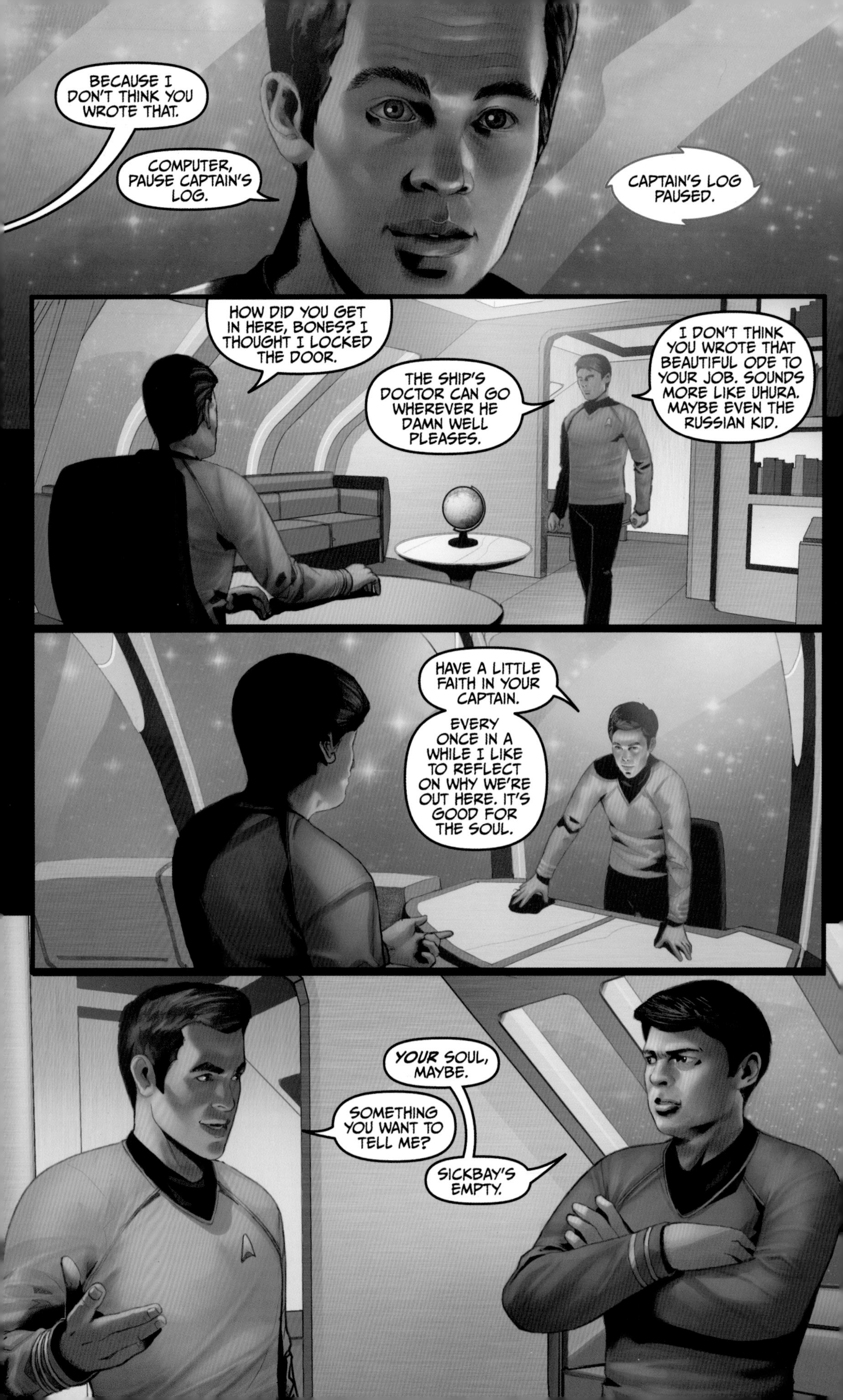
BECAUSE I DON'T THINK YOU WROTE THAT.
COMPUTER, PAUSE CAPTAIN'S LOG.
CAPTAIN'S LOG PAUSED.
HOW DID YOU GET IN HERE, BONES? I THOUGHT I LOCKED THE DOOR.
THE SHIP'S DOCTOR CAN GO WHEREVER HE DAMN WELL PLEASES.
I DON'T THINK YOU WROTE THAT BEAUTIFUL ODE TO YOUR JOB. SOUNDS MORE LIKE UHURA. MAYBE EVEN THE RUSSIAN KID.
HAVE A LITTLE FAITH IN YOUR CAPTAIN.
EVERY ONCE IN A WHILE I LIKE TO REFLECT ON WHY WE'RE OUT HERE. IT'S GOOD FOR THE SOUL.
YOUR SOUL, MAYBE.
SOMETHING YOU WANT TO TELL ME?
SICKBAY'S EMPTY.

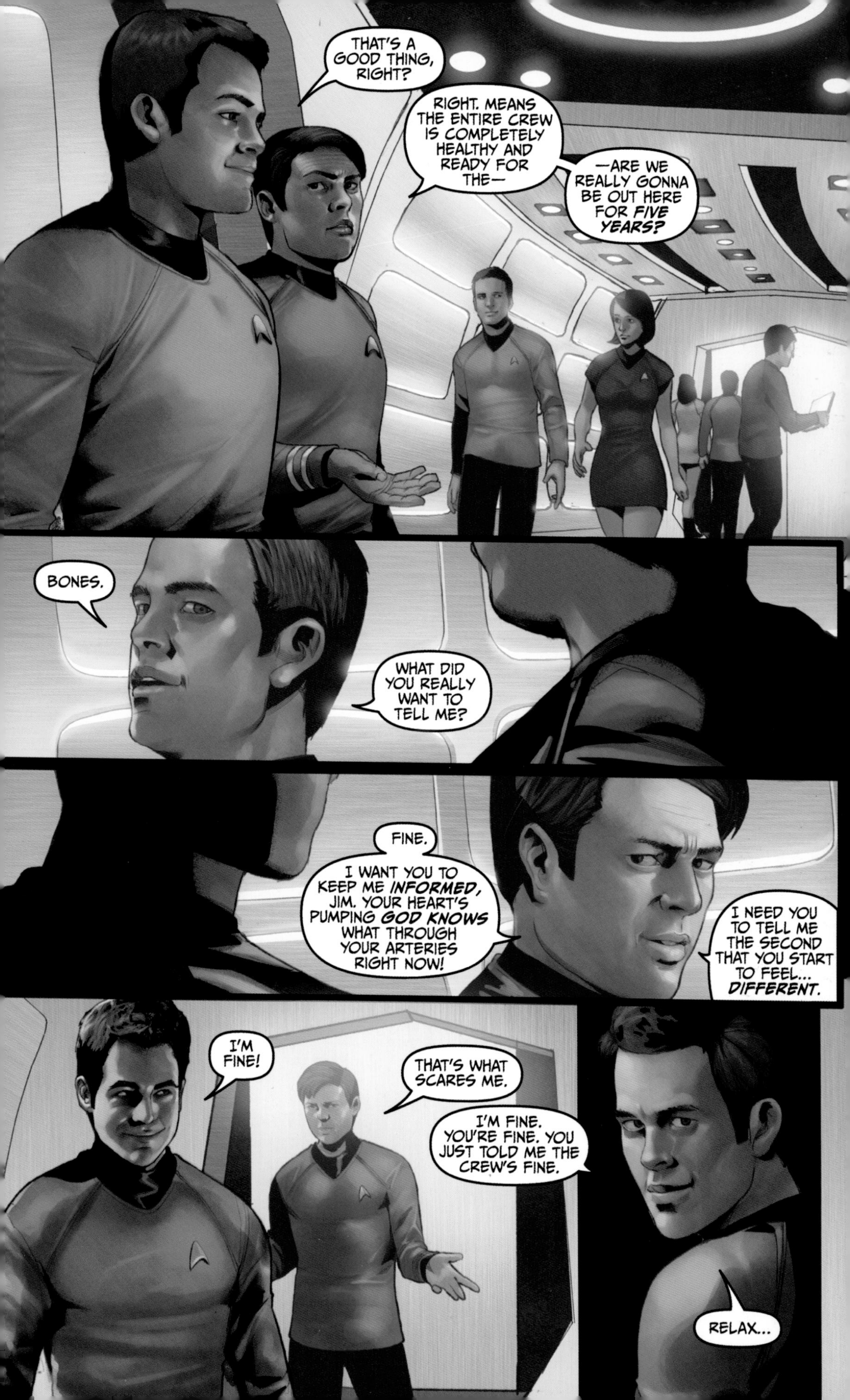
THAT'S A GOOD THING, RIGHT?
RIGHT. MEANS THE ENTIRE CREW IS COMPLETELY HEALTHY AND READY FOR THE—
—ARE WE REALLY GONNA BE OUT HERE FOR *FIVE YEARS?*
BONES.
WHAT DID YOU REALLY WANT TO TELL ME?
FINE.
I WANT YOU TO KEEP ME *INFORMED*, JIM. YOUR HEART'S PUMPING *GOD KNOWS* WHAT THROUGH YOUR ARTERIES RIGHT NOW!
I NEED YOU TO TELL ME THE SECOND THAT YOU START TO FEEL... *DIFFERENT*.
I'M FINE!
THAT'S WHAT SCARES ME.
I'M FINE. YOU'RE FINE. YOU JUST TOLD ME THE CREW'S FINE.
RELAX...

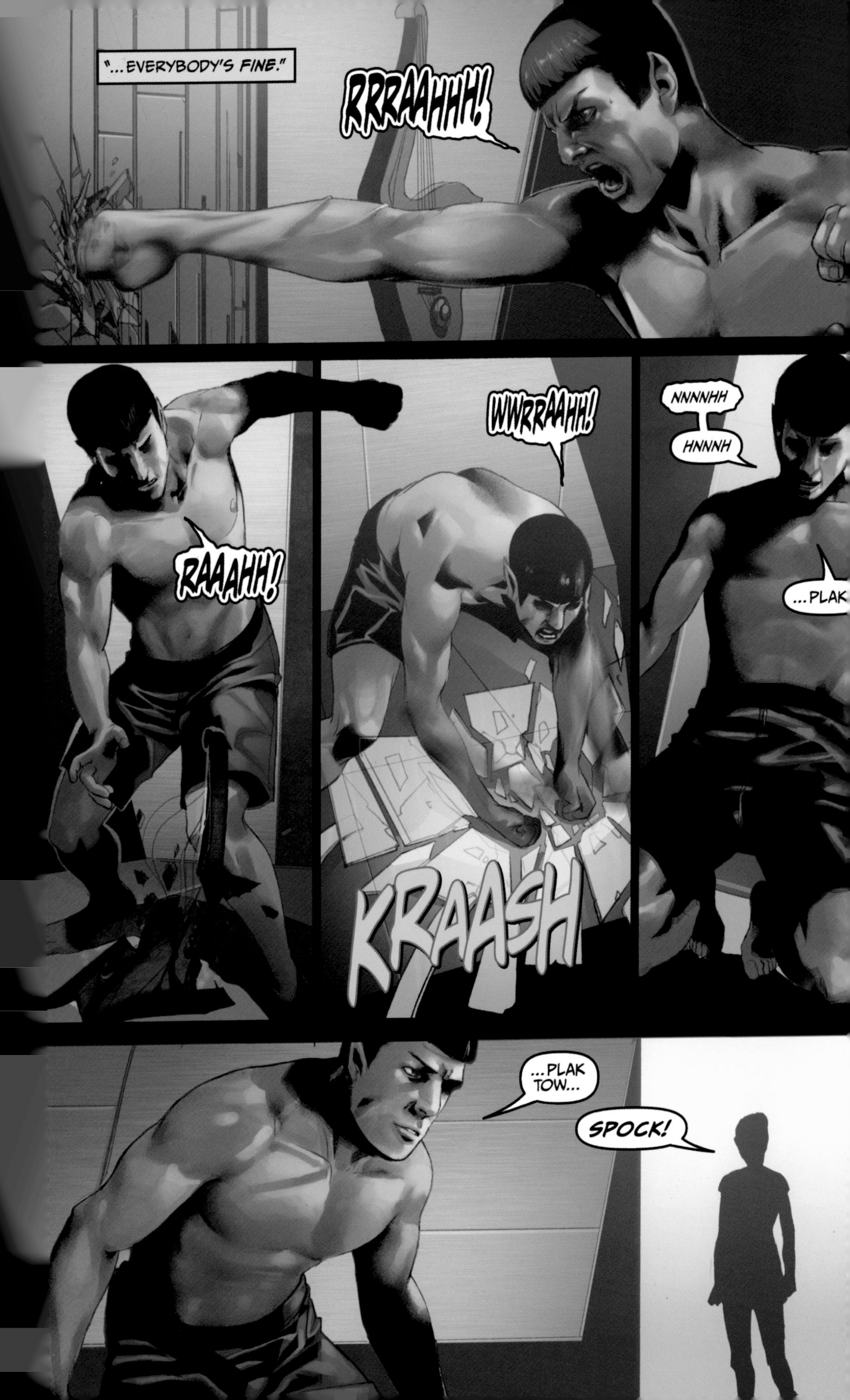
"...EVERYBODY'S FINE."
RRRAAHHH!
RAAAHH!
WWRRAAHH!
KRAASH
NNNNHH
HNNNH
...PLAK
...PLAK TOW...
SPOCK!

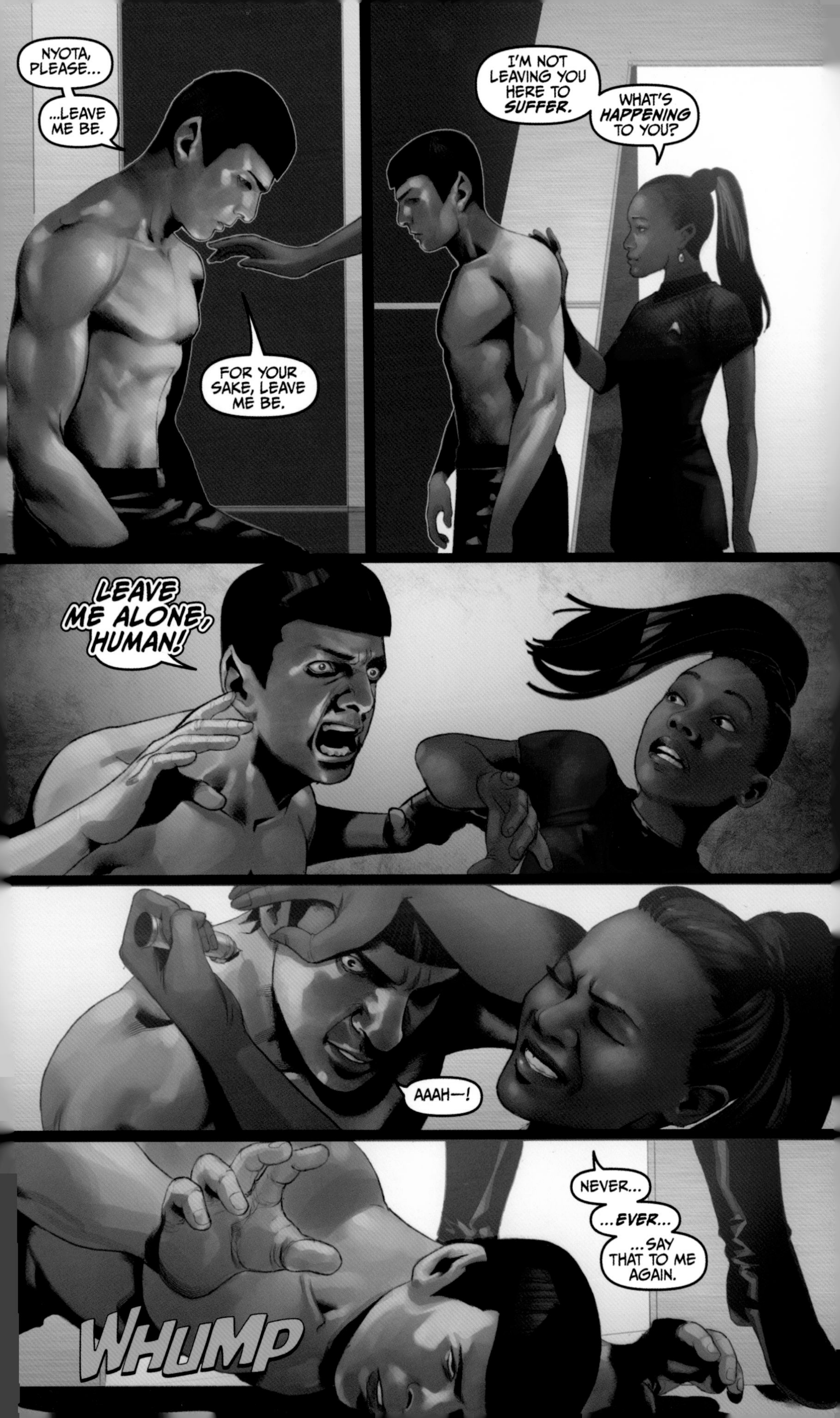
NYOTA, PLEASE...
...LEAVE ME BE.
FOR YOUR SAKE, LEAVE ME BE.
I'M NOT LEAVING YOU HERE TO SUFFER.
WHAT'S HAPPENING TO YOU?
LEAVE ME ALONE, HUMAN!
AAAH—!
NEVER...
...EVER...
...SAY THAT TO ME AGAIN.
WHUMP

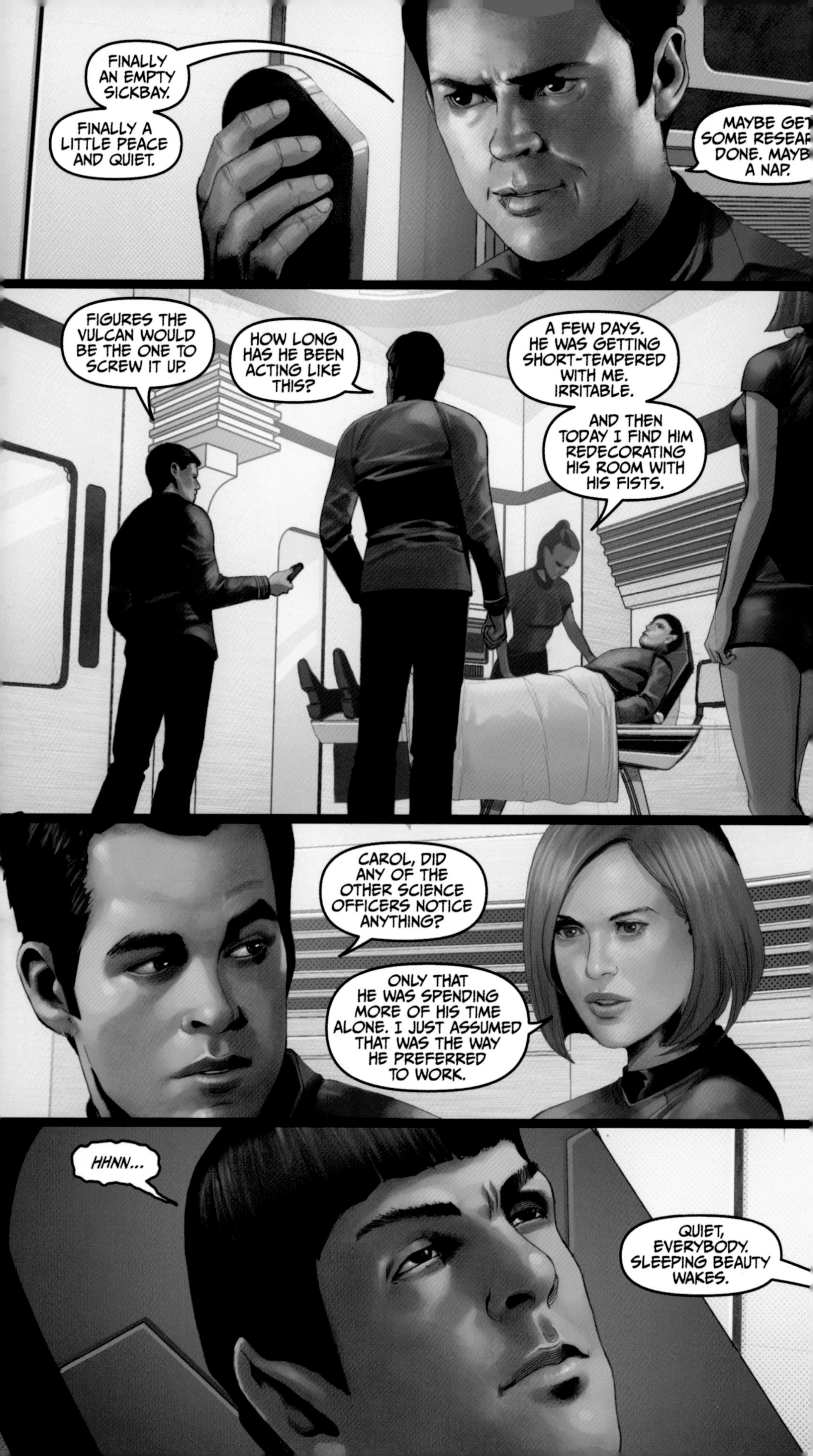
FINALLY AN EMPTY SICKBAY.
FINALLY A LITTLE PEACE AND QUIET.
MAYBE GET SOME RESEAR DONE. MAYB A NAP.
FIGURES THE VULCAN WOULD BE THE ONE TO SCREW IT UP.
HOW LONG HAS HE BEEN ACTING LIKE THIS?
A FEW DAYS. HE WAS GETTING SHORT-TEMPERED WITH ME. IRRITABLE.
AND THEN TODAY I FIND HIM REDECORATING HIS ROOM WITH HIS FISTS.
CAROL, DID ANY OF THE OTHER SCIENCE OFFICERS NOTICE ANYTHING?
ONLY THAT HE WAS SPENDING MORE OF HIS TIME ALONE. I JUST ASSUMED THAT WAS THE WAY HE PREFERRED TO WORK.
HHNN...
QUIET, EVERYBODY. SLEEPING BEAUTY WAKES.

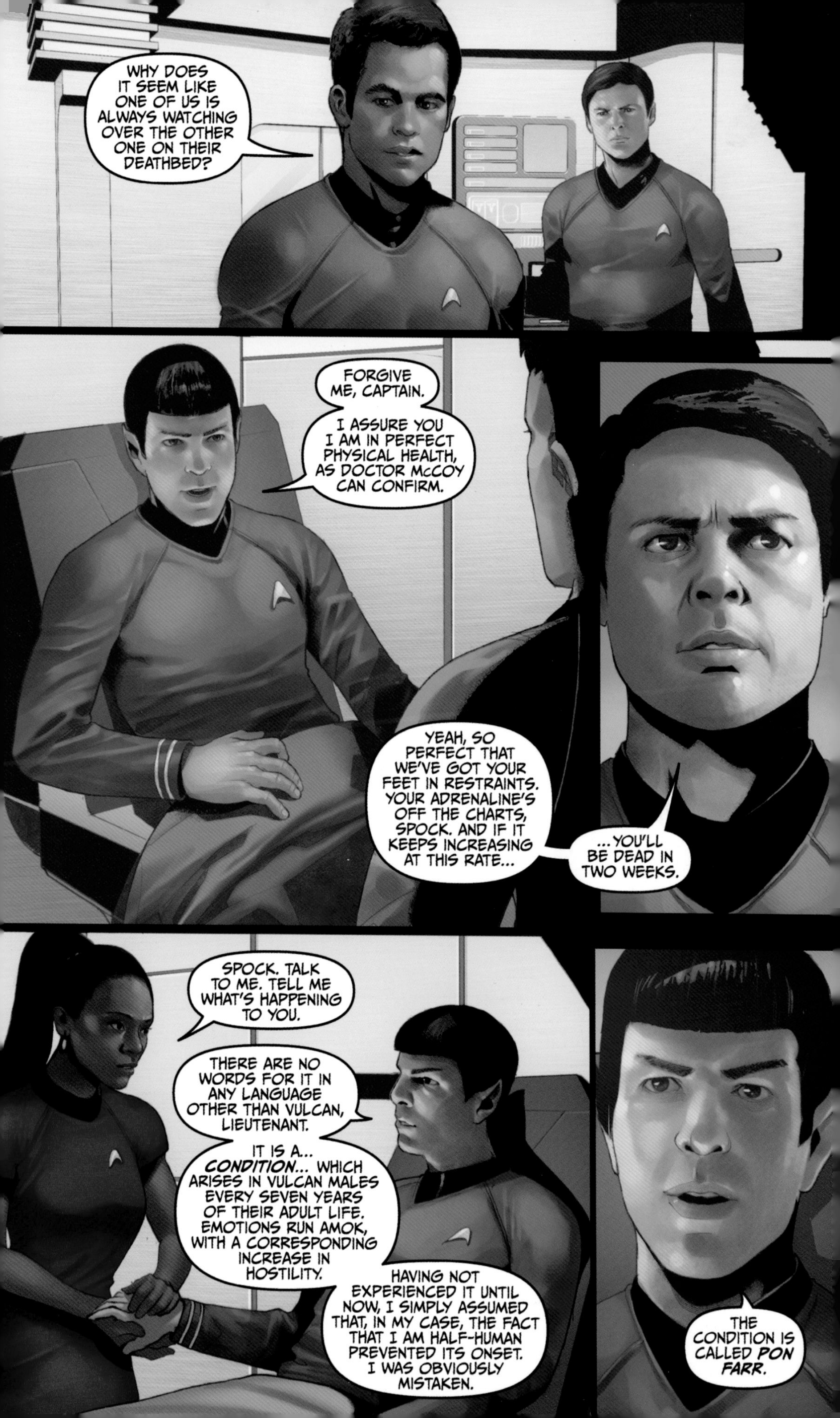
WHY DOES IT SEEM LIKE ONE OF US IS ALWAYS WATCHING OVER THE OTHER ONE ON THEIR DEATHBED?
FORGIVE ME, CAPTAIN.
I ASSURE YOU I AM IN PERFECT PHYSICAL HEALTH, AS DOCTOR McCOY CAN CONFIRM.
YEAH, SO PERFECT THAT WE'VE GOT YOUR FEET IN RESTRAINTS. YOUR ADRENALINE'S OFF THE CHARTS, SPOCK. AND IF IT KEEPS INCREASING AT THIS RATE...
...YOU'LL BE DEAD IN TWO WEEKS.
SPOCK. TALK TO ME. TELL ME WHAT'S HAPPENING TO YOU.
THERE ARE NO WORDS FOR IT IN ANY LANGUAGE OTHER THAN VULCAN, LIEUTENANT.
IT IS A... *CONDITION*... WHICH ARISES IN VULCAN MALES EVERY SEVEN YEARS OF THEIR ADULT LIFE. EMOTIONS RUN AMOK, WITH A CORRESPONDING INCREASE IN HOSTILITY.
HAVING NOT EXPERIENCED IT UNTIL NOW, I SIMPLY ASSUMED THAT, IN MY CASE, THE FACT THAT I AM HALF-HUMAN PREVENTED ITS ONSET. I WAS OBVIOUSLY MISTAKEN.
THE CONDITION IS CALLED *PON FARR*.

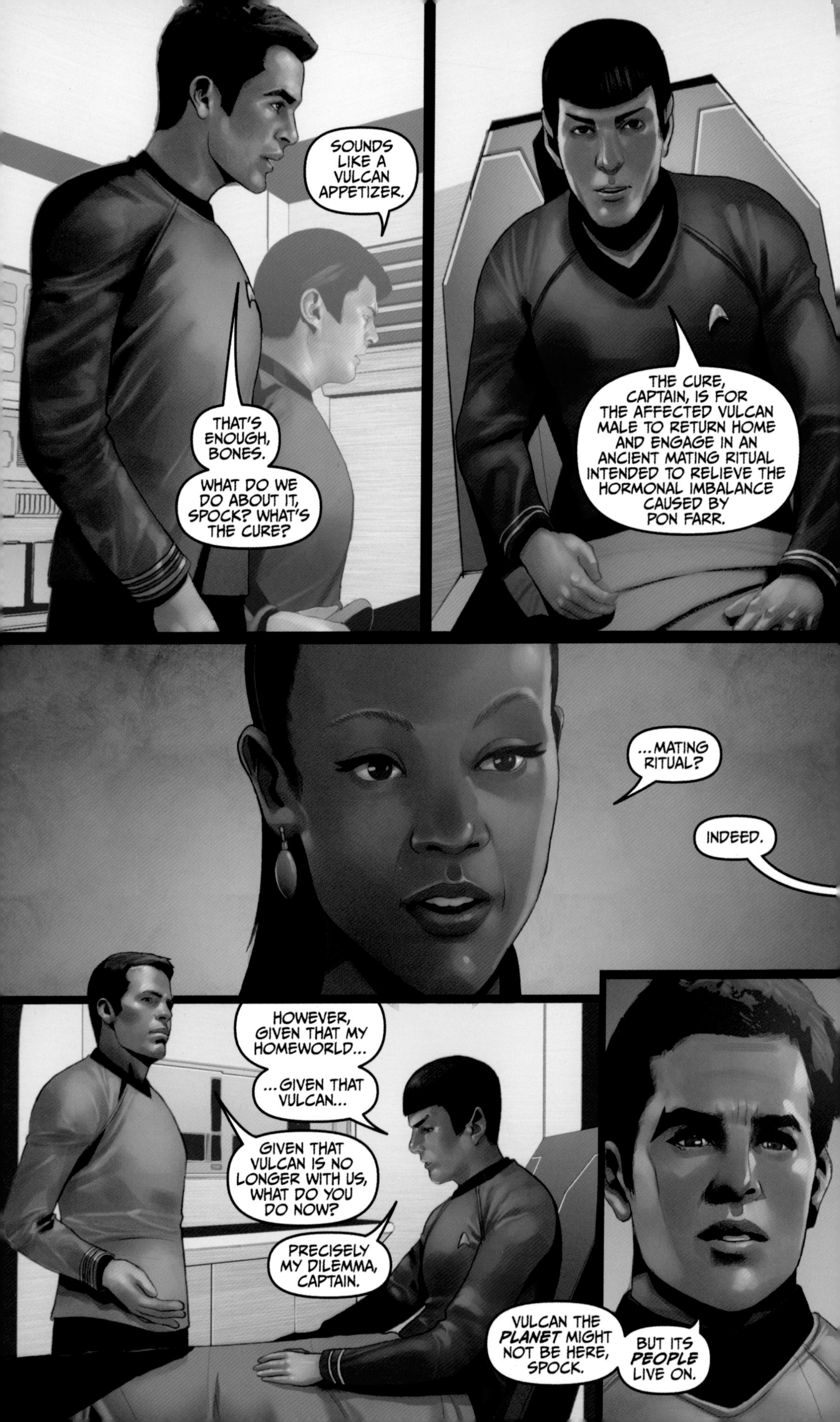
SOUNDS LIKE A VULCAN APPETIZER.
THAT'S ENOUGH, BONES.
WHAT DO WE DO ABOUT IT, SPOCK? WHAT'S THE CURE?
THE CURE, CAPTAIN, IS FOR THE AFFECTED VULCAN MALE TO RETURN HOME AND ENGAGE IN AN ANCIENT MATING RITUAL INTENDED TO RELIEVE THE HORMONAL IMBALANCE CAUSED BY PON FARR.
...MATING RITUAL?
INDEED.
HOWEVER, GIVEN THAT MY HOMEWORLD...
...GIVEN THAT VULCAN...
GIVEN THAT VULCAN IS NO LONGER WITH US, WHAT DO YOU DO NOW?
PRECISELY MY DILEMMA, CAPTAIN.
VULCAN THE *PLANET* MIGHT NOT BE HERE, SPOCK.
BUT ITS *PEOPLE* LIVE ON.

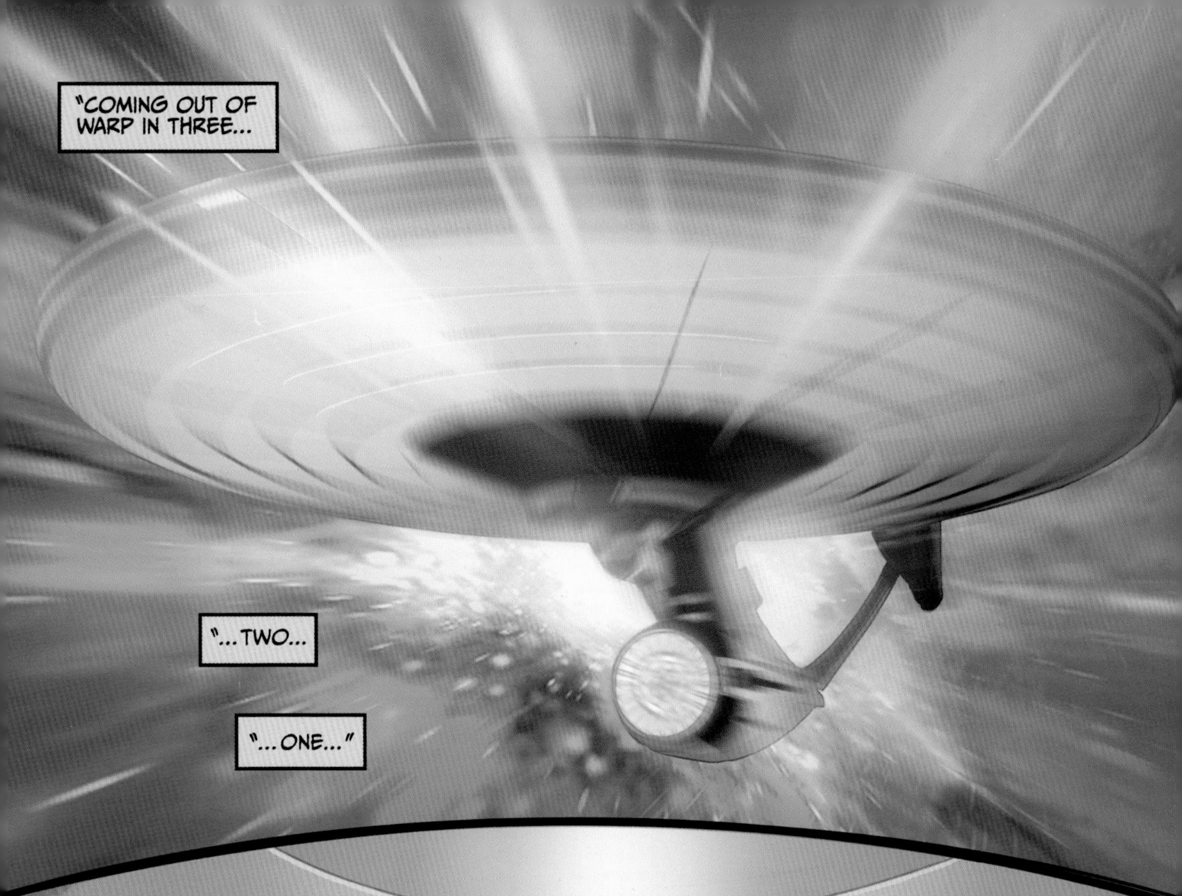
"COMING OUT OF WARP IN THREE...
"...TWO...
"...ONE..."

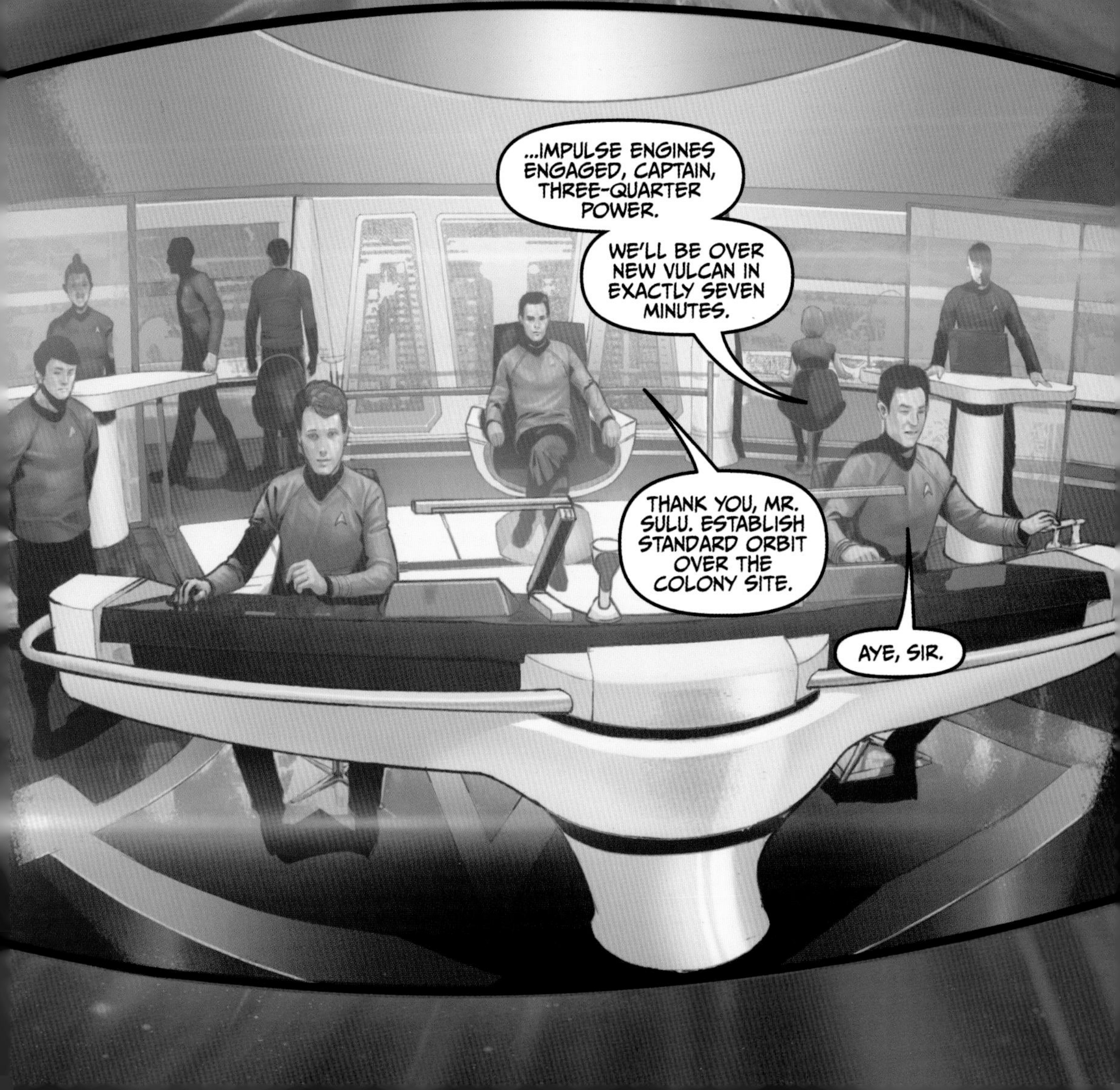
...IMPULSE ENGINES ENGAGED, CAPTAIN, THREE-QUARTER POWER.
WE'LL BE OVER NEW VULCAN IN EXACTLY SEVEN MINUTES.
THANK YOU, MR. SULU. ESTABLISH STANDARD ORBIT OVER THE COLONY SITE.
AYE, SIR.

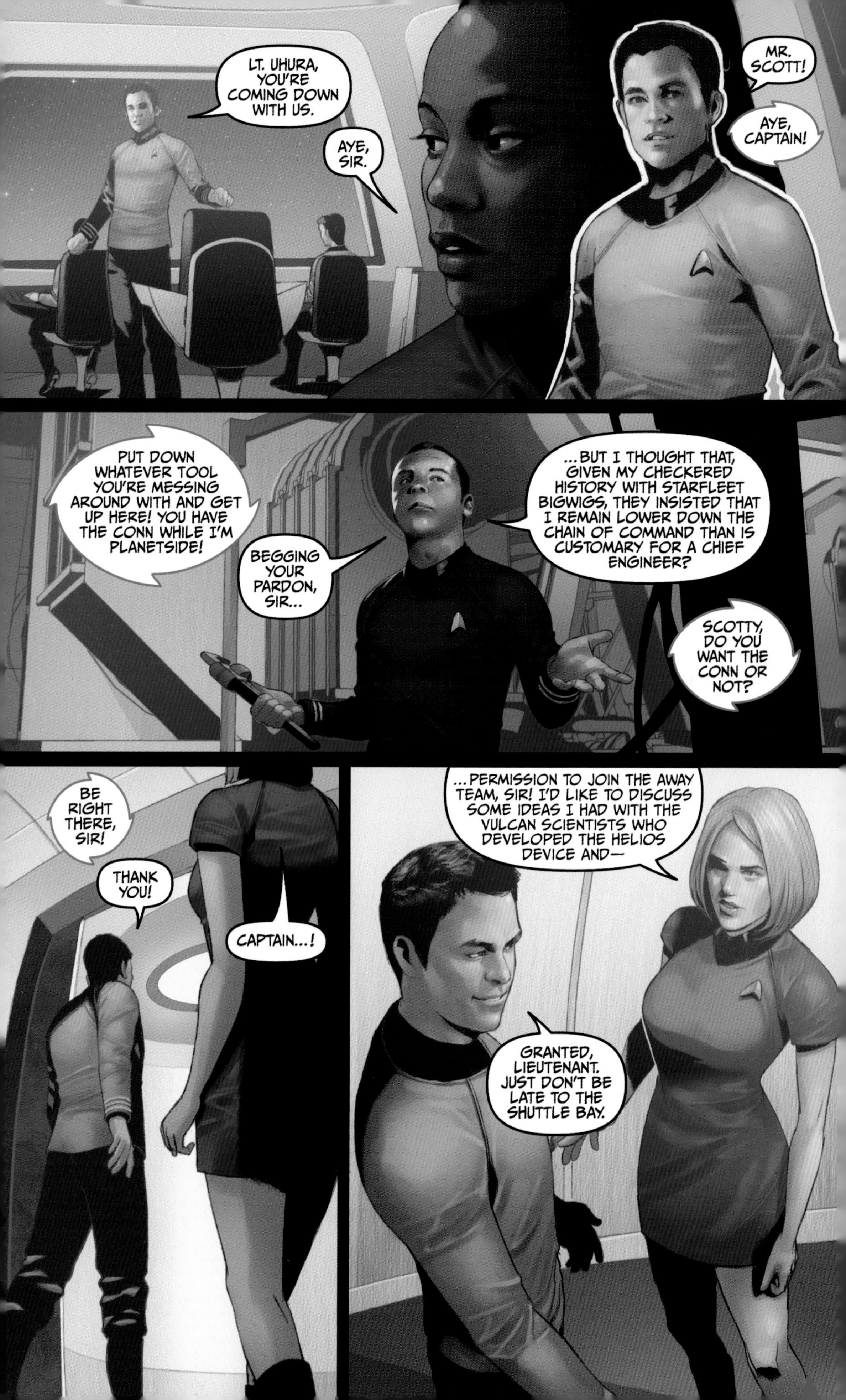
LT. UHURA, YOU'RE COMING DOWN WITH US.
AYE, SIR.
MR. SCOTT!
AYE, CAPTAIN!
PUT DOWN WHATEVER TOOL YOU'RE MESSING AROUND WITH AND GET UP HERE! YOU HAVE THE CONN WHILE I'M PLANETSIDE!
BEGGING YOUR PARDON, SIR...
...BUT I THOUGHT THAT, GIVEN MY CHECKERED HISTORY WITH STARFLEET BIGWIGS, THEY INSISTED THAT I REMAIN LOWER DOWN THE CHAIN OF COMMAND THAN IS CUSTOMARY FOR A CHIEF ENGINEER?
SCOTTY, DO YOU WANT THE CONN OR NOT?
BE RIGHT THERE, SIR!
THANK YOU!
CAPTAIN...!
...PERMISSION TO JOIN THE AWAY TEAM, SIR! I'D LIKE TO DISCUSS SOME IDEAS I HAD WITH THE VULCAN SCIENTISTS WHO DEVELOPED THE HELIOS DEVICE AND—
GRANTED, LIEUTENANT. JUST DON'T BE LATE TO THE SHUTTLE BAY.

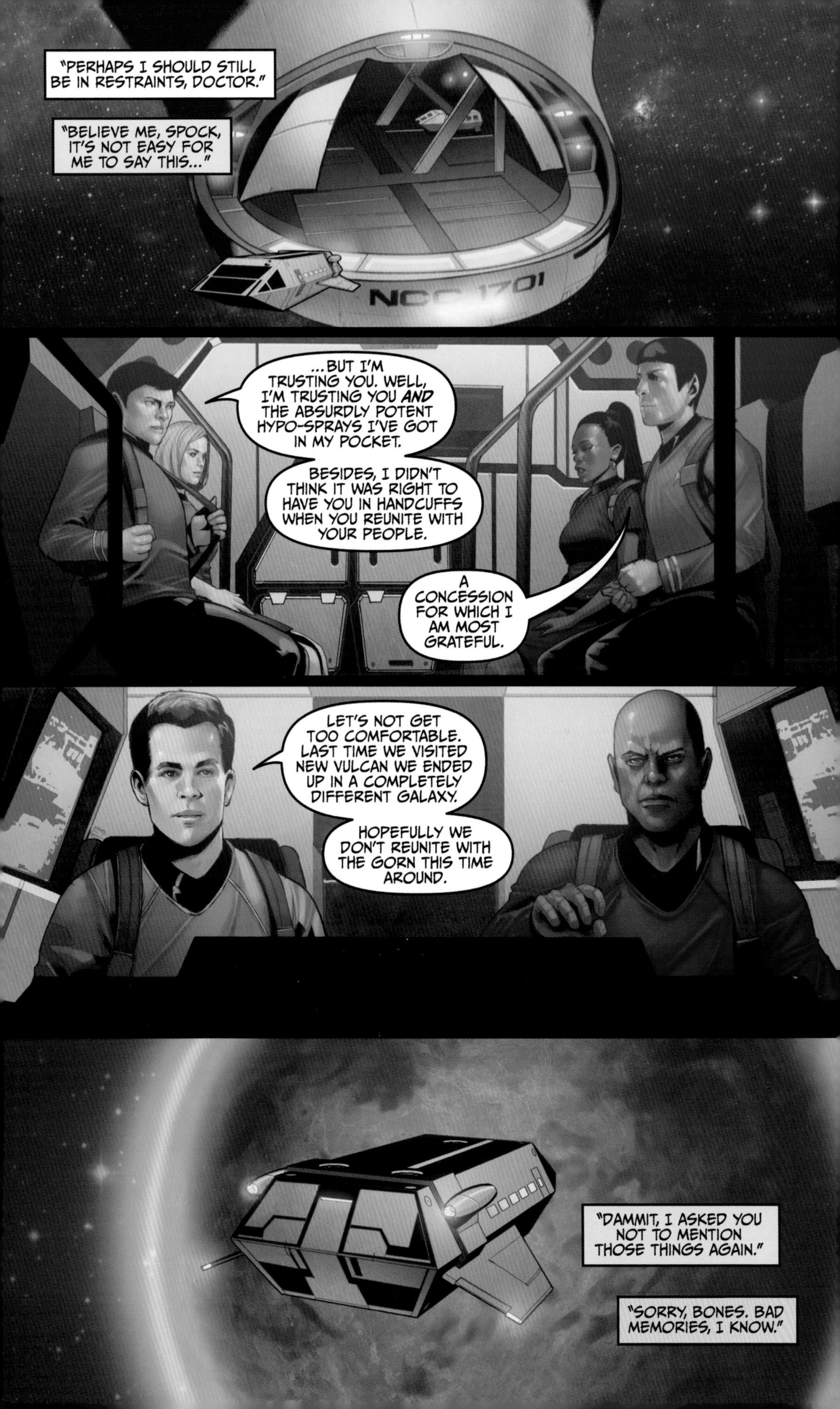
"PERHAPS I SHOULD STILL BE IN RESTRAINTS, DOCTOR."
"BELIEVE ME, SPOCK, IT'S NOT EASY FOR ME TO SAY THIS..."
NCC-1701
...BUT I'M TRUSTING YOU. WELL, I'M TRUSTING YOU AND THE ABSURDLY POTENT HYPO-SPRAYS I'VE GOT IN MY POCKET.
BESIDES, I DIDN'T THINK IT WAS RIGHT TO HAVE YOU IN HANDCUFFS WHEN YOU REUNITE WITH YOUR PEOPLE.
A CONCESSION FOR WHICH I AM MOST GRATEFUL.
LET'S NOT GET TOO COMFORTABLE. LAST TIME WE VISITED NEW VULCAN WE ENDED UP IN A COMPLETELY DIFFERENT GALAXY.
HOPEFULLY WE DON'T REUNITE WITH THE GORN THIS TIME AROUND.
"DAMMIT, I ASKED YOU NOT TO MENTION THOSE THINGS AGAIN."
"SORRY, BONES. BAD MEMORIES, I KNOW."

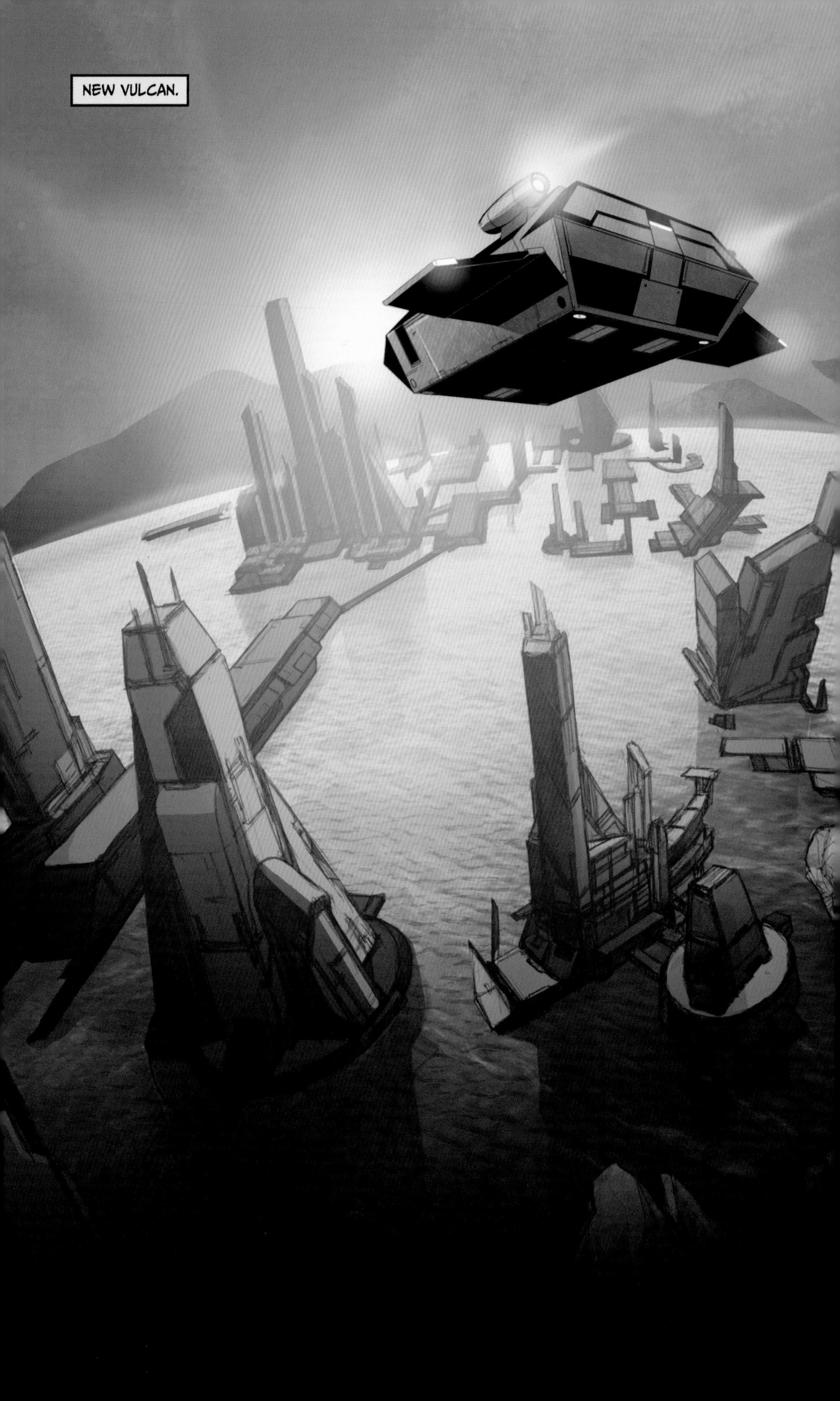
NEW VULCAN.

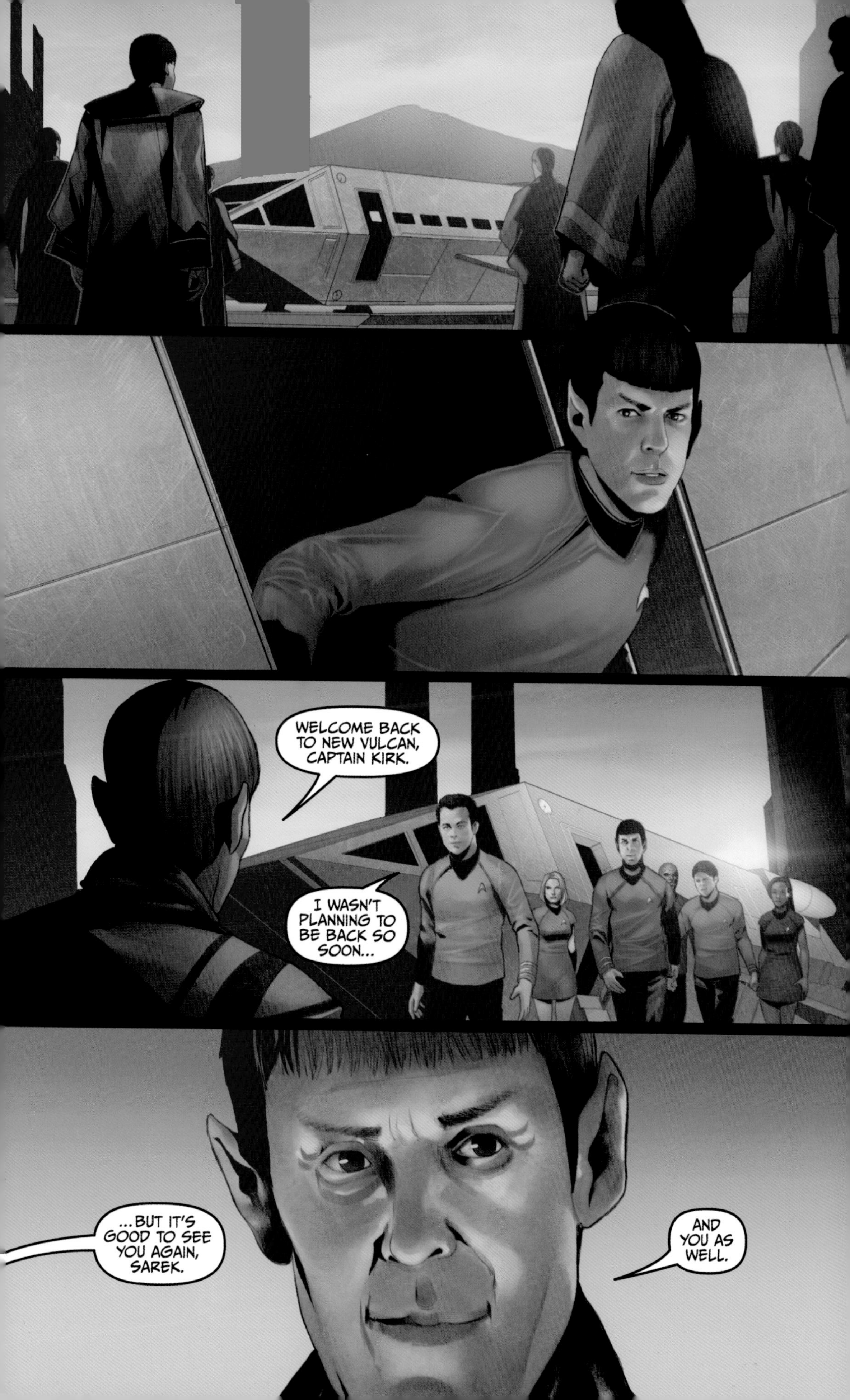
WELCOME BACK TO NEW VULCAN, CAPTAIN KIRK.
I WASN'T PLANNING TO BE BACK SO SOON...
...BUT IT'S GOOD TO SEE YOU AGAIN, SAREK.
AND YOU AS WELL.

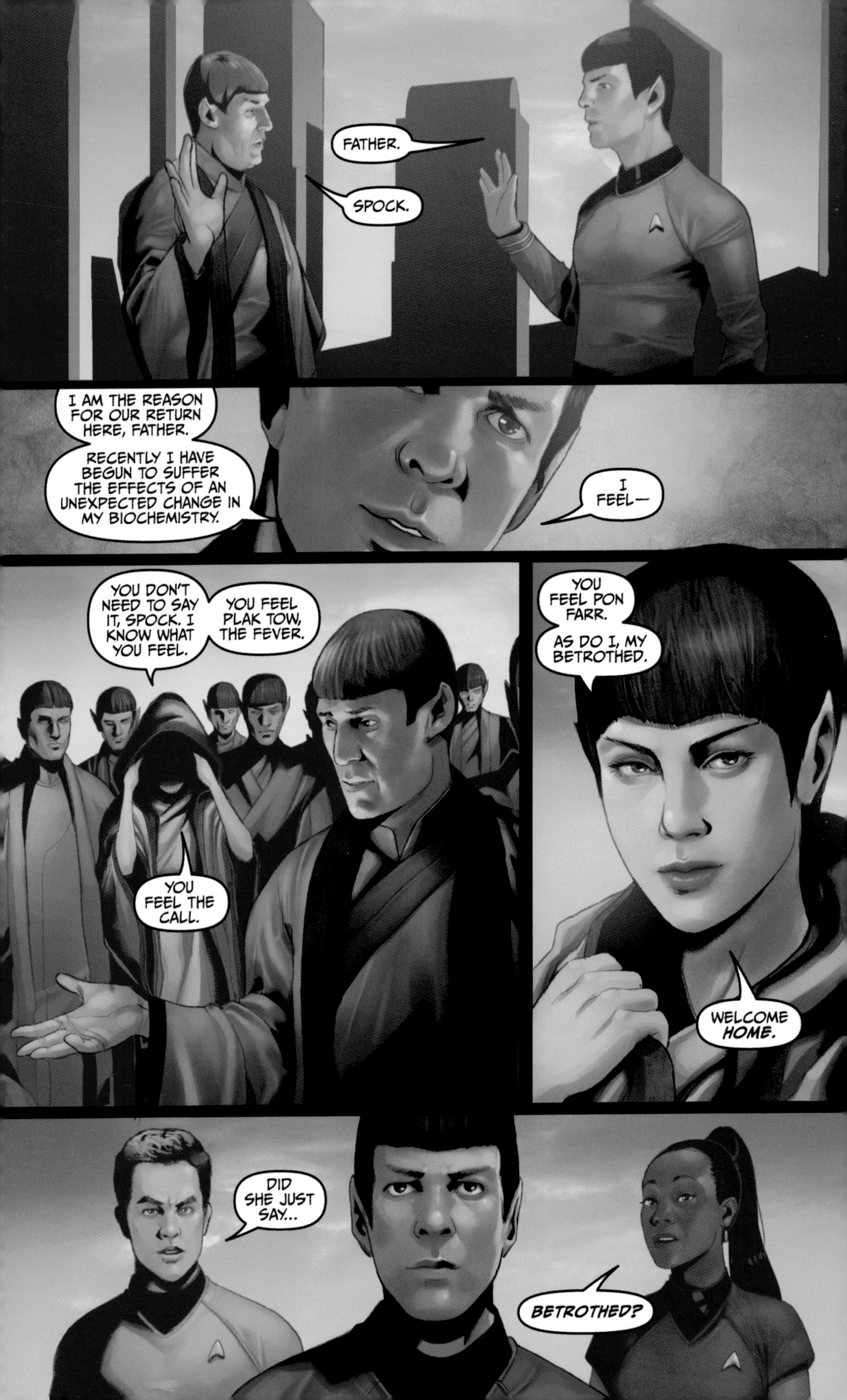

FATHER.
SPOCK.
I AM THE REASON FOR OUR RETURN HERE, FATHER.
RECENTLY I HAVE BEGUN TO SUFFER THE EFFECTS OF AN UNEXPECTED CHANGE IN MY BIOCHEMISTRY.
I FEEL—
YOU DON'T NEED TO SAY IT, SPOCK. I KNOW WHAT YOU FEEL.
YOU FEEL PLAK TOW, THE FEVER.
YOU FEEL THE CALL.
YOU FEEL PON FARR.
AS DO I, MY BETROTHED.
WELCOME *HOME.*
DID SHE JUST SAY...
BETROTHED?

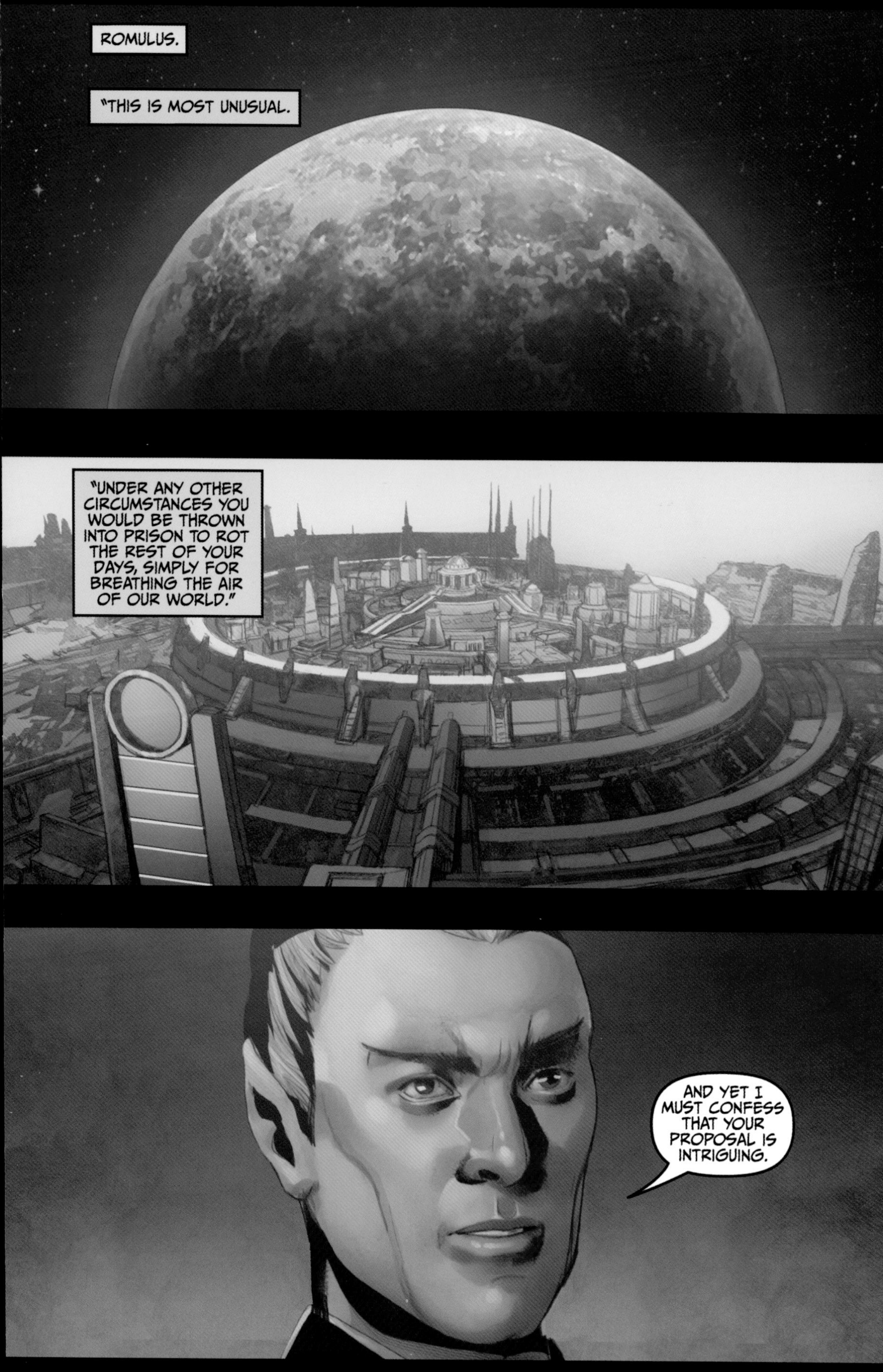
ROMULUS.
"THIS IS MOST UNUSUAL.
"UNDER ANY OTHER CIRCUMSTANCES YOU WOULD BE THROWN INTO PRISON TO ROT THE REST OF YOUR DAYS, SIMPLY FOR BREATHING THE AIR OF OUR WORLD."
AND YET I MUST CONFESS THAT YOUR PROPOSAL IS INTRIGUING.

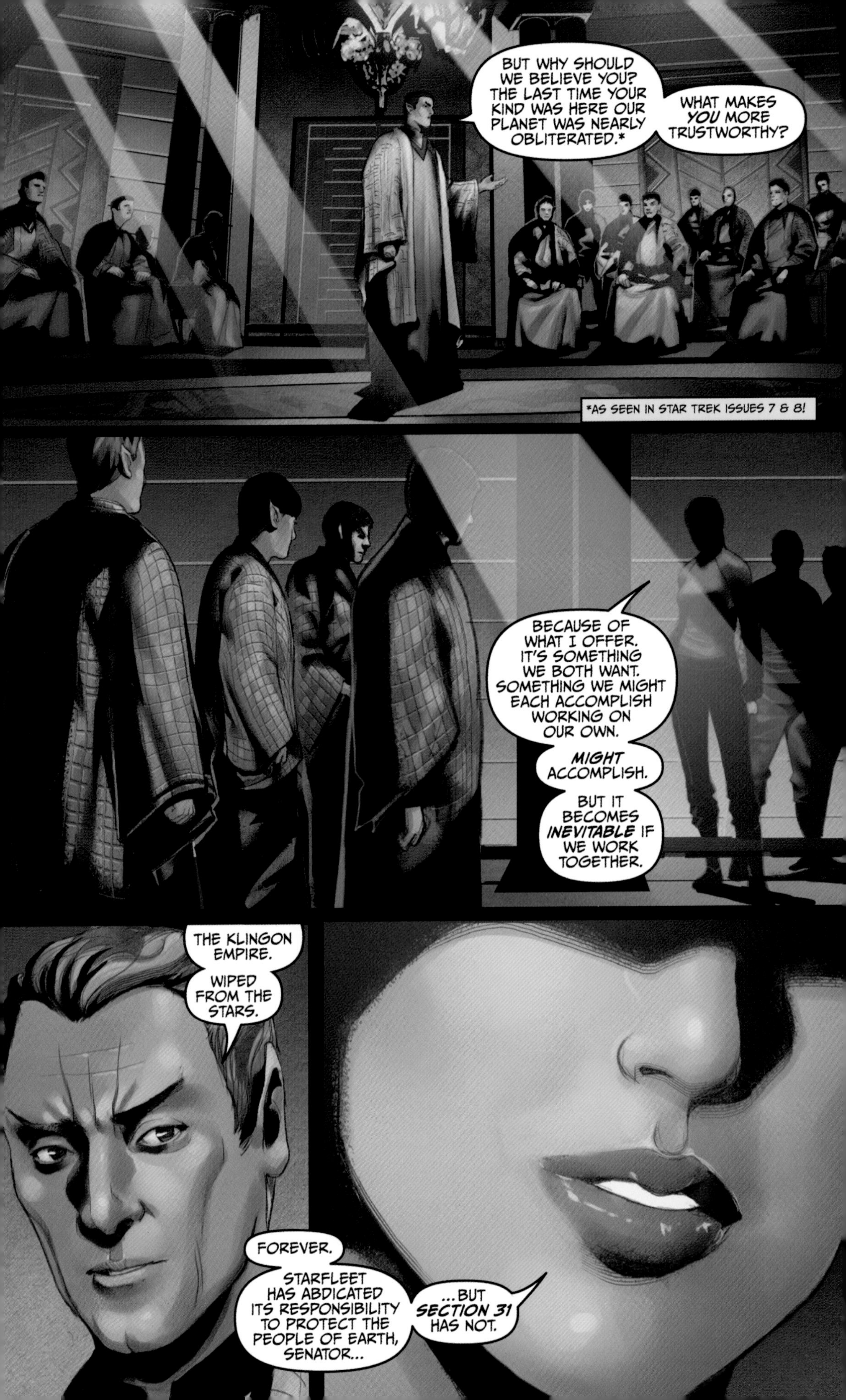
BUT WHY SHOULD WE BELIEVE YOU? THE LAST TIME YOUR KIND WAS HERE OUR PLANET WAS NEARLY OBLITERATED.*
WHAT MAKES *YOU* MORE TRUSTWORTHY?
*AS SEEN IN STAR TREK ISSUES 7 & 8!
BECAUSE OF WHAT I OFFER. IT'S SOMETHING WE BOTH WANT. SOMETHING WE MIGHT EACH ACCOMPLISH WORKING ON OUR OWN.
MIGHT ACCOMPLISH.
BUT IT BECOMES *INEVITABLE* IF WE WORK TOGETHER.
THE KLINGON EMPIRE.
WIPED FROM THE STARS.
FOREVER.
STARFLEET HAS ABDICATED ITS RESPONSIBILITY TO PROTECT THE PEOPLE OF EARTH, SENATOR...
...BUT *SECTION 31* HAS NOT.

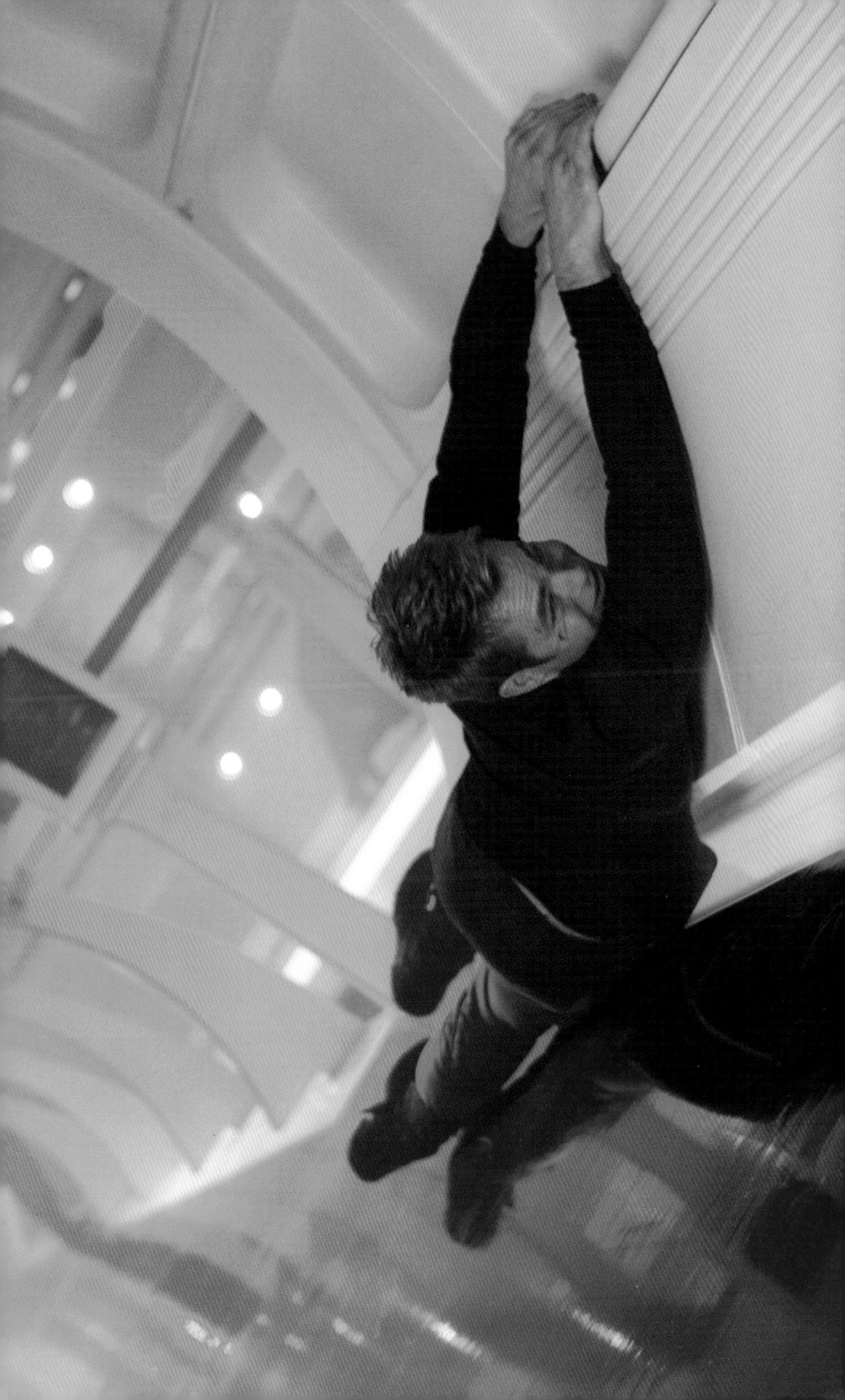

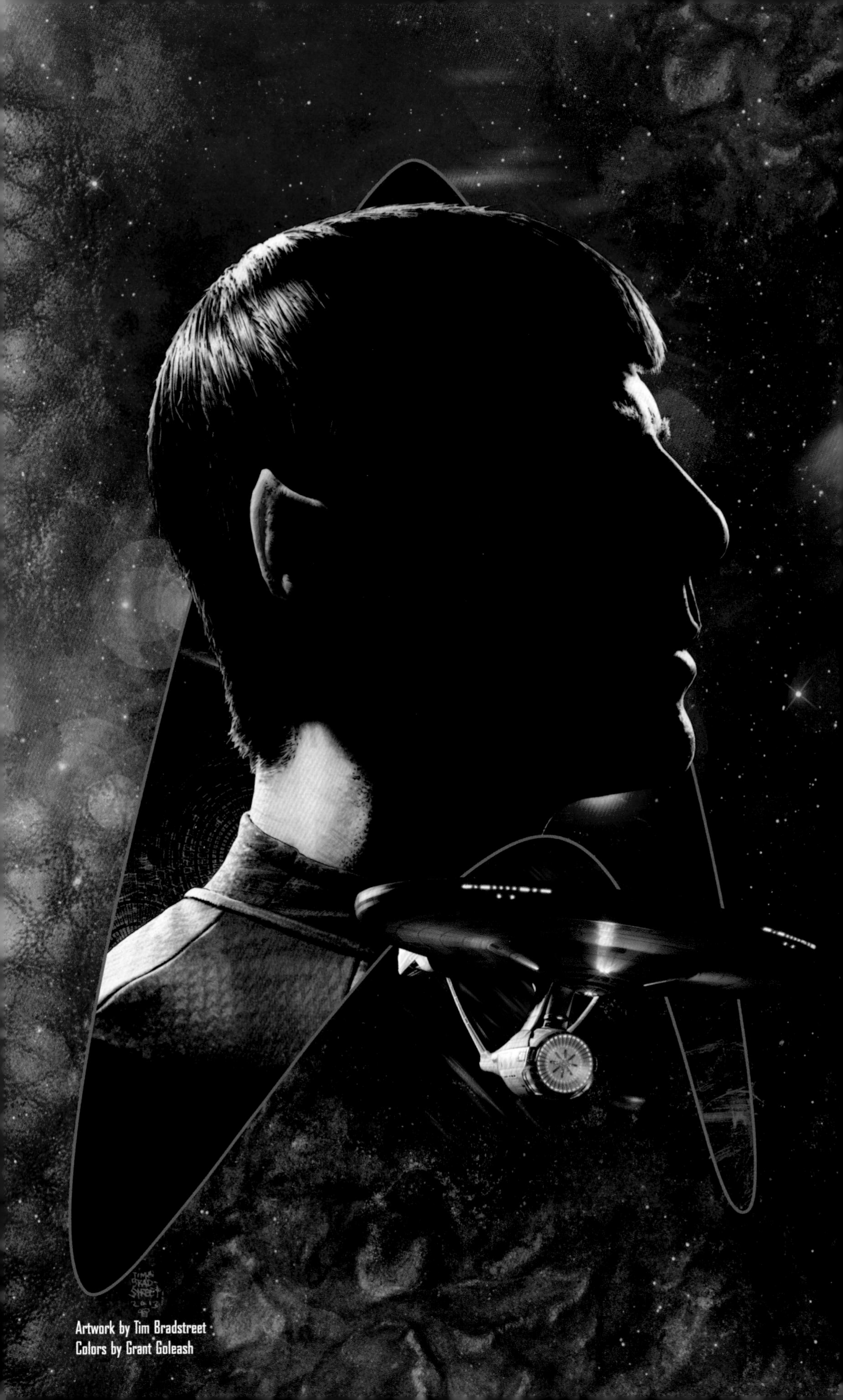

Artwork by Tim Bradstreet
Colors by Grant Goleash

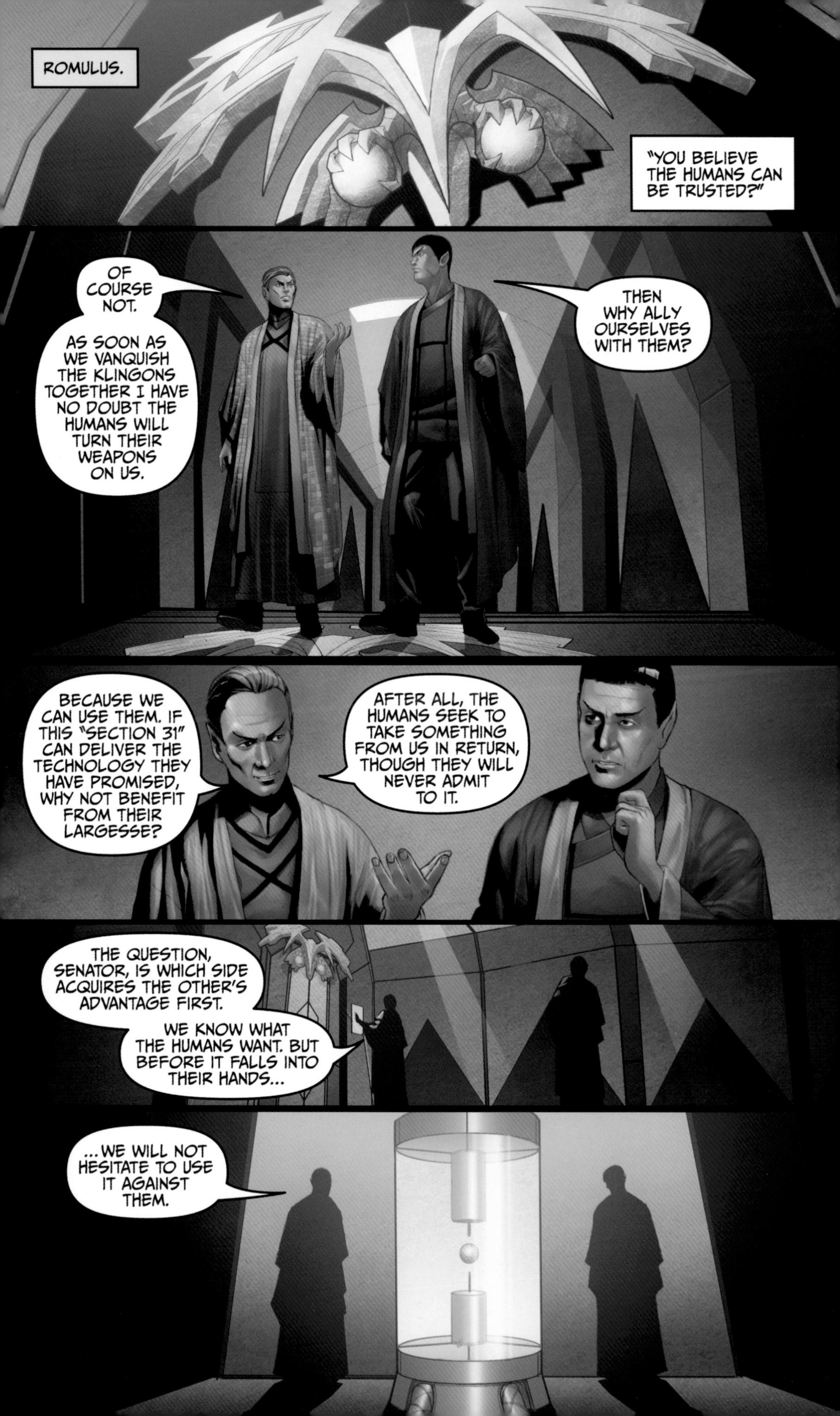
ROMULUS.
"YOU BELIEVE THE HUMANS CAN BE TRUSTED?"
OF COURSE NOT.
AS SOON AS WE VANQUISH THE KLINGONS TOGETHER I HAVE NO DOUBT THE HUMANS WILL TURN THEIR WEAPONS ON US.
THEN WHY ALLY OURSELVES WITH THEM?
BECAUSE WE CAN USE THEM. IF THIS "SECTION 31" CAN DELIVER THE TECHNOLOGY THEY HAVE PROMISED, WHY NOT BENEFIT FROM THEIR LARGESSE?
AFTER ALL, THE HUMANS SEEK TO TAKE SOMETHING FROM US IN RETURN, THOUGH THEY WILL NEVER ADMIT TO IT.
THE QUESTION, SENATOR, IS WHICH SIDE ACQUIRES THE OTHER'S ADVANTAGE FIRST.
WE KNOW WHAT THE HUMANS WANT. BUT BEFORE IT FALLS INTO THEIR HANDS...
...WE WILL NOT HESITATE TO USE IT AGAINST THEM.

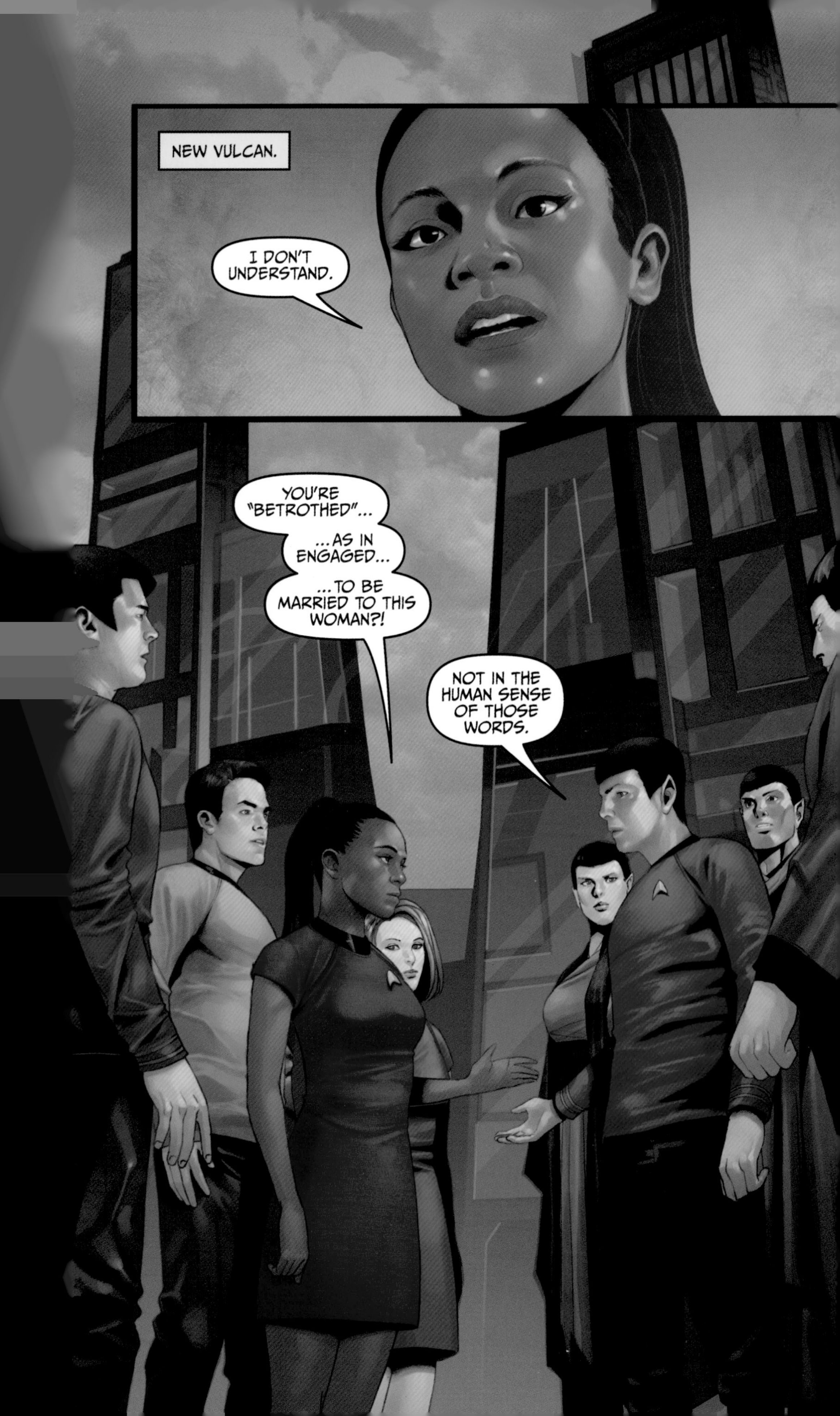
NEW VULCAN.
I DON'T UNDERSTAND.
YOU'RE "BETROTHED"...
...AS IN ENGAGED...
...TO BE MARRIED TO THIS WOMAN?!
NOT IN THE HUMAN SENSE OF THOSE WORDS.

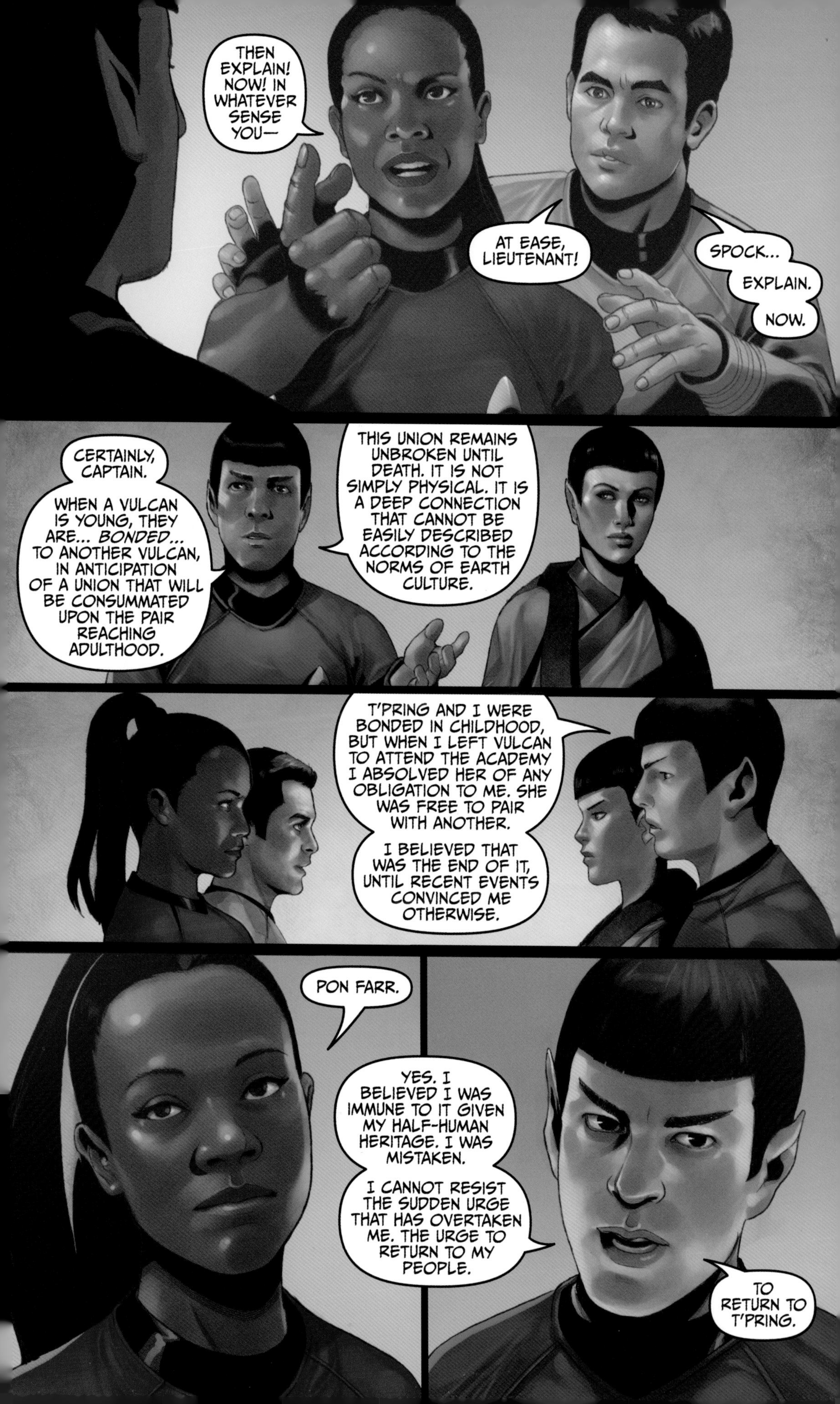
THEN EXPLAIN! NOW! IN WHATEVER SENSE YOU—
AT EASE, LIEUTENANT!
SPOCK...
EXPLAIN.
NOW.
CERTAINLY, CAPTAIN.
WHEN A VULCAN IS YOUNG, THEY ARE... *BONDED*... TO ANOTHER VULCAN, IN ANTICIPATION OF A UNION THAT WILL BE CONSUMMATED UPON THE PAIR REACHING ADULTHOOD.
THIS UNION REMAINS UNBROKEN UNTIL DEATH. IT IS NOT SIMPLY PHYSICAL. IT IS A DEEP CONNECTION THAT CANNOT BE EASILY DESCRIBED ACCORDING TO THE NORMS OF EARTH CULTURE.
T'PRING AND I WERE BONDED IN CHILDHOOD, BUT WHEN I LEFT VULCAN TO ATTEND THE ACADEMY I ABSOLVED HER OF ANY OBLIGATION TO ME. SHE WAS FREE TO PAIR WITH ANOTHER.
I BELIEVED THAT WAS THE END OF IT, UNTIL RECENT EVENTS CONVINCED ME OTHERWISE.
PON FARR.
YES. I BELIEVED I WAS IMMUNE TO IT GIVEN MY HALF-HUMAN HERITAGE. I WAS MISTAKEN.
I CANNOT RESIST THE SUDDEN URGE THAT HAS OVERTAKEN ME. THE URGE TO RETURN TO MY PEOPLE.
TO RETURN TO T'PRING.

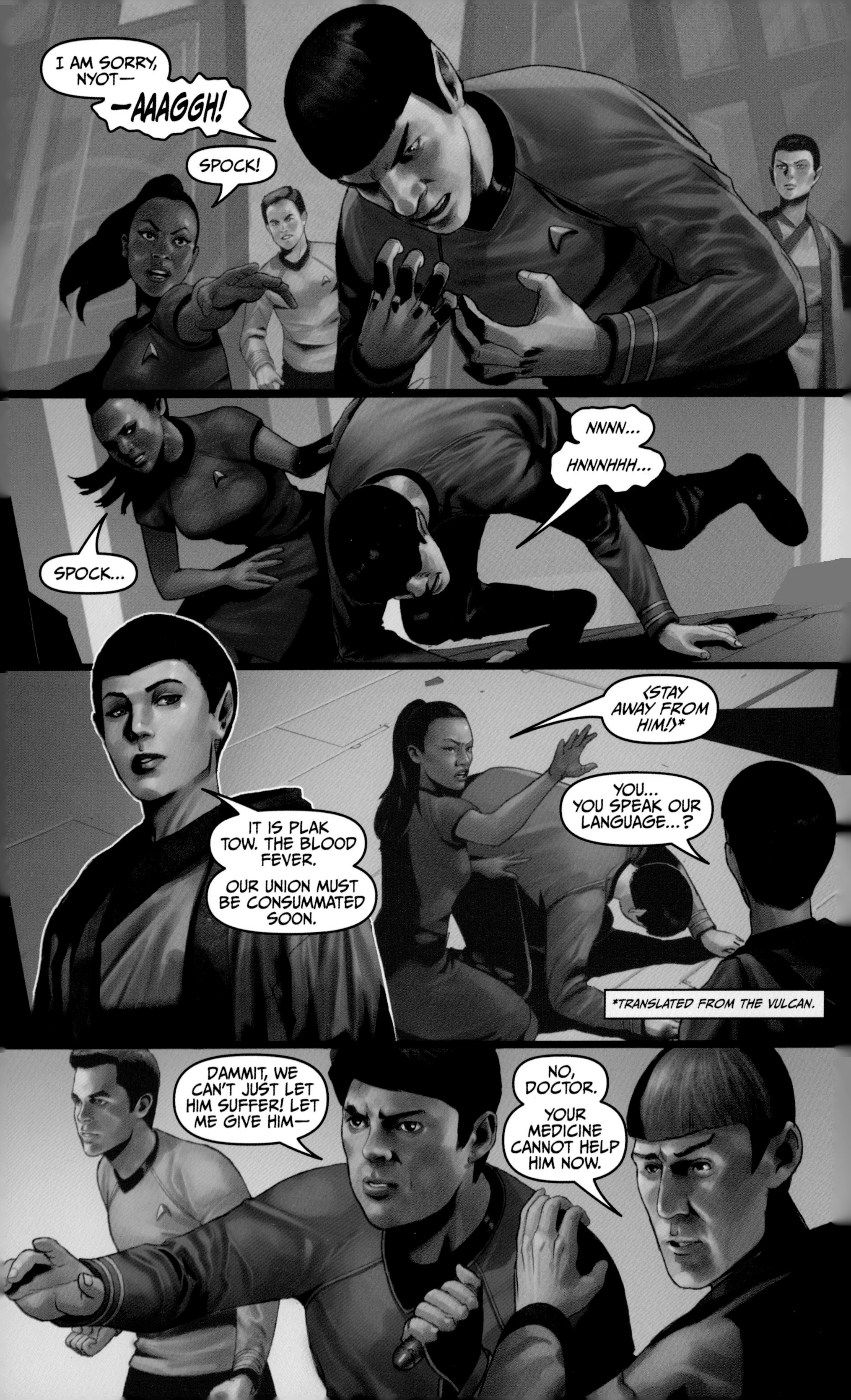

I AM SORRY, NYOT—
—AAAGGH!
SPOCK!
NNNN...
HNNNHHH...
SPOCK...
<STAY AWAY FROM HIM!>*
IT IS PLAK TOW. THE BLOOD FEVER.
OUR UNION MUST BE CONSUMMATED SOON.
YOU... YOU SPEAK OUR LANGUAGE...?
*TRANSLATED FROM THE VULCAN.
DAMMIT, WE CAN'T JUST LET HIM SUFFER! LET ME GIVE HIM—
NO, DOCTOR.
YOUR MEDICINE CANNOT HELP HIM NOW.

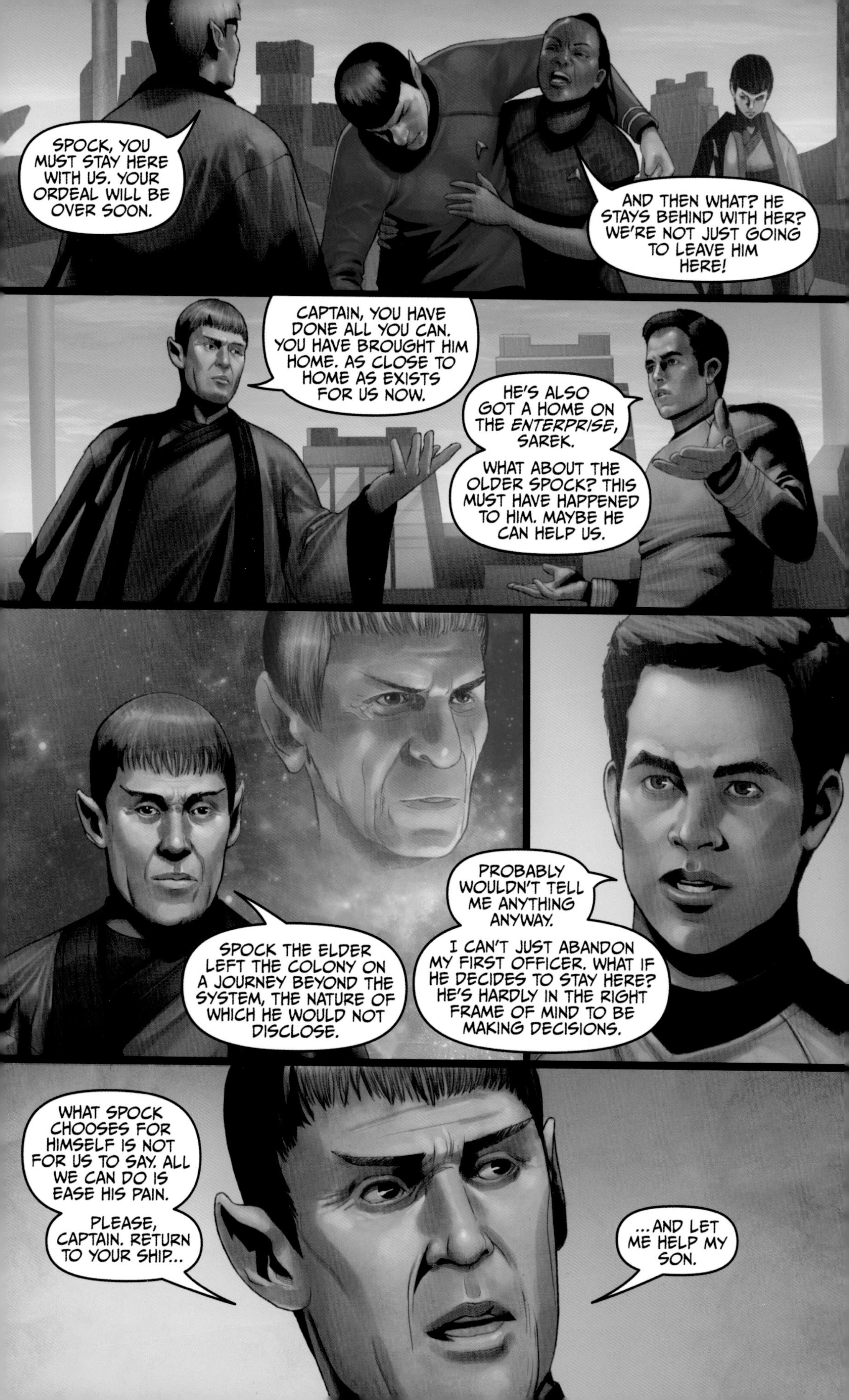
SPOCK, YOU MUST STAY HERE WITH US. YOUR ORDEAL WILL BE OVER SOON.
AND THEN WHAT? HE STAYS BEHIND WITH HER? WE'RE NOT JUST GOING TO LEAVE HIM HERE!
CAPTAIN, YOU HAVE DONE ALL YOU CAN. YOU HAVE BROUGHT HIM HOME. AS CLOSE TO HOME AS EXISTS FOR US NOW.
HE'S ALSO GOT A HOME ON THE *ENTERPRISE*, SAREK.
WHAT ABOUT THE OLDER SPOCK? THIS MUST HAVE HAPPENED TO HIM. MAYBE HE CAN HELP US.
SPOCK THE ELDER LEFT THE COLONY ON A JOURNEY BEYOND THE SYSTEM, THE NATURE OF WHICH HE WOULD NOT DISCLOSE.
PROBABLY WOULDN'T TELL ME ANYTHING ANYWAY.
I CAN'T JUST ABANDON MY FIRST OFFICER. WHAT IF HE DECIDES TO STAY HERE? HE'S HARDLY IN THE RIGHT FRAME OF MIND TO BE MAKING DECISIONS.
WHAT SPOCK CHOOSES FOR HIMSELF IS NOT FOR US TO SAY. ALL WE CAN DO IS EASE HIS PAIN.
PLEASE, CAPTAIN. RETURN TO YOUR SHIP...
...AND LET ME HELP MY SON.

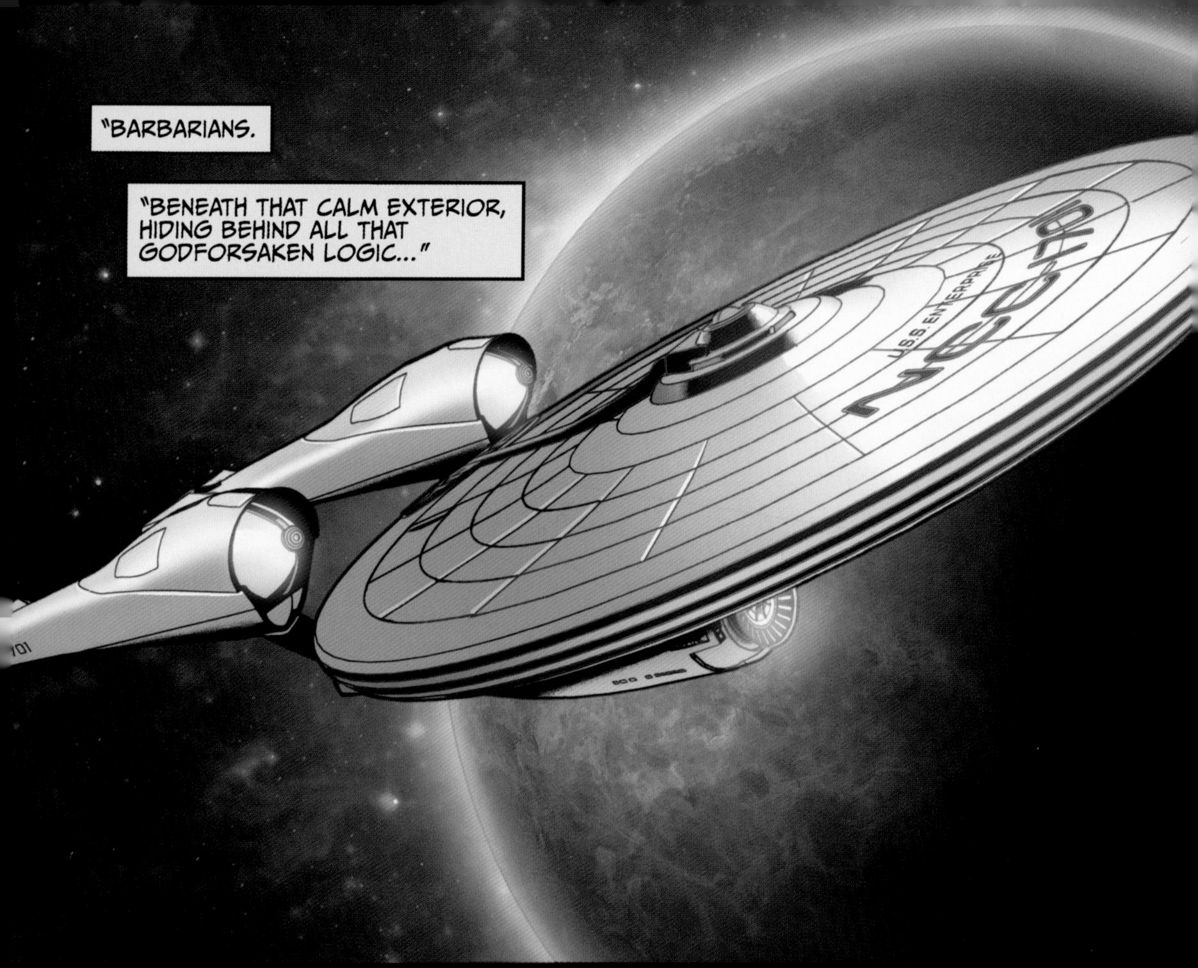
"BARBARIANS.
"BENEATH THAT CALM EXTERIOR, HIDING BEHIND ALL THAT GODFORSAKEN LOGIC..."
NCC-1701
U.S.S. ENTERPRISE

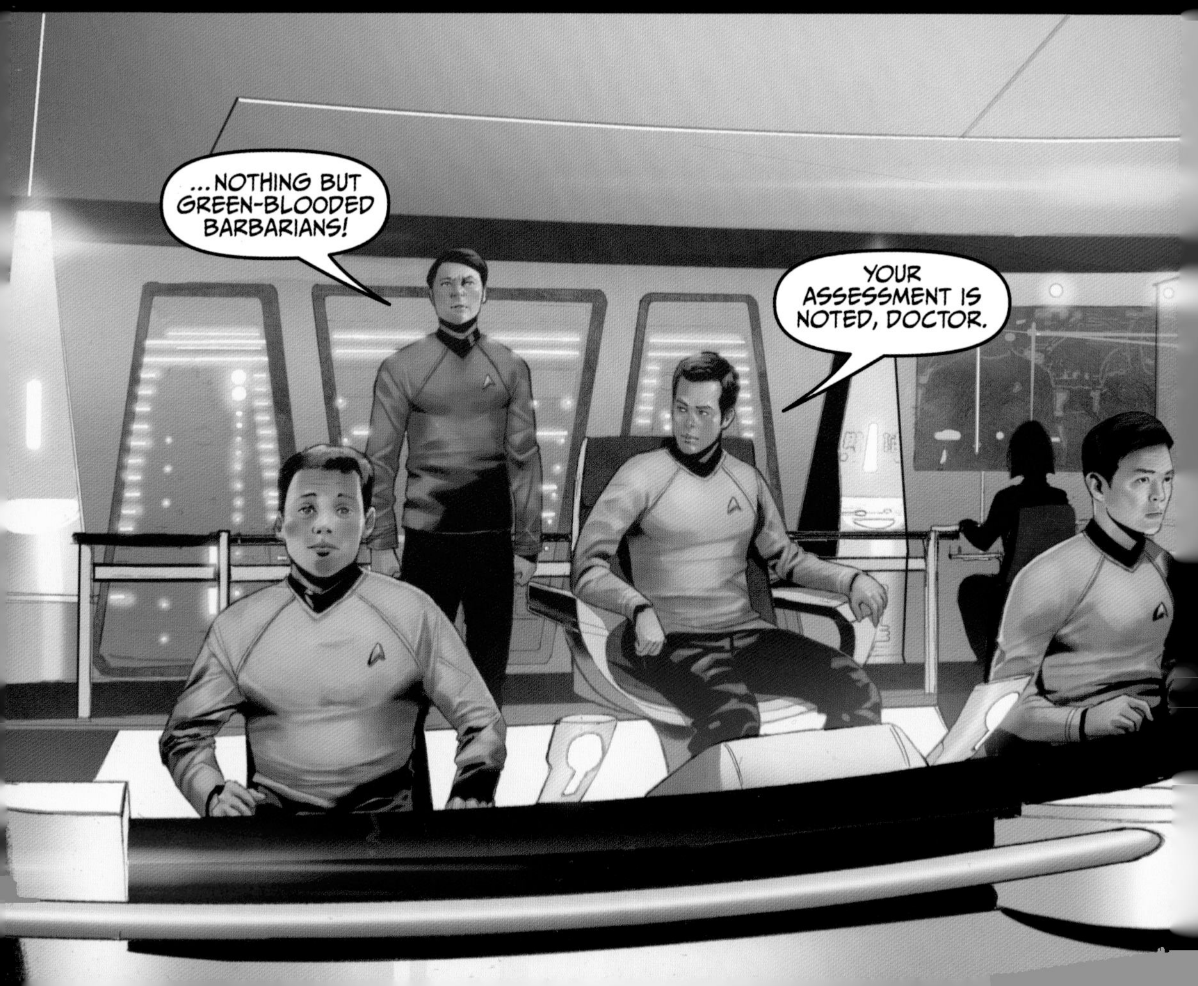
...NOTHING BUT GREEN-BLOODED BARBARIANS!
YOUR ASSESSMENT IS NOTED, DOCTOR.

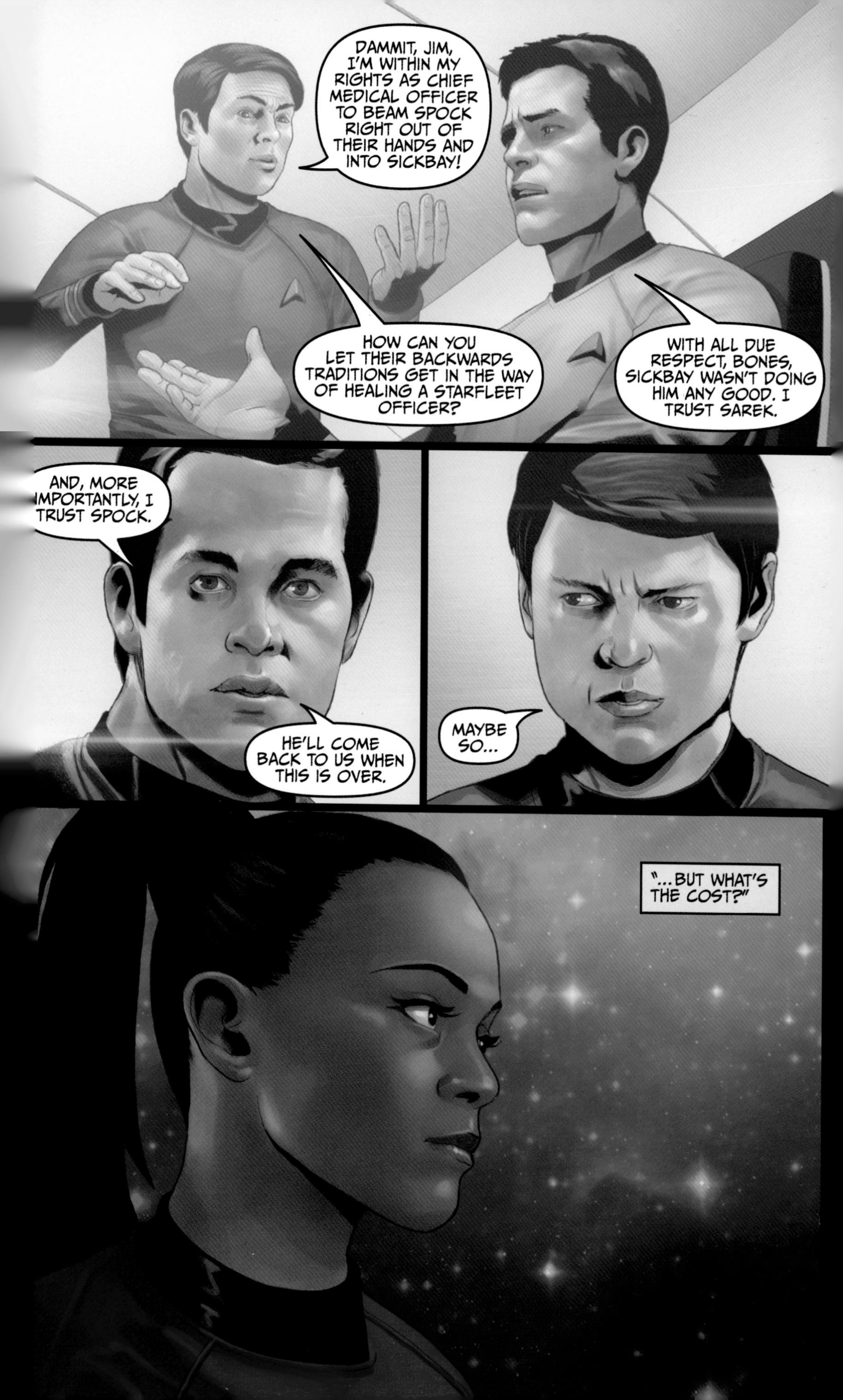

DAMMIT, JIM, I'M WITHIN MY RIGHTS AS CHIEF MEDICAL OFFICER TO BEAM SPOCK RIGHT OUT OF THEIR HANDS AND INTO SICKBAY!
HOW CAN YOU LET THEIR BACKWARDS TRADITIONS GET IN THE WAY OF HEALING A STARFLEET OFFICER?
WITH ALL DUE RESPECT, BONES, SICKBAY WASN'T DOING HIM ANY GOOD. I TRUST SAREK.
AND, MORE IMPORTANTLY, I TRUST SPOCK.
HE'LL COME BACK TO US WHEN THIS IS OVER.
MAYBE SO...
"...BUT WHAT'S THE COST?"

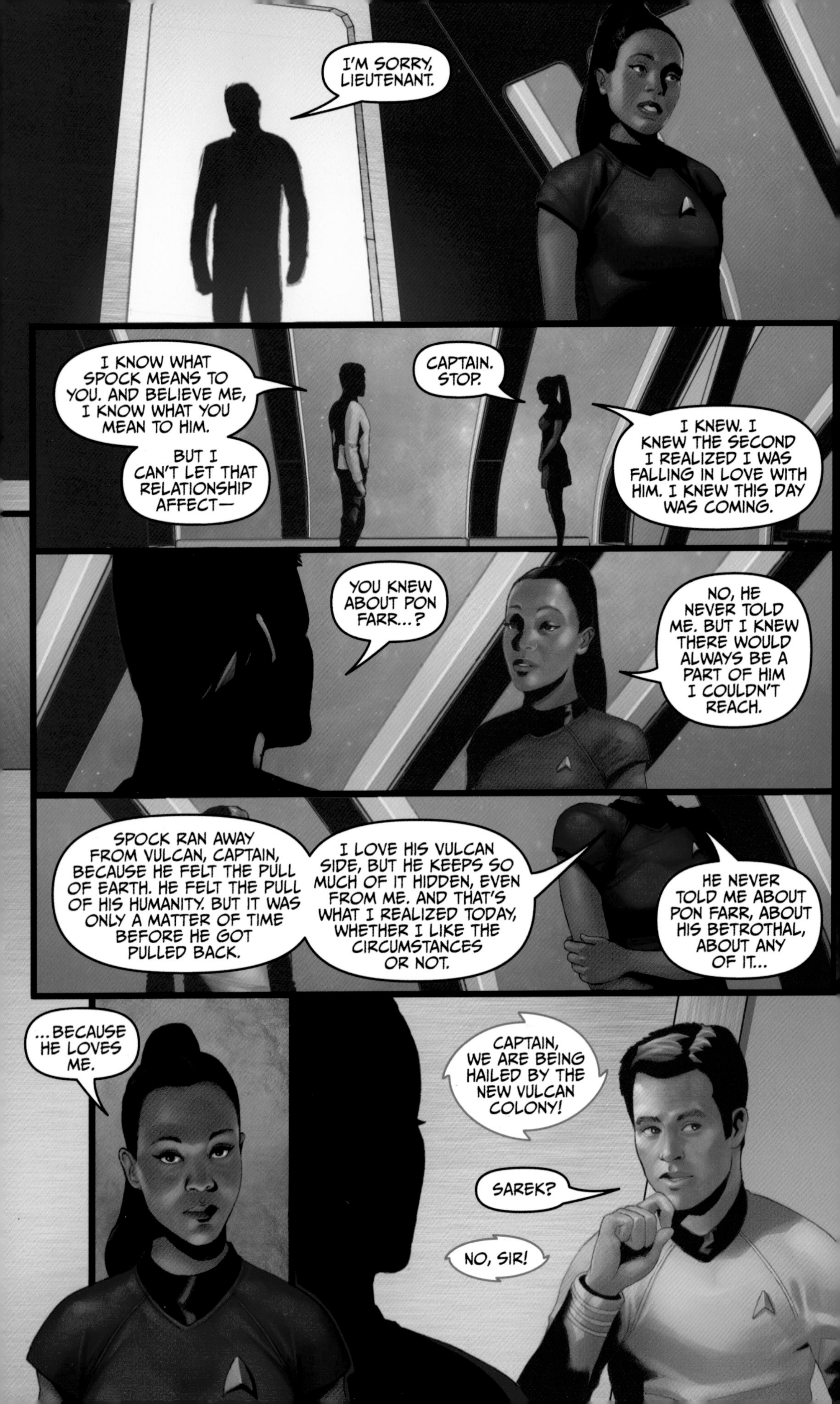
I'M SORRY, LIEUTENANT.
I KNOW WHAT SPOCK MEANS TO YOU. AND BELIEVE ME, I KNOW WHAT YOU MEAN TO HIM.
BUT I CAN'T LET THAT RELATIONSHIP AFFECT—
CAPTAIN. STOP.
I KNEW. I KNEW THE SECOND I REALIZED I WAS FALLING IN LOVE WITH HIM. I KNEW THIS DAY WAS COMING.
YOU KNEW ABOUT PON FARR...?
NO, HE NEVER TOLD ME. BUT I KNEW THERE WOULD ALWAYS BE A PART OF HIM I COULDN'T REACH.
SPOCK RAN AWAY FROM VULCAN, CAPTAIN, BECAUSE HE FELT THE PULL OF EARTH. HE FELT THE PULL OF HIS HUMANITY. BUT IT WAS ONLY A MATTER OF TIME BEFORE HE GOT PULLED BACK.
I LOVE HIS VULCAN SIDE, BUT HE KEEPS SO MUCH OF IT HIDDEN, EVEN FROM ME. AND THAT'S WHAT I REALIZED TODAY, WHETHER I LIKE THE CIRCUMSTANCES OR NOT.
HE NEVER TOLD ME ABOUT PON FARR, ABOUT HIS BETROTHAL, ABOUT ANY OF IT...
...BECAUSE HE LOVES ME.
CAPTAIN, WE ARE BEING HAILED BY THE NEW VULCAN COLONY!
SAREK?
NO, SIR!

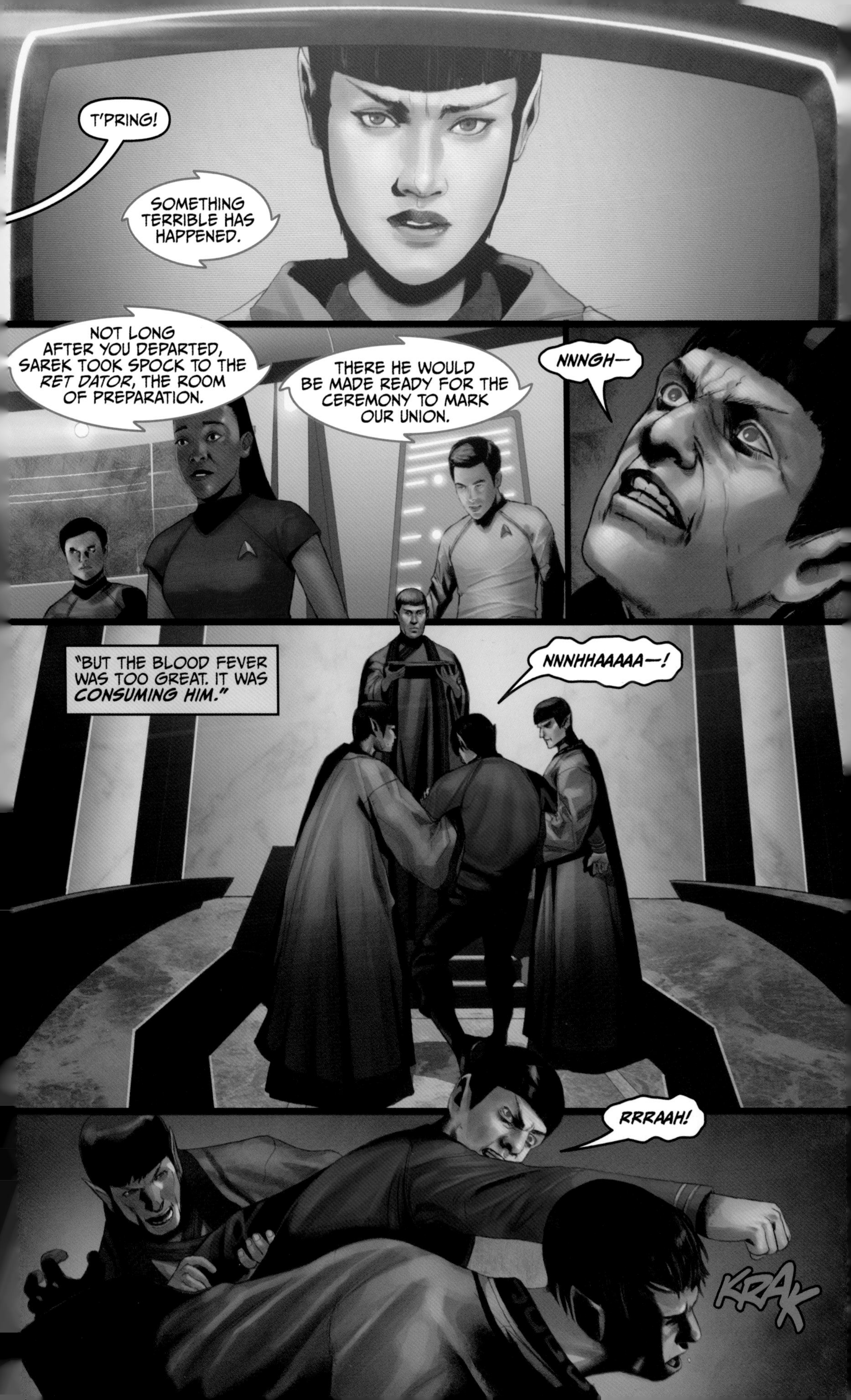
T'PRING!
SOMETHING TERRIBLE HAS HAPPENED.
NOT LONG AFTER YOU DEPARTED, SAREK TOOK SPOCK TO THE *RET DATOR*, THE ROOM OF PREPARATION.
THERE HE WOULD BE MADE READY FOR THE CEREMONY TO MARK OUR UNION.
NNNGH—
"BUT THE BLOOD FEVER WAS TOO GREAT. IT WAS *CONSUMING HIM.*"
NNNHHAAAAA—!
RRRAAH!
KRAK

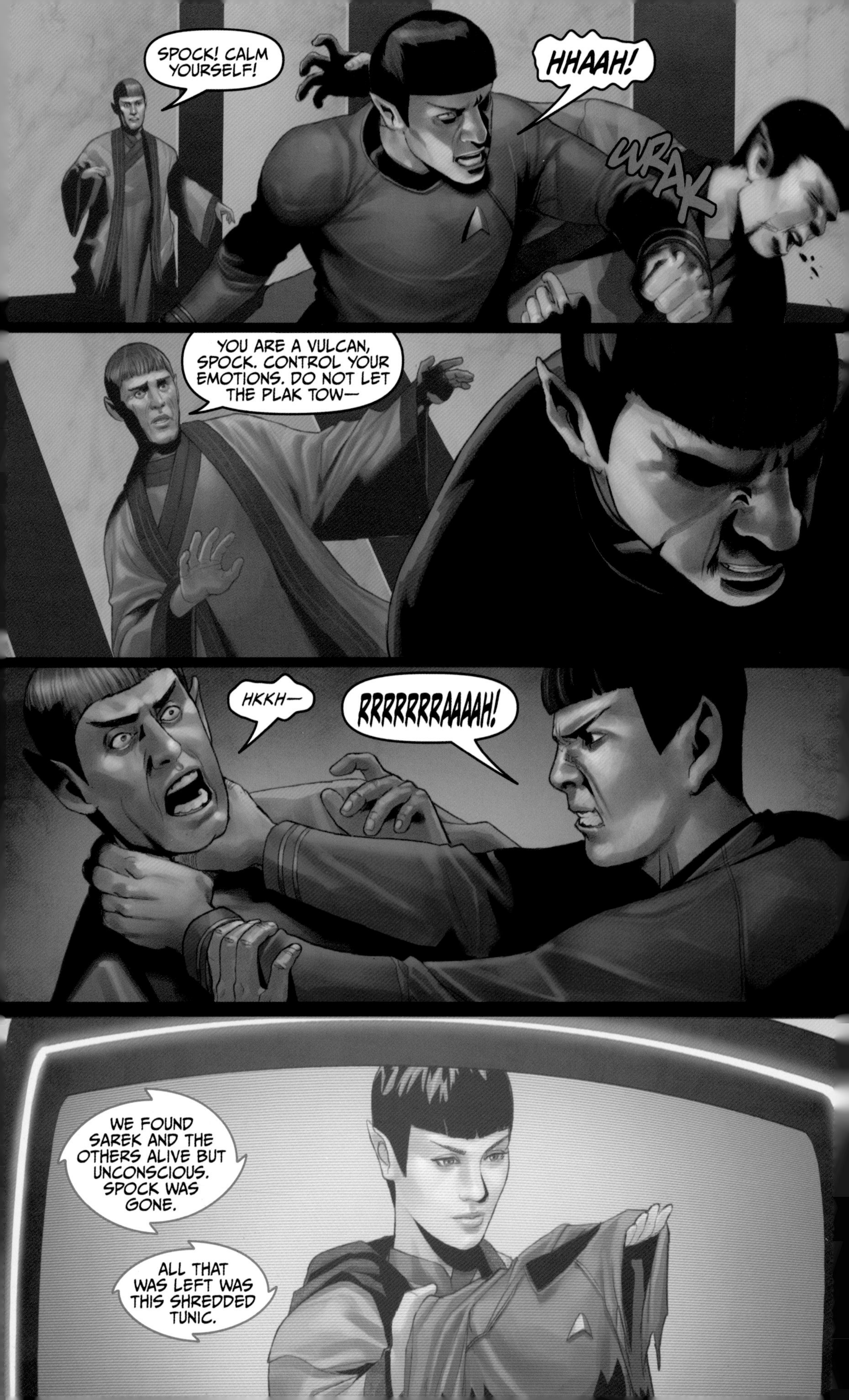
SPOCK! CALM YOURSELF!
HHAAH!
WRAK
YOU ARE A VULCAN, SPOCK. CONTROL YOUR EMOTIONS. DO NOT LET THE PLAK TOW—
HKKH—
RRRRRRRAAAAH!
WE FOUND SAREK AND THE OTHERS ALIVE BUT UNCONSCIOUS. SPOCK WAS GONE.
ALL THAT WAS LEFT WAS THIS SHREDDED TUNIC.

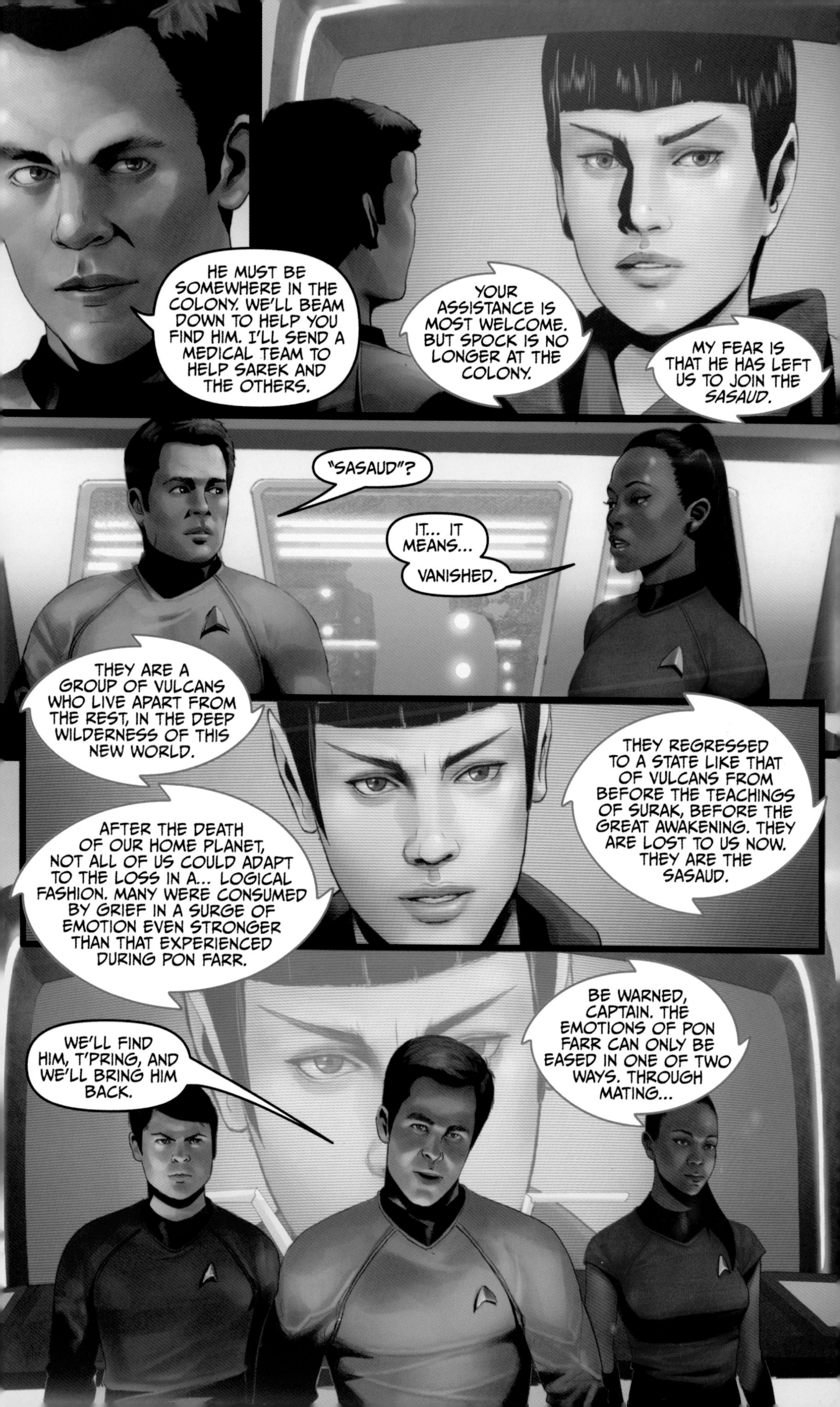
HE MUST BE SOMEWHERE IN THE COLONY. WE'LL BEAM DOWN TO HELP YOU FIND HIM. I'LL SEND A MEDICAL TEAM TO HELP SAREK AND THE OTHERS.
YOUR ASSISTANCE IS MOST WELCOME. BUT SPOCK IS NO LONGER AT THE COLONY.
MY FEAR IS THAT HE HAS LEFT US TO JOIN THE *SASAUD*.
"SASAUD"?
IT... IT MEANS...
VANISHED.
THEY ARE A GROUP OF VULCANS WHO LIVE APART FROM THE REST, IN THE DEEP WILDERNESS OF THIS NEW WORLD.
AFTER THE DEATH OF OUR HOME PLANET, NOT ALL OF US COULD ADAPT TO THE LOSS IN A... LOGICAL FASHION. MANY WERE CONSUMED BY GRIEF IN A SURGE OF EMOTION EVEN STRONGER THAN THAT EXPERIENCED DURING PON FARR.
THEY REGRESSED TO A STATE LIKE THAT OF VULCANS FROM BEFORE THE TEACHINGS OF SURAK, BEFORE THE GREAT AWAKENING. THEY ARE LOST TO US NOW. THEY ARE THE SASAUD.
WE'LL FIND HIM, T'PRING, AND WE'LL BRING HIM BACK.
BE WARNED, CAPTAIN. THE EMOTIONS OF PON FARR CAN ONLY BE EASED IN ONE OF TWO WAYS. THROUGH MATING...

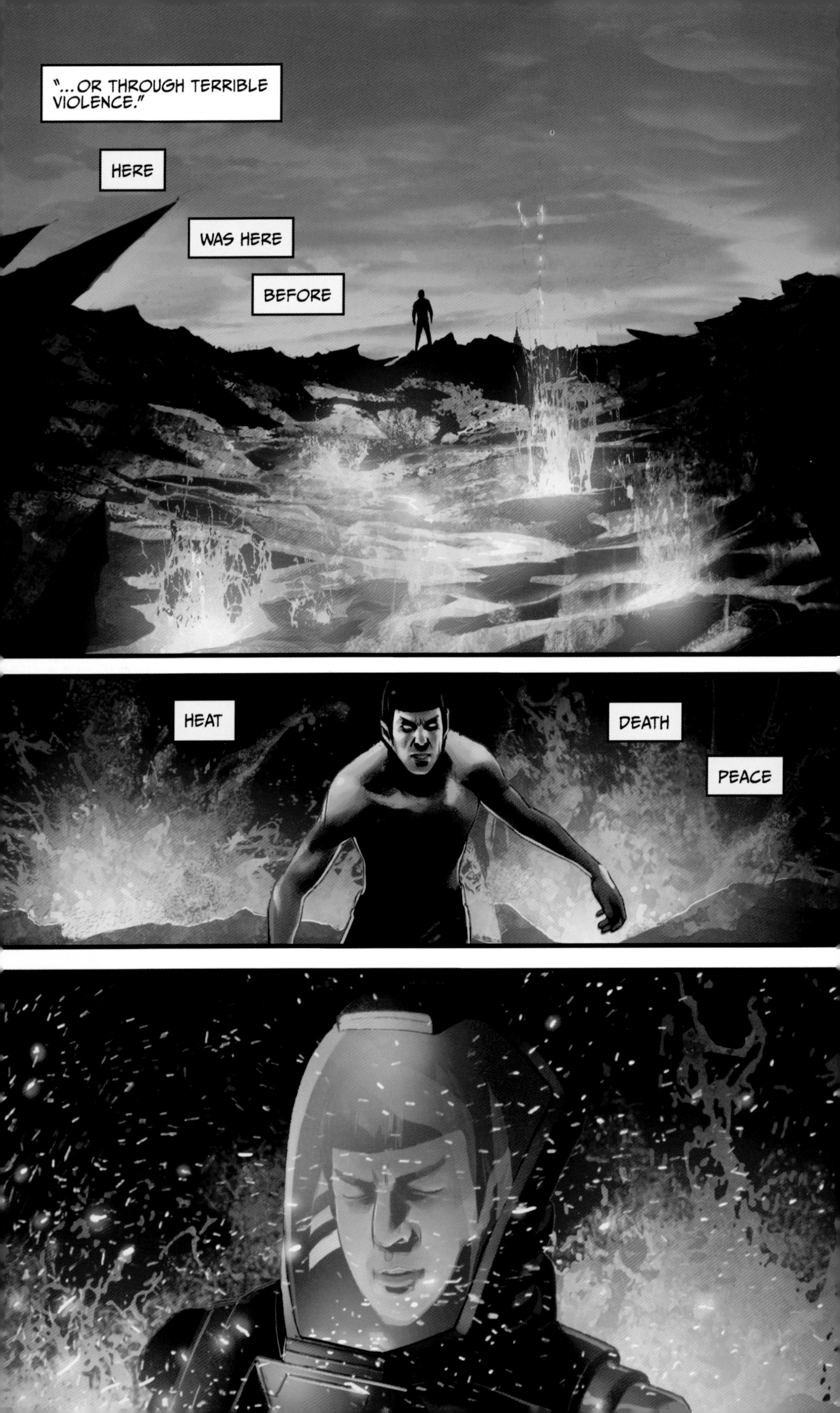
"...OR THROUGH TERRIBLE VIOLENCE."
HERE
WAS HERE
BEFORE
HEAT
DEATH
PEACE

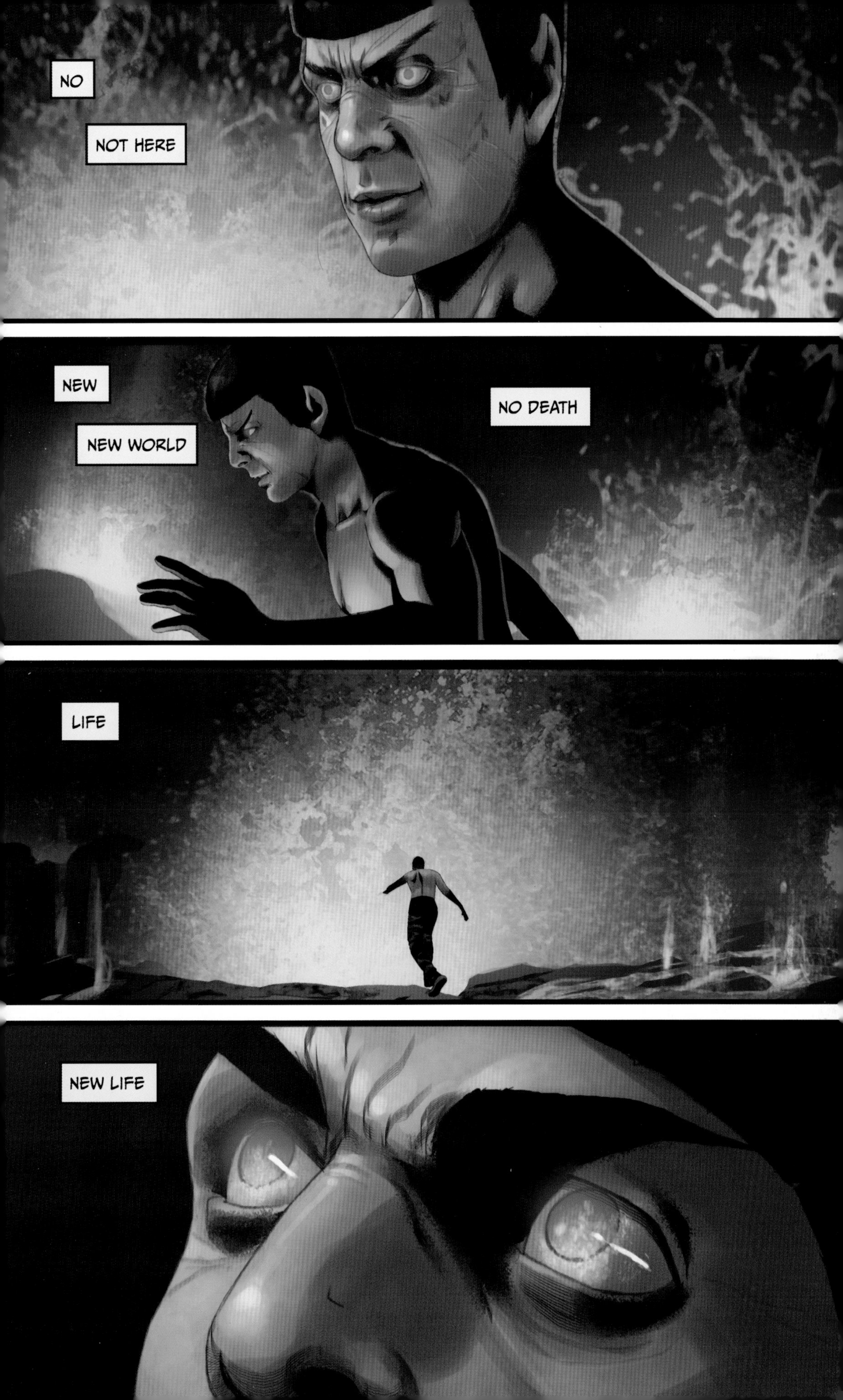
NO
NOT HERE
NEW
NEW WORLD
NO DEATH
LIFE
NEW LIFE

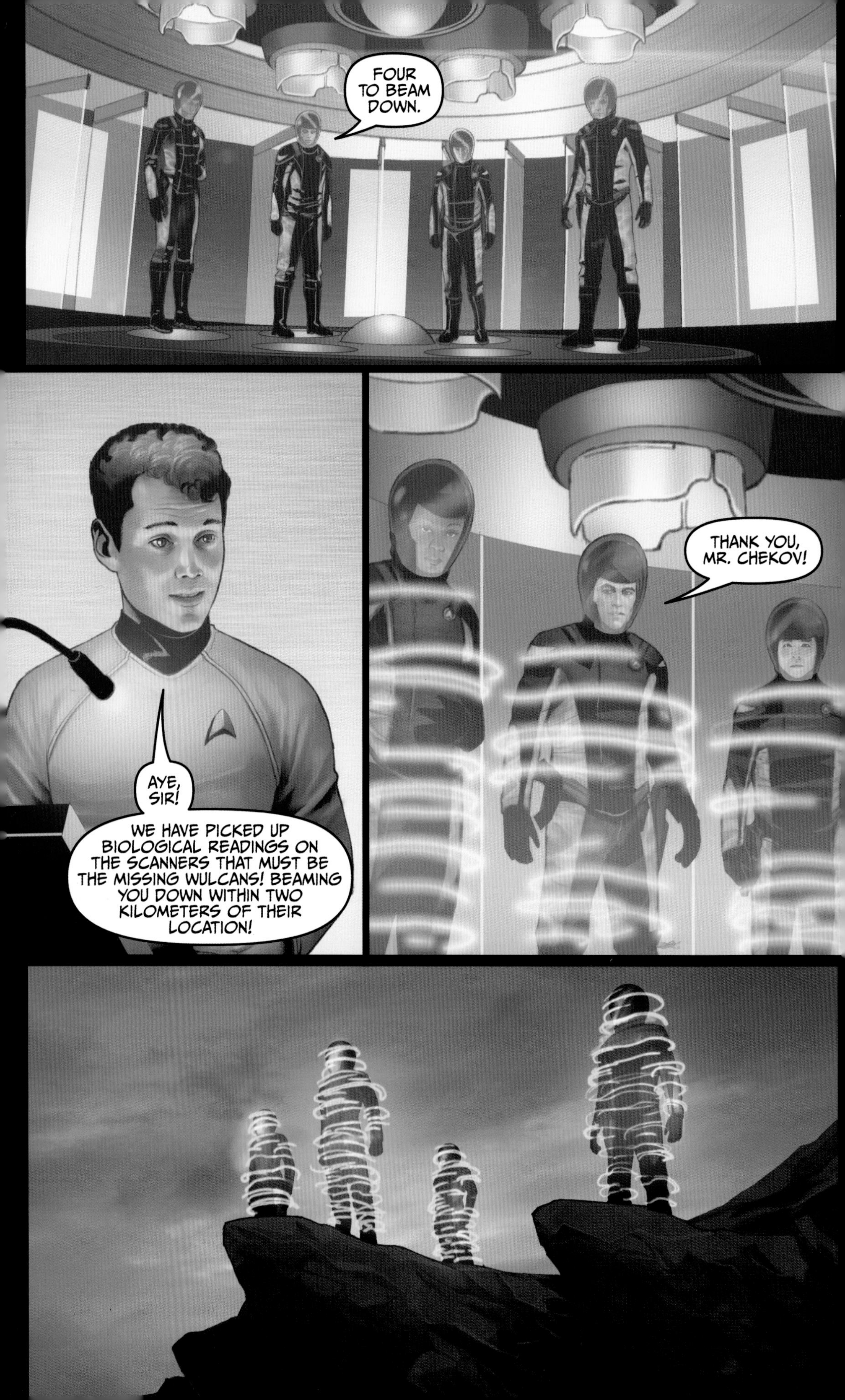
FOUR TO BEAM DOWN.
AYE, SIR!
WE HAVE PICKED UP BIOLOGICAL READINGS ON THE SCANNERS THAT MUST BE THE MISSING WULCANS! BEAMING YOU DOWN WITHIN TWO KILOMETERS OF THEIR LOCATION!
THANK YOU, MR. CHEKOV!

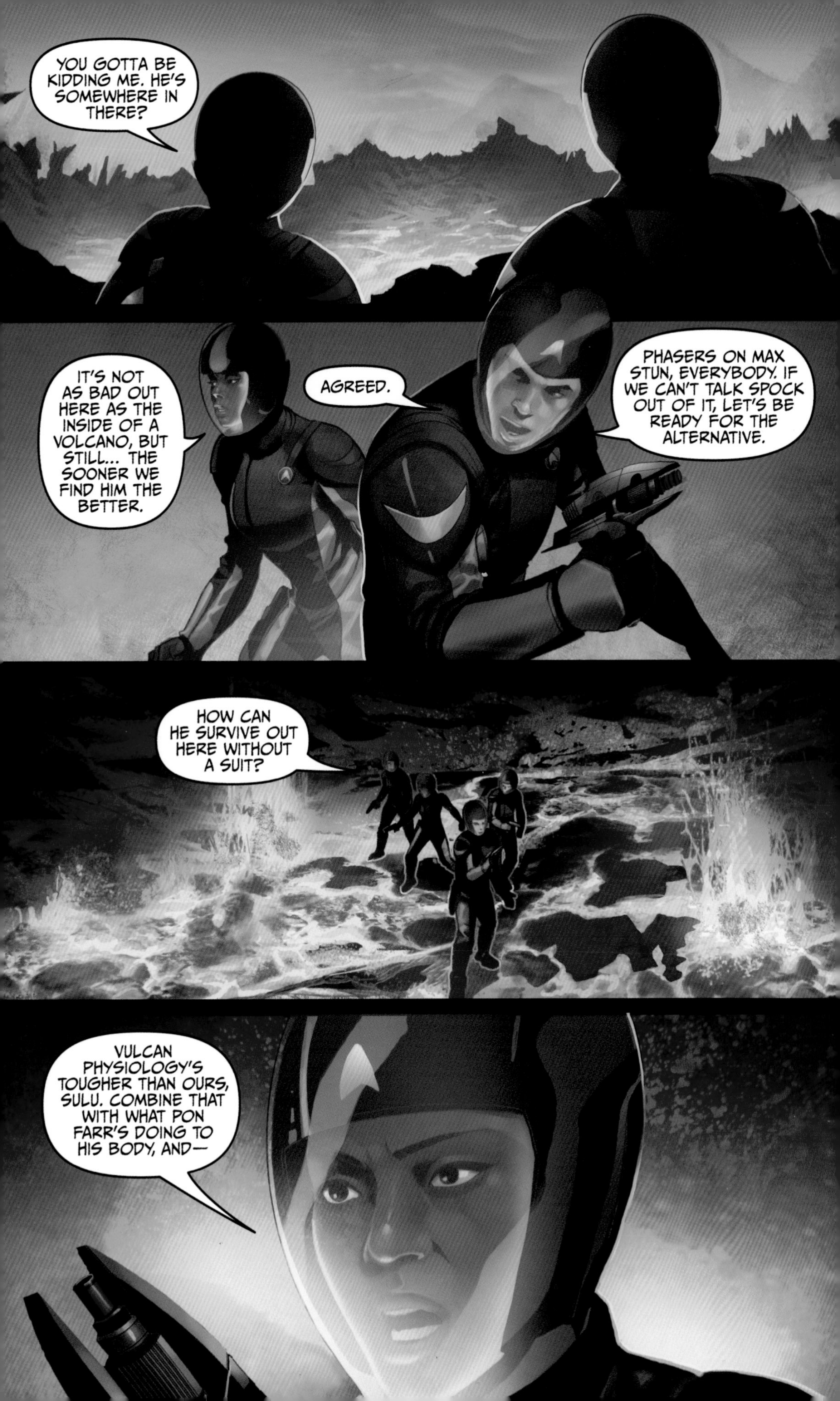

YOU GOTTA BE KIDDING ME. HE'S SOMEWHERE IN THERE?
IT'S NOT AS BAD OUT HERE AS THE INSIDE OF A VOLCANO, BUT STILL... THE SOONER WE FIND HIM THE BETTER.
AGREED.
PHASERS ON MAX STUN, EVERYBODY. IF WE CAN'T TALK SPOCK OUT OF IT, LET'S BE READY FOR THE ALTERNATIVE.
HOW CAN HE SURVIVE OUT HERE WITHOUT A SUIT?
VULCAN PHYSIOLOGY'S TOUGHER THAN OURS, SULU. COMBINE THAT WITH WHAT PON FARR'S DOING TO HIS BODY, AND—

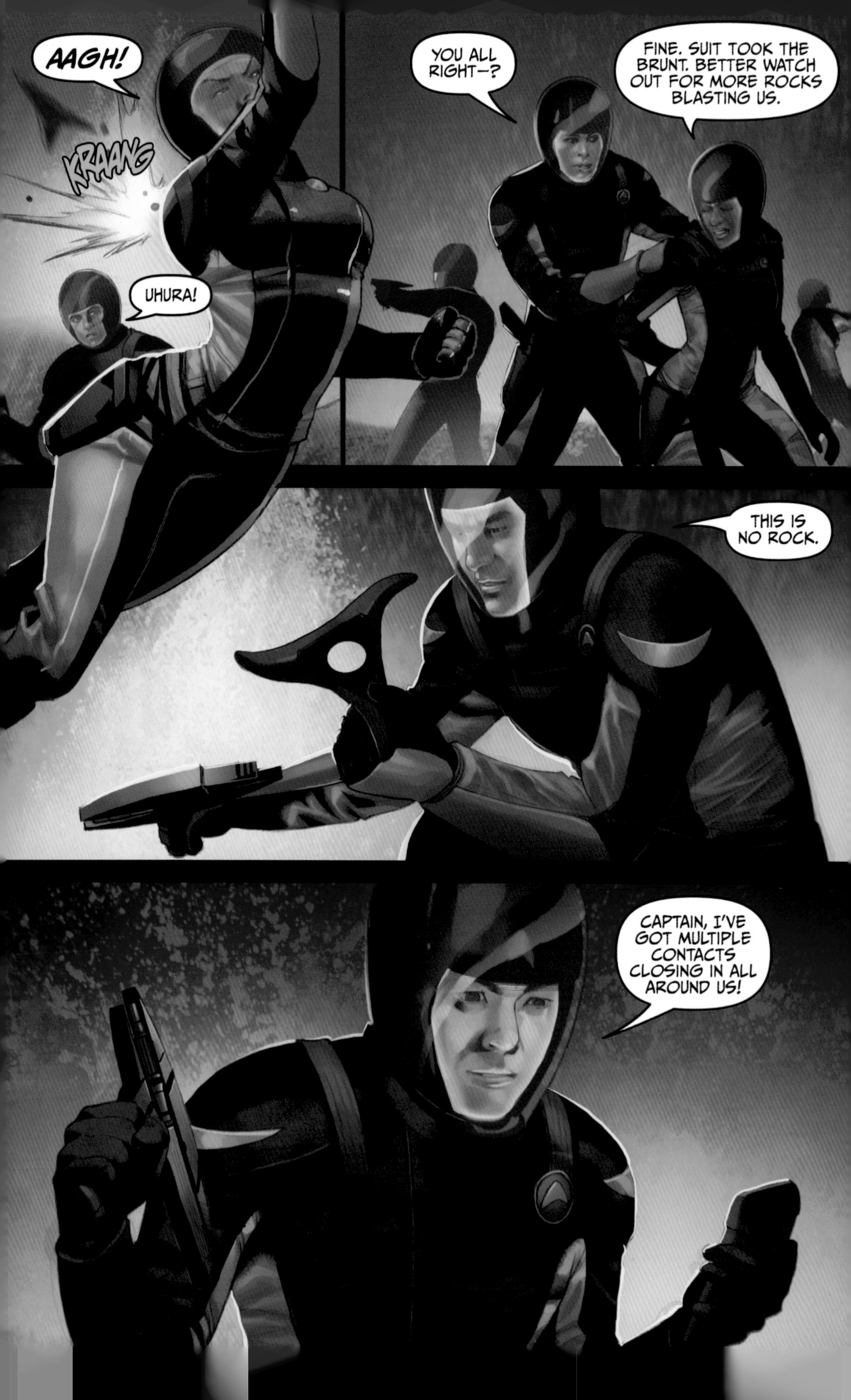
AAGH!
KRAANG
UHURA!
YOU ALL RIGHT—?
FINE. SUIT TOOK THE BRUNT. BETTER WATCH OUT FOR MORE ROCKS BLASTING US.
THIS IS NO ROCK.
CAPTAIN, I'VE GOT MULTIPLE CONTACTS CLOSING IN ALL AROUND US!

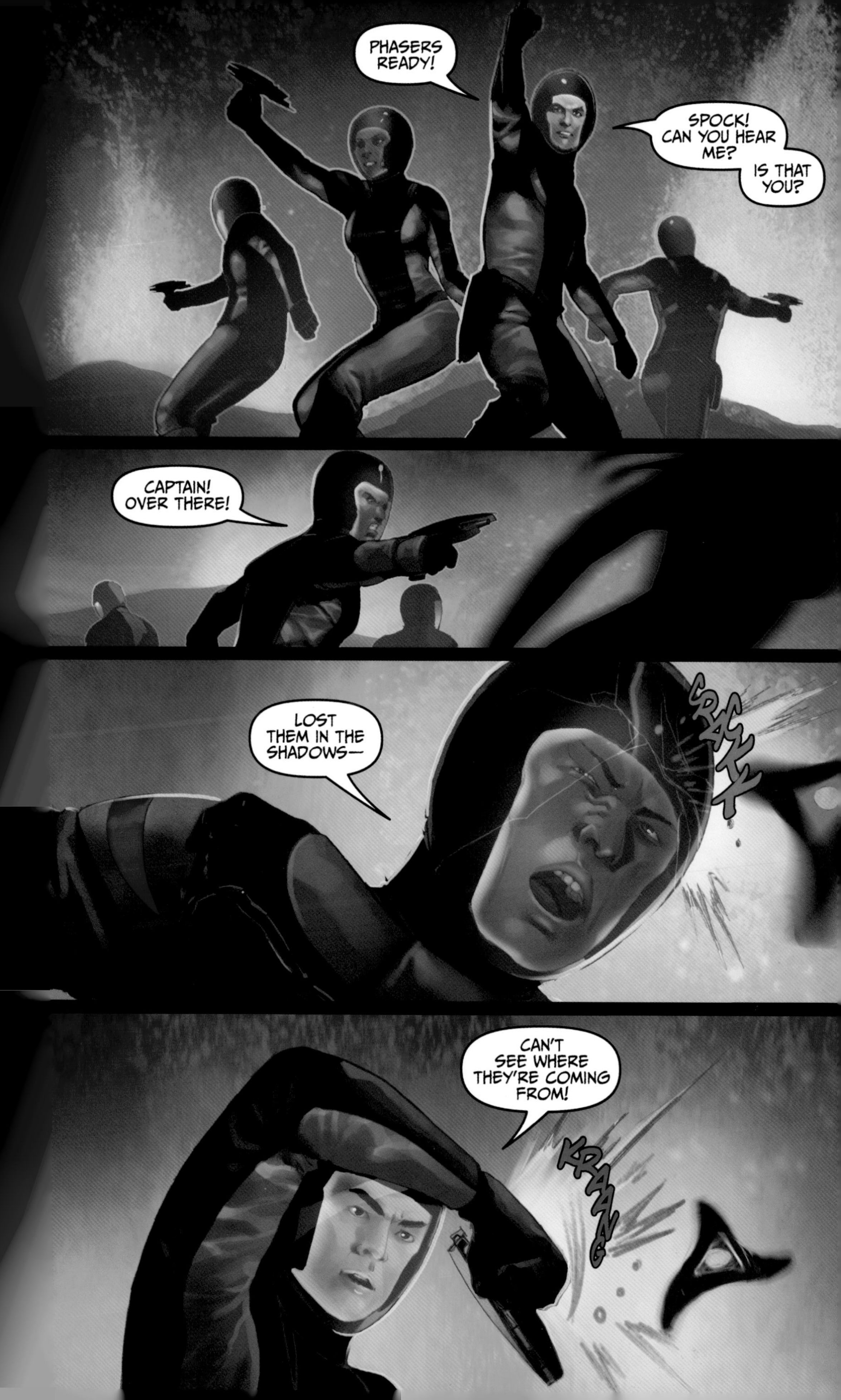
PHASERS READY!
SPOCK! CAN YOU HEAR ME?
IS THAT YOU?
CAPTAIN! OVER THERE!
LOST THEM IN THE SHADOWS—
CRACKK
CAN'T SEE WHERE THEY'RE COMING FROM!
KRAAANG

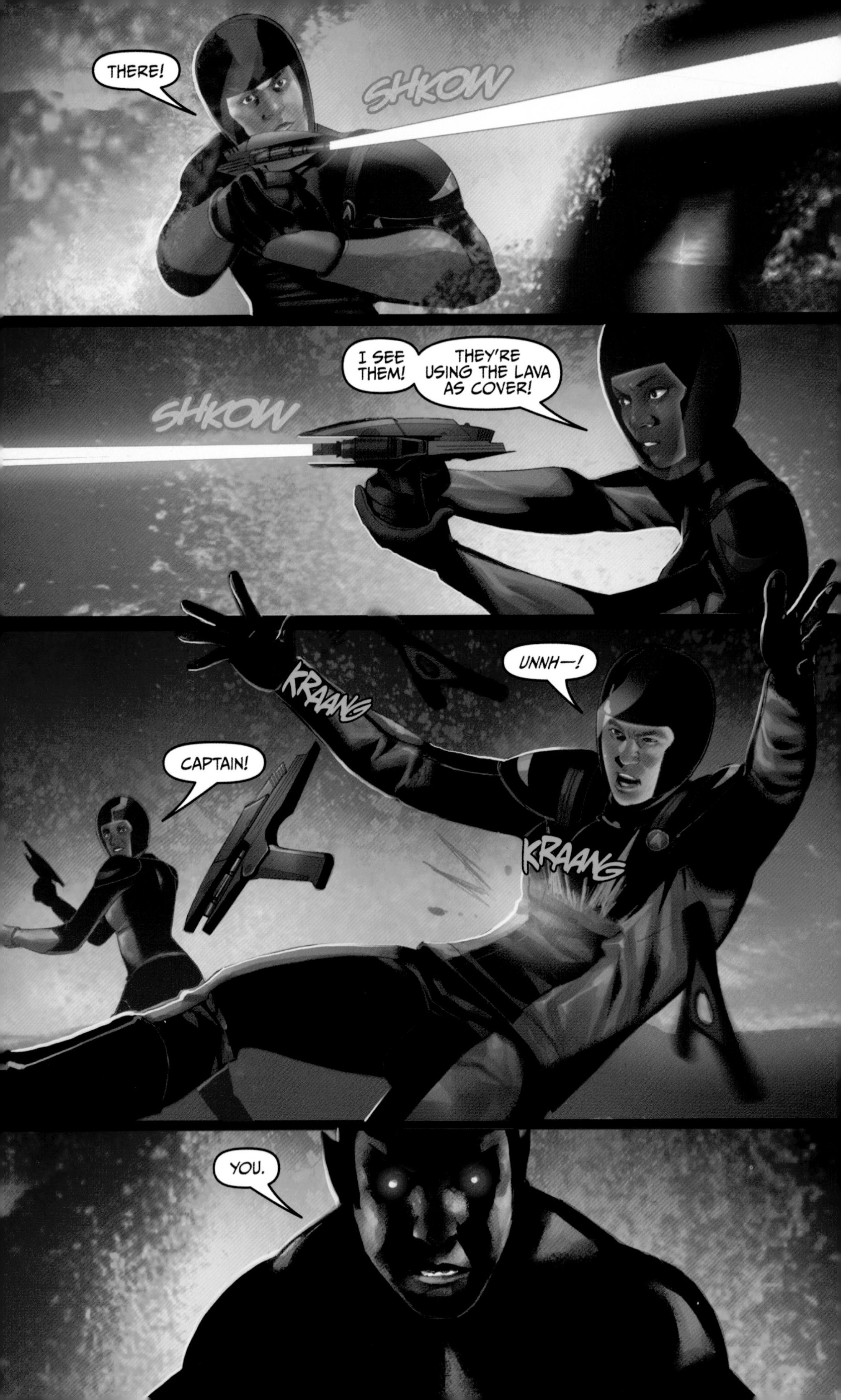

THERE!
SHKOW
I SEE THEM!
THEY'RE USING THE LAVA AS COVER!
SHKOW
UNNH—!
KRAANG
CAPTAIN!
KRAANG
YOU.

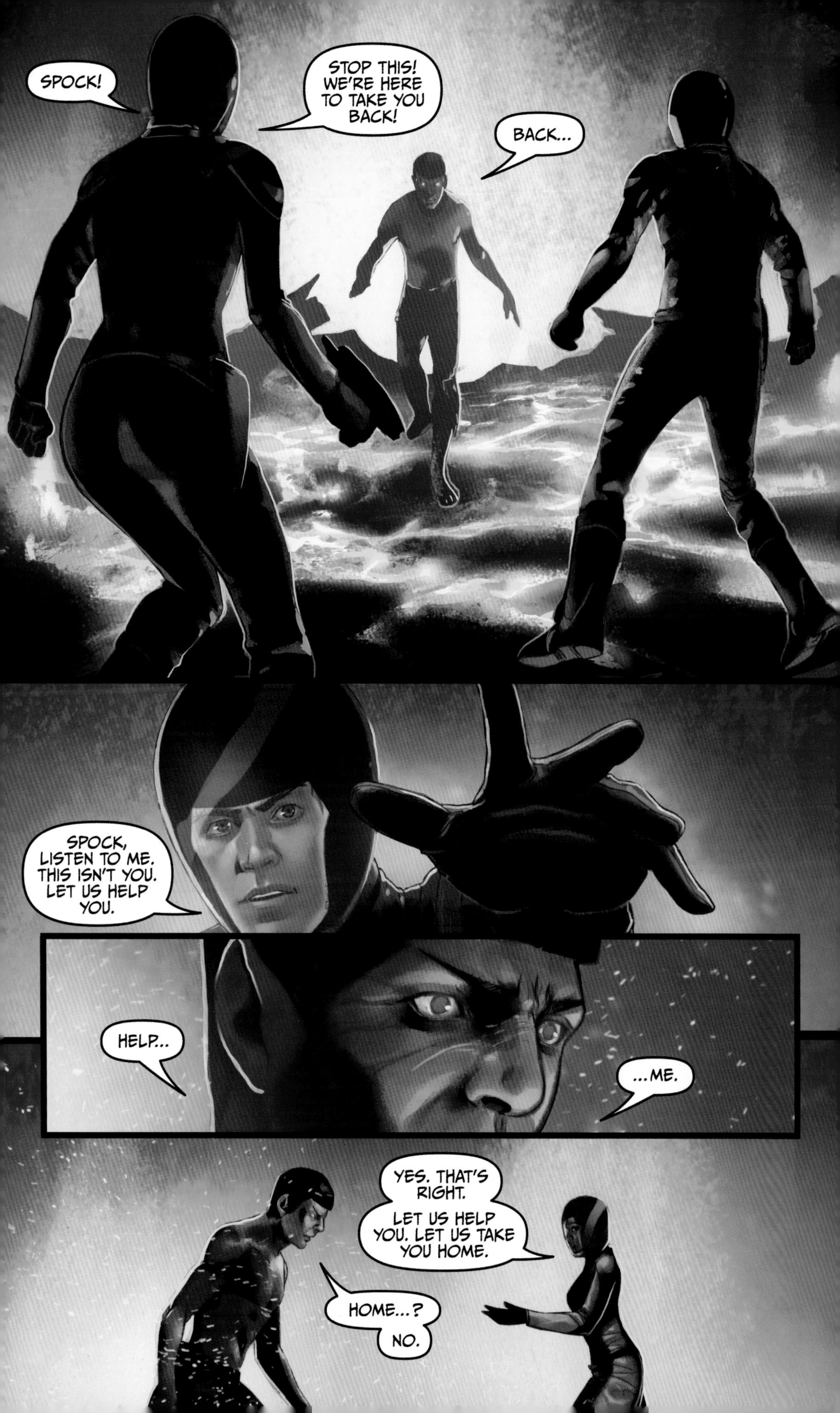
SPOCK!
STOP THIS! WE'RE HERE TO TAKE YOU BACK!
BACK...
SPOCK, LISTEN TO ME. THIS ISN'T YOU. LET US HELP YOU.
HELP...
...ME.
YES. THAT'S RIGHT.
LET US HELP YOU. LET US TAKE YOU HOME.
HOME...?
NO.

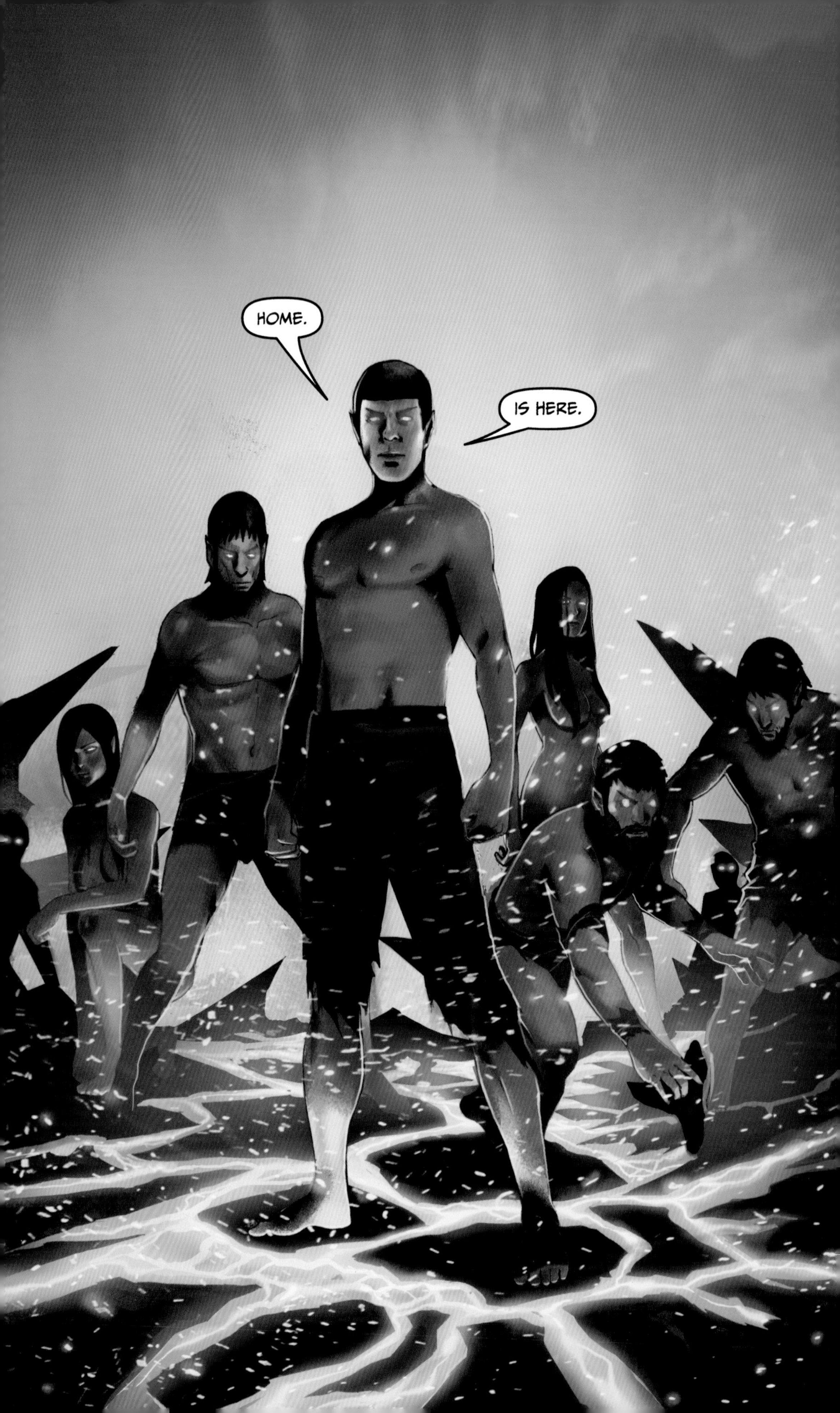
HOME.
IS HERE.

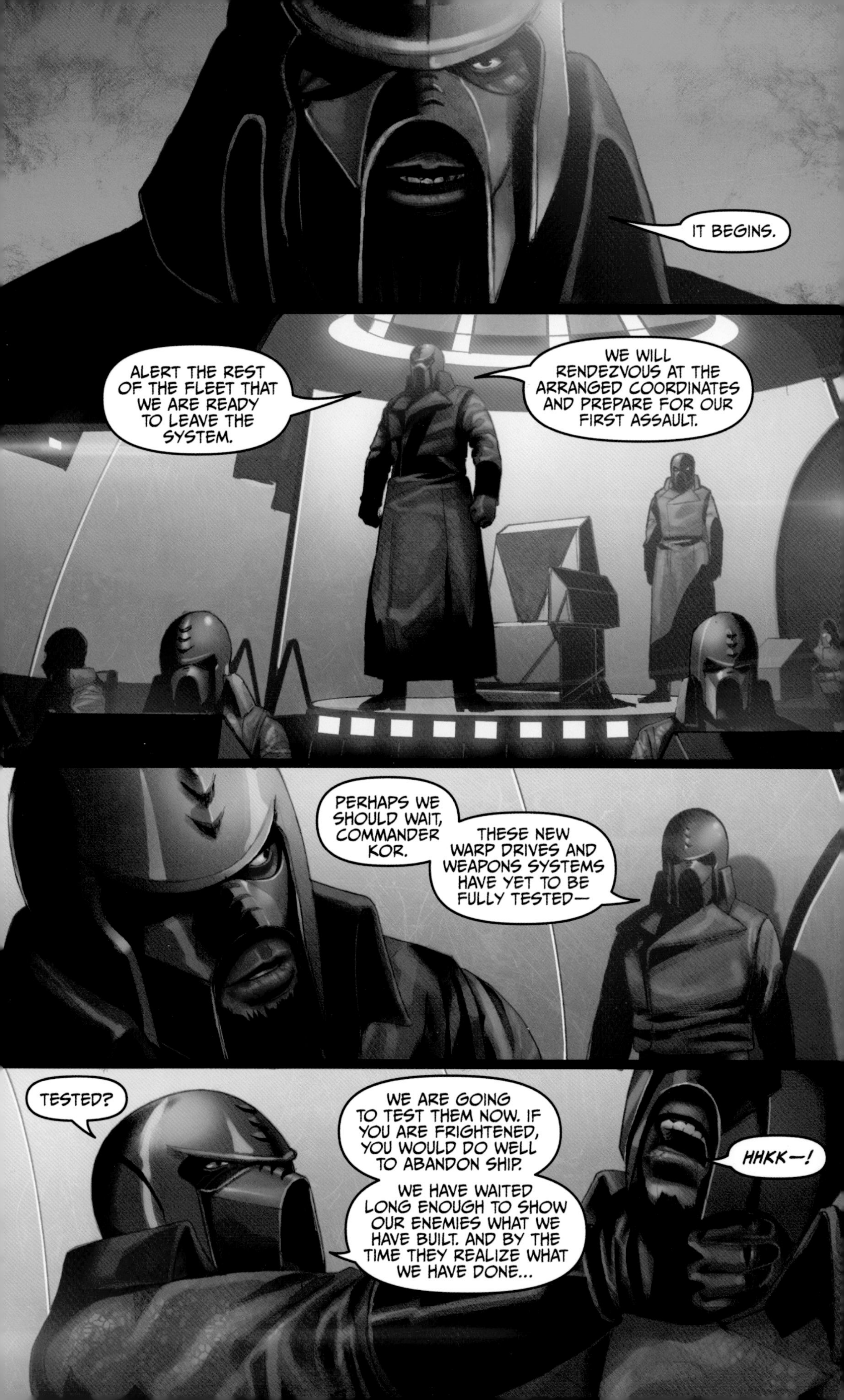
IT BEGINS.
ALERT THE REST OF THE FLEET THAT WE ARE READY TO LEAVE THE SYSTEM.
WE WILL RENDEZVOUS AT THE ARRANGED COORDINATES AND PREPARE FOR OUR FIRST ASSAULT.
PERHAPS WE SHOULD WAIT, COMMANDER KOR.
THESE NEW WARP DRIVES AND WEAPONS SYSTEMS HAVE YET TO BE FULLY TESTED—
TESTED?
WE ARE GOING TO TEST THEM NOW. IF YOU ARE FRIGHTENED, YOU WOULD DO WELL TO ABANDON SHIP.
HHKK—!
WE HAVE WAITED LONG ENOUGH TO SHOW OUR ENEMIES WHAT WE HAVE BUILT. AND BY THE TIME THEY REALIZE WHAT WE HAVE DONE...

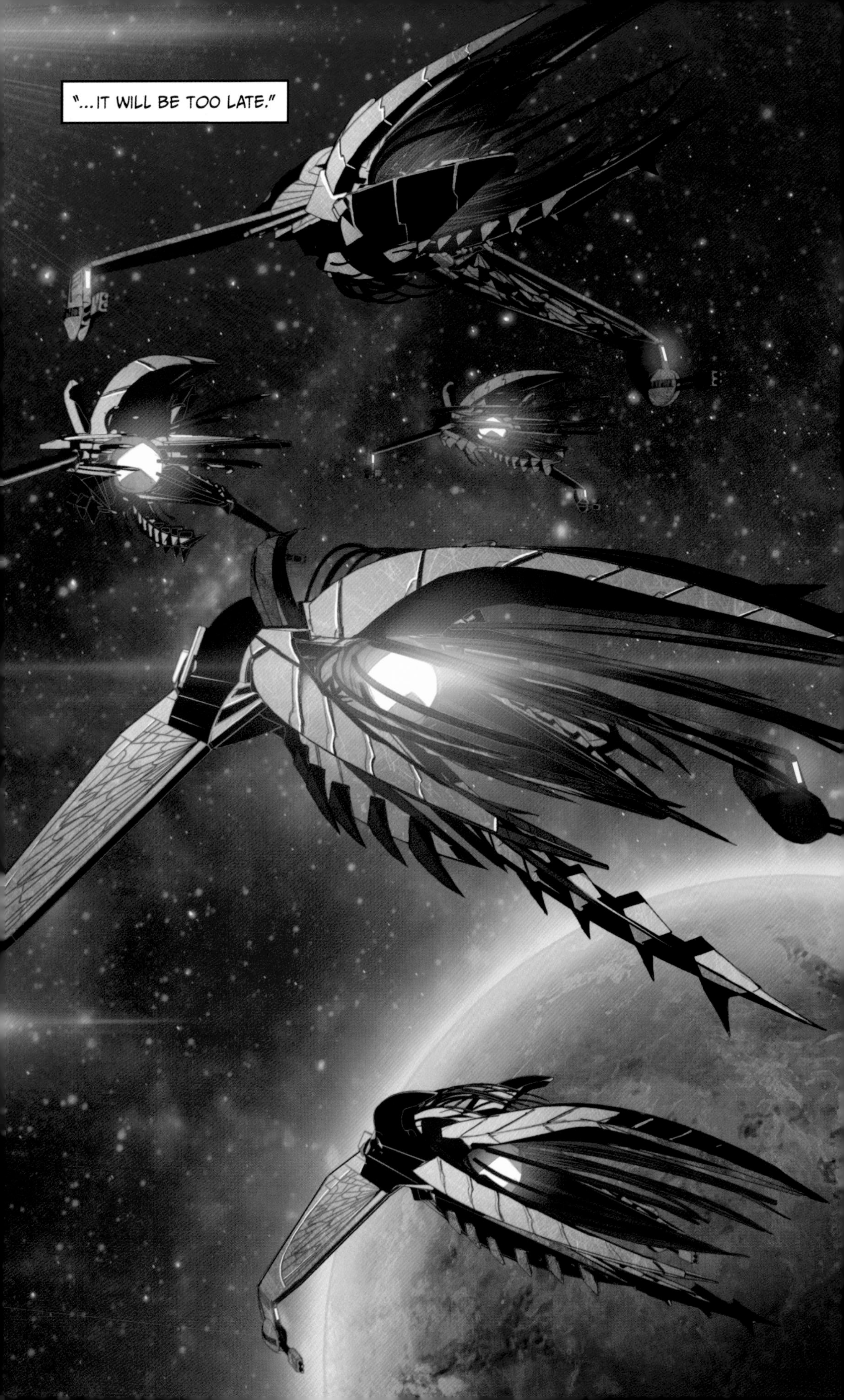
"...IT WILL BE TOO LATE."

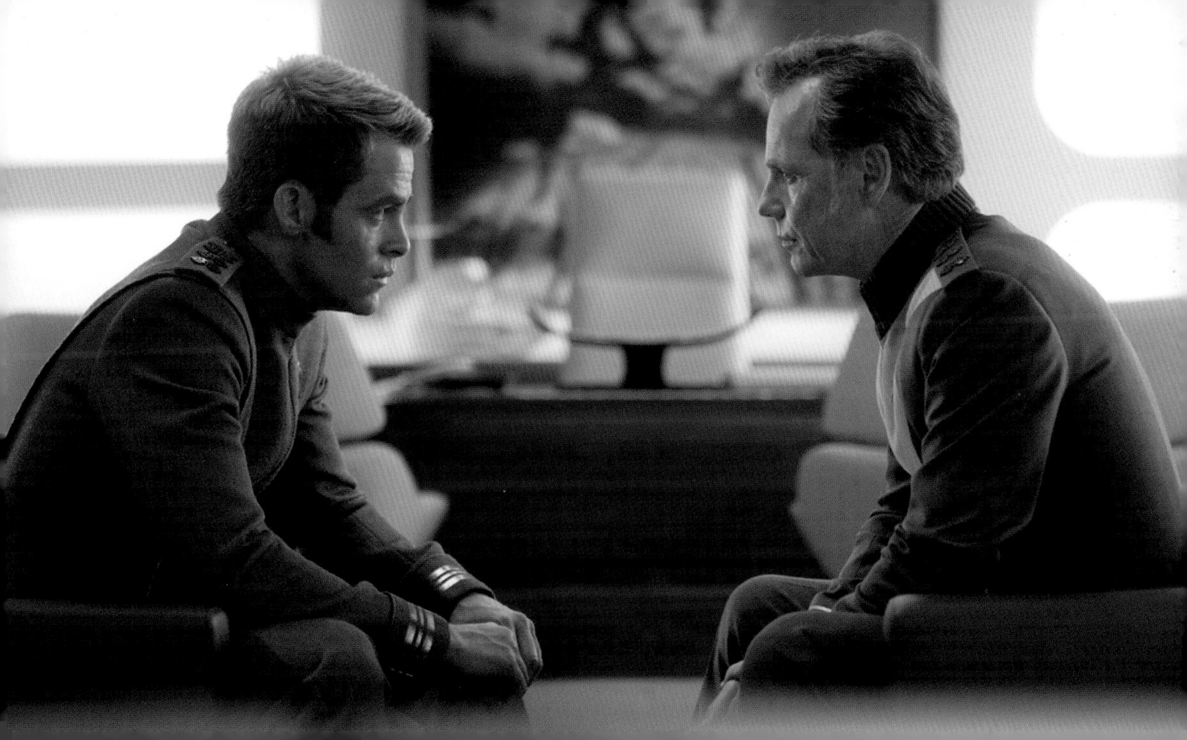

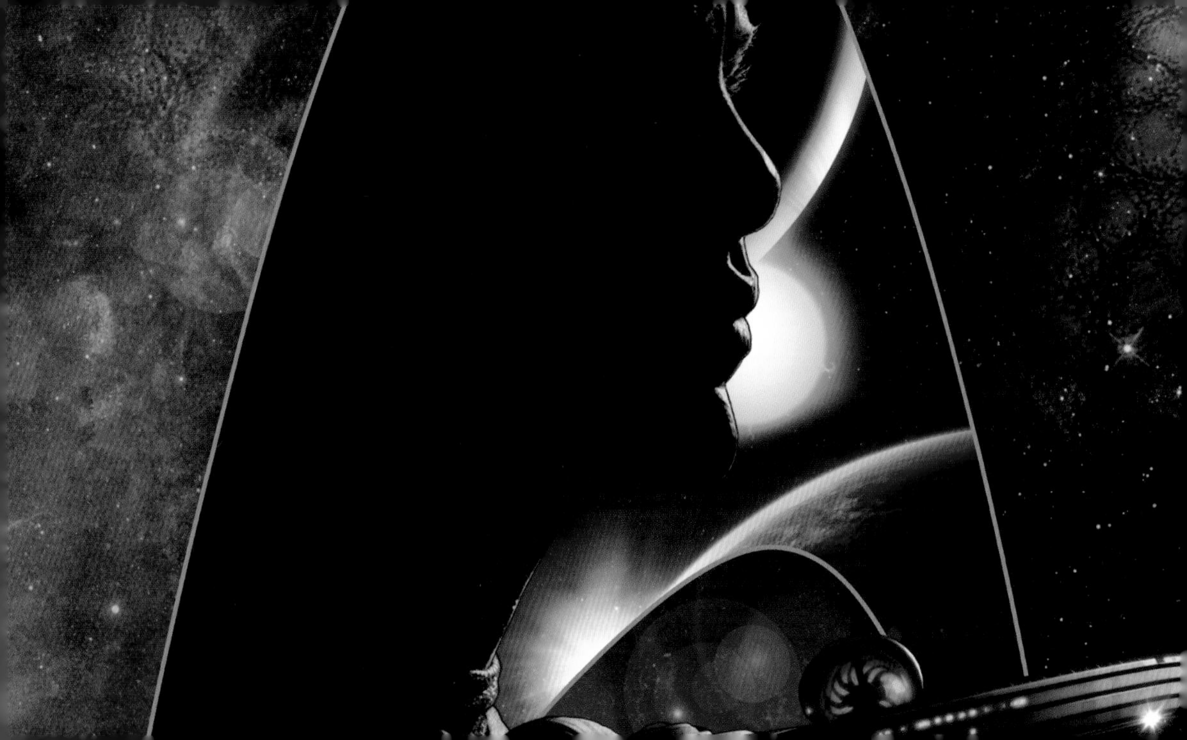

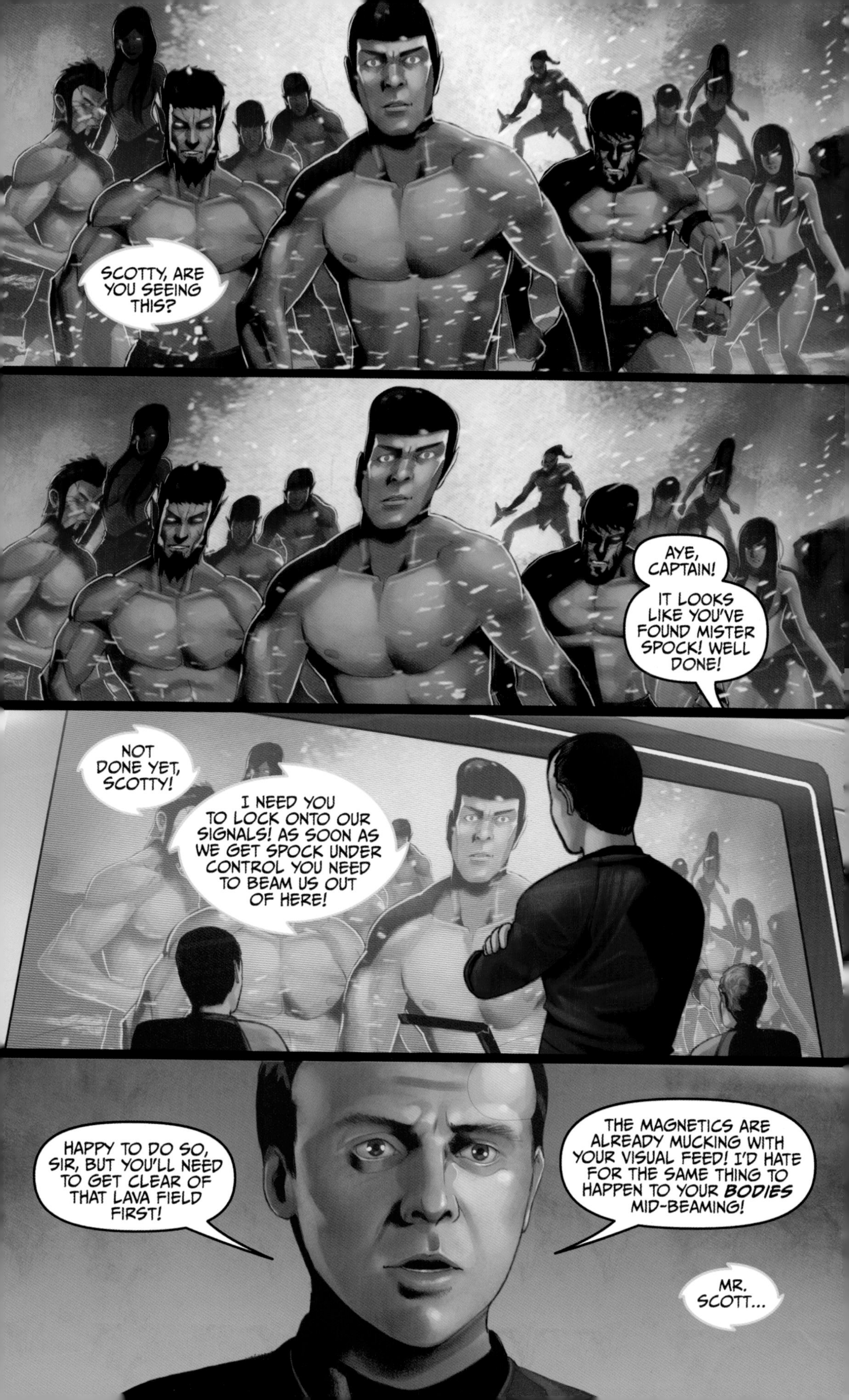
SCOTTY, ARE YOU SEEING THIS?
AYE, CAPTAIN!
IT LOOKS LIKE YOU'VE FOUND MISTER SPOCK! WELL DONE!
NOT DONE YET, SCOTTY!
I NEED YOU TO LOCK ONTO OUR SIGNALS! AS SOON AS WE GET SPOCK UNDER CONTROL YOU NEED TO BEAM US OUT OF HERE!
HAPPY TO DO SO, SIR, BUT YOU'LL NEED TO GET CLEAR OF THAT LAVA FIELD FIRST!
THE MAGNETICS ARE ALREADY MUCKING WITH YOUR VISUAL FEED! I'D HATE FOR THE SAME THING TO HAPPEN TO YOUR *BODIES* MID-BEAMING!
MR. SCOTT...

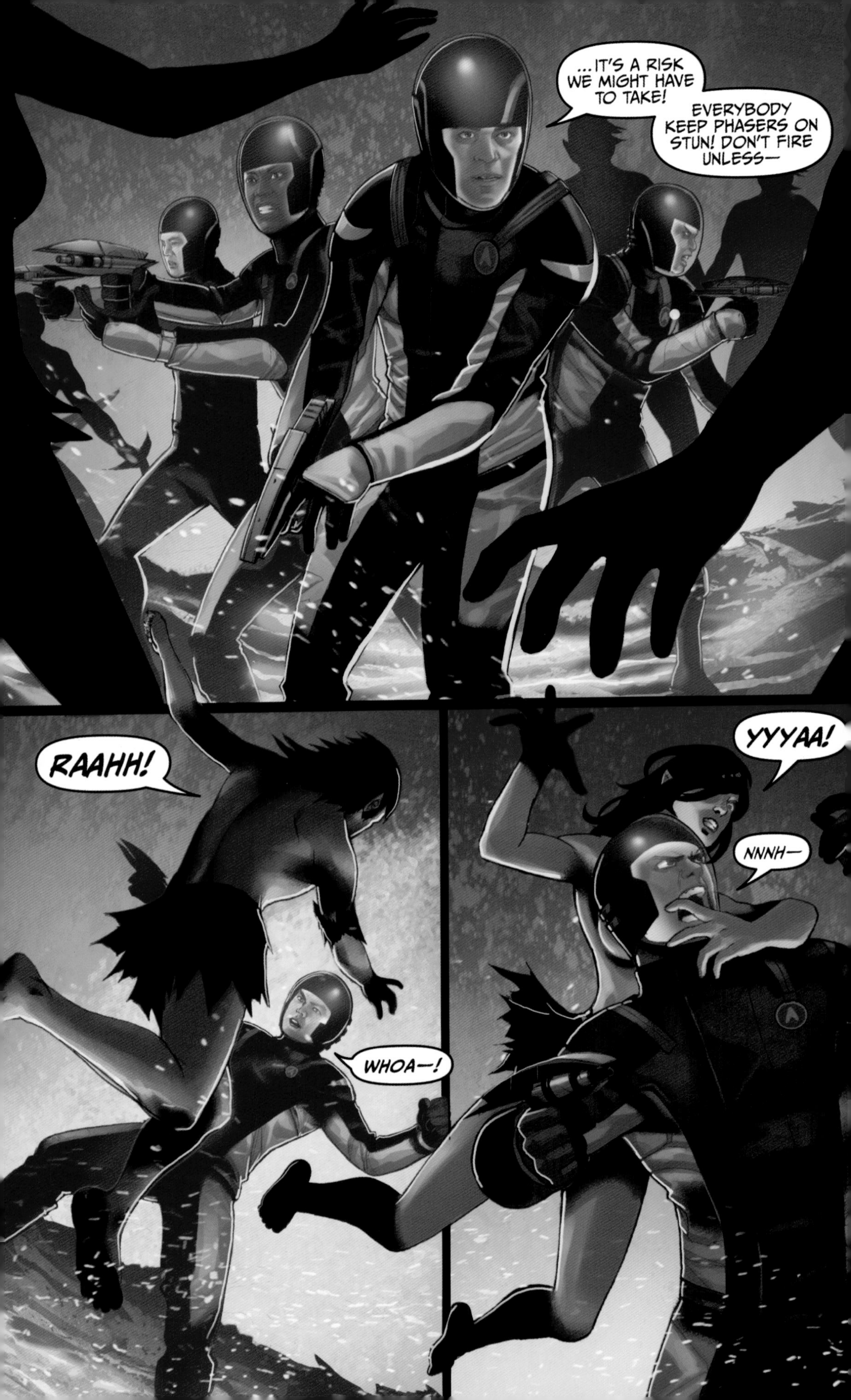
...IT'S A RISK WE MIGHT HAVE TO TAKE!
EVERYBODY KEEP PHASERS ON STUN! DON'T FIRE UNLESS—
RAAHH!
WHOA—!
YYYAA!
NNNH—

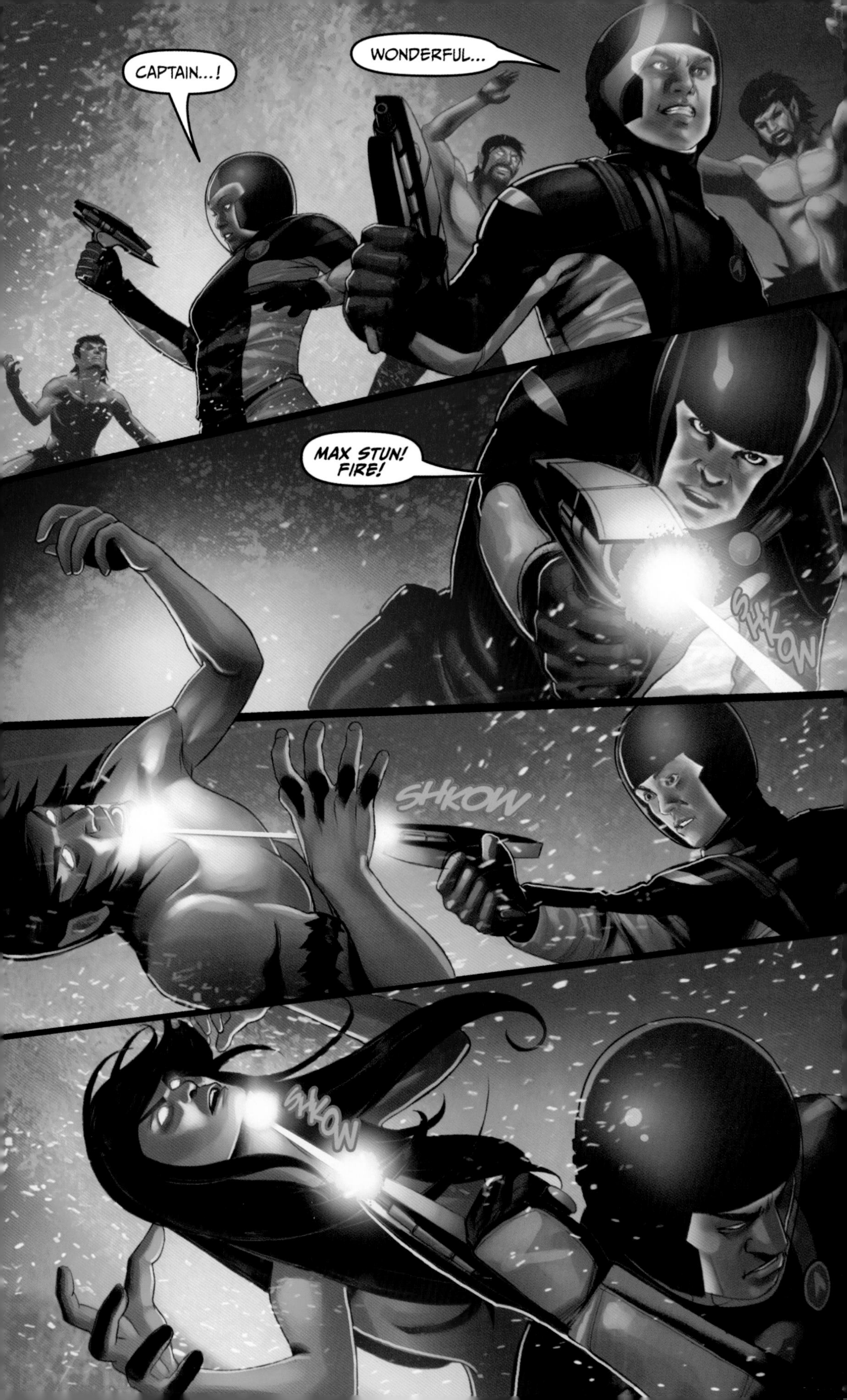
CAPTAIN...!
WONDERFUL...
MAX STUN! FIRE!
SHKOW
SHKOW
SHKOW

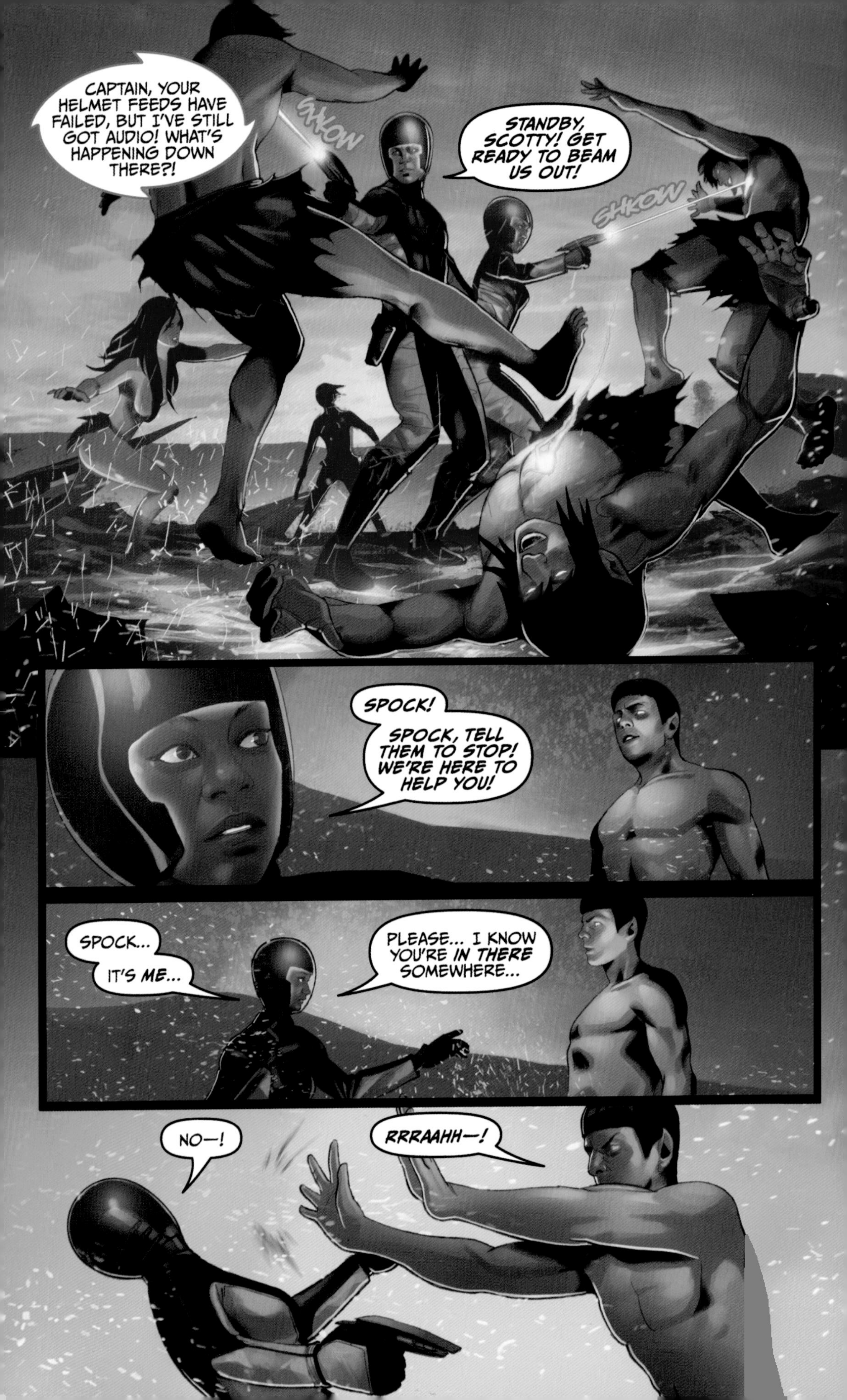
CAPTAIN, YOUR HELMET FEEDS HAVE FAILED, BUT I'VE STILL GOT AUDIO! WHAT'S HAPPENING DOWN THERE?!
SHKOW
STANDBY, SCOTTY! GET READY TO BEAM US OUT!
SHKOW
SPOCK!
SPOCK, TELL THEM TO STOP! WE'RE HERE TO HELP YOU!
SPOCK...
IT'S ME...
PLEASE... I KNOW YOU'RE IN THERE SOMEWHERE...
NO—!
RRRAAHH—!

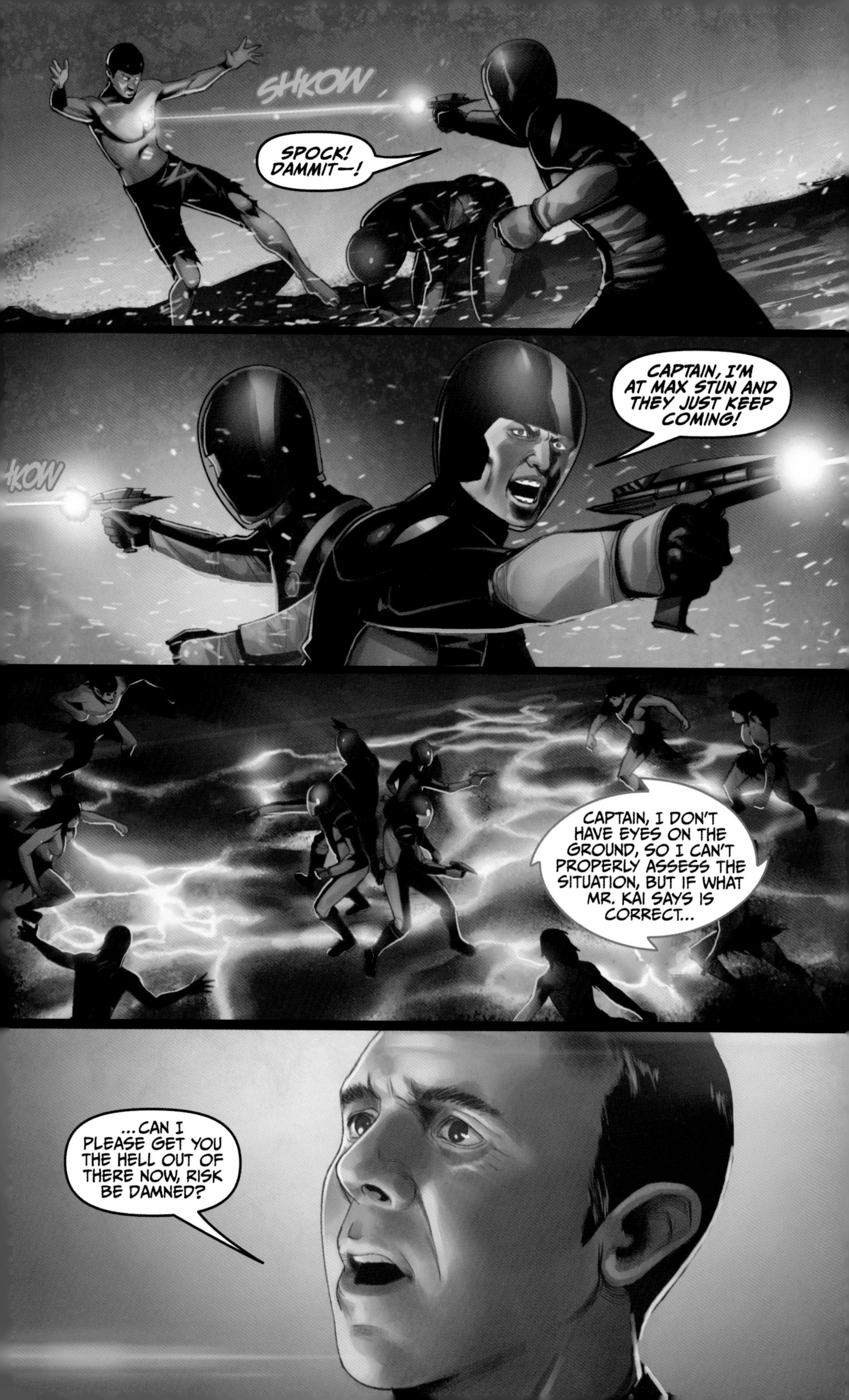
SHKOW
SPOCK! DAMMIT—!
CAPTAIN, I'M AT MAX STUN AND THEY JUST KEEP COMING!
KOW
CAPTAIN, I DON'T HAVE EYES ON THE GROUND, SO I CAN'T PROPERLY ASSESS THE SITUATION, BUT IF WHAT MR. KAI SAYS IS CORRECT...
...CAN I PLEASE GET YOU THE HELL OUT OF THERE NOW, RISK BE DAMNED?

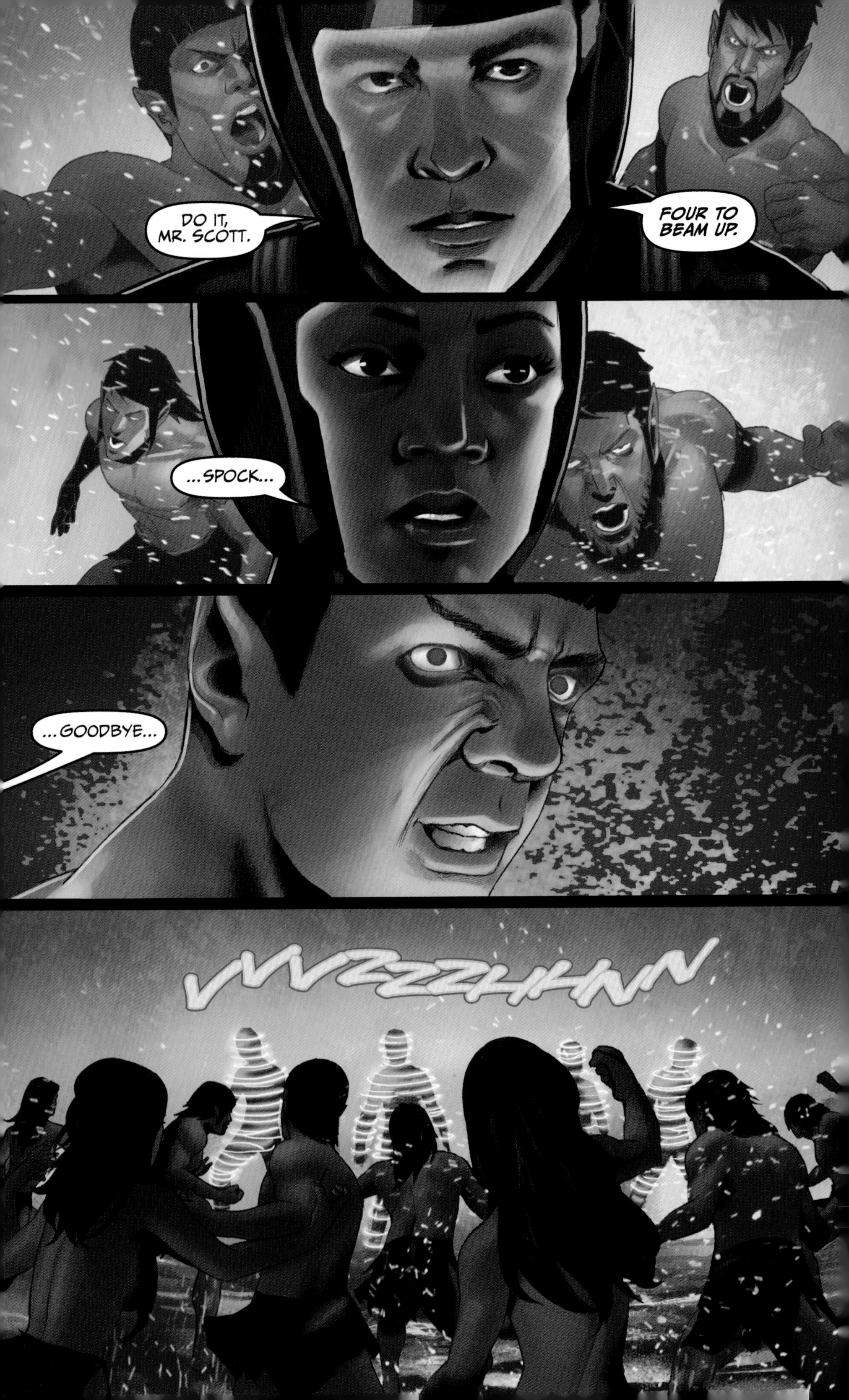
DO IT, MR. SCOTT.
FOUR TO BEAM UP.
...SPOCK...
...GOODBYE...
VVVZZZHHNN

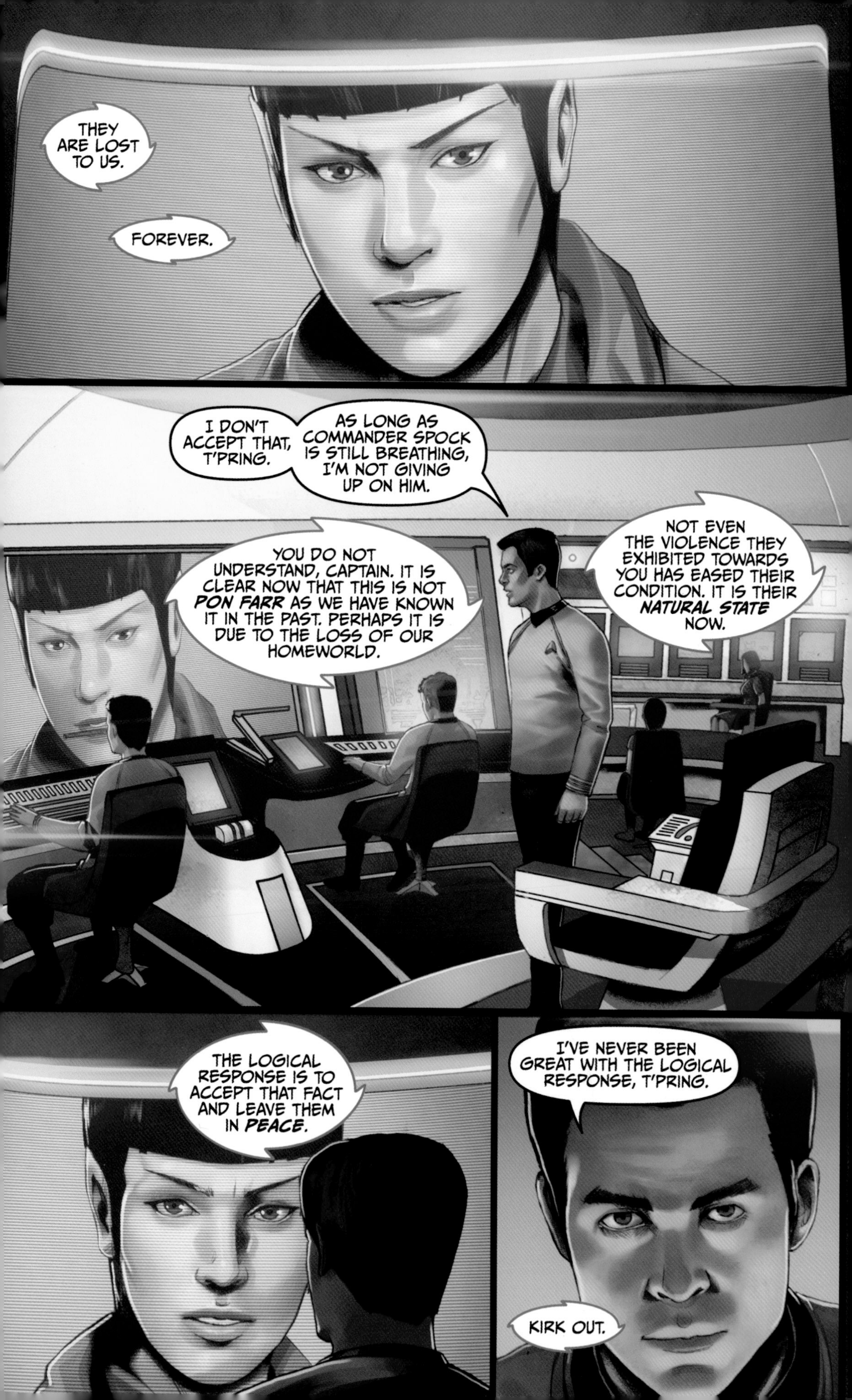
THEY ARE LOST TO US.
FOREVER.
I DON'T ACCEPT THAT, T'PRING.
AS LONG AS COMMANDER SPOCK IS STILL BREATHING, I'M NOT GIVING UP ON HIM.
YOU DO NOT UNDERSTAND, CAPTAIN. IT IS CLEAR NOW THAT THIS IS NOT PON FARR AS WE HAVE KNOWN IT IN THE PAST. PERHAPS IT IS DUE TO THE LOSS OF OUR HOMEWORLD.
NOT EVEN THE VIOLENCE THEY EXHIBITED TOWARDS YOU HAS EASED THEIR CONDITION. IT IS THEIR NATURAL STATE NOW.
THE LOGICAL RESPONSE IS TO ACCEPT THAT FACT AND LEAVE THEM IN PEACE.
I'VE NEVER BEEN GREAT WITH THE LOGICAL RESPONSE, T'PRING.
KIRK OUT.

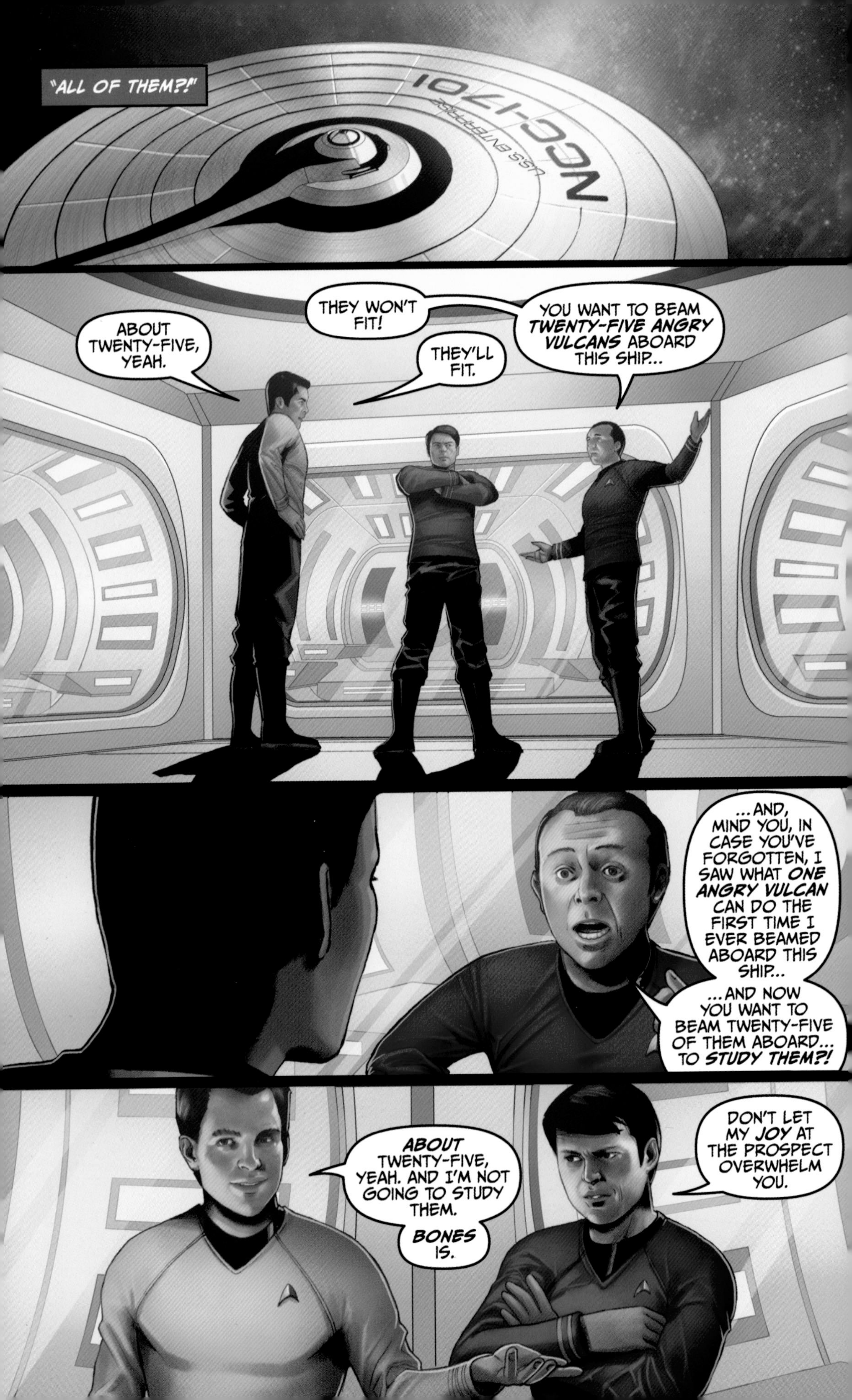
"ALL OF THEM?!"
NCC-1701
U.S.S. ENTERPRISE
ABOUT TWENTY-FIVE, YEAH.
THEY WON'T FIT!
THEY'LL FIT.
YOU WANT TO BEAM *TWENTY-FIVE ANGRY VULCANS* ABOARD THIS SHIP...
...AND, MIND YOU, IN CASE YOU'VE FORGOTTEN, I SAW WHAT *ONE ANGRY VULCAN* CAN DO THE FIRST TIME I EVER BEAMED ABOARD THIS SHIP...
...AND NOW YOU WANT TO BEAM TWENTY-FIVE OF THEM ABOARD... TO *STUDY THEM?!*
ABOUT TWENTY-FIVE, YEAH. AND I'M NOT GOING TO STUDY THEM.
BONES IS.
DON'T LET MY *JOY* AT THE PROSPECT OVERWHELM YOU.

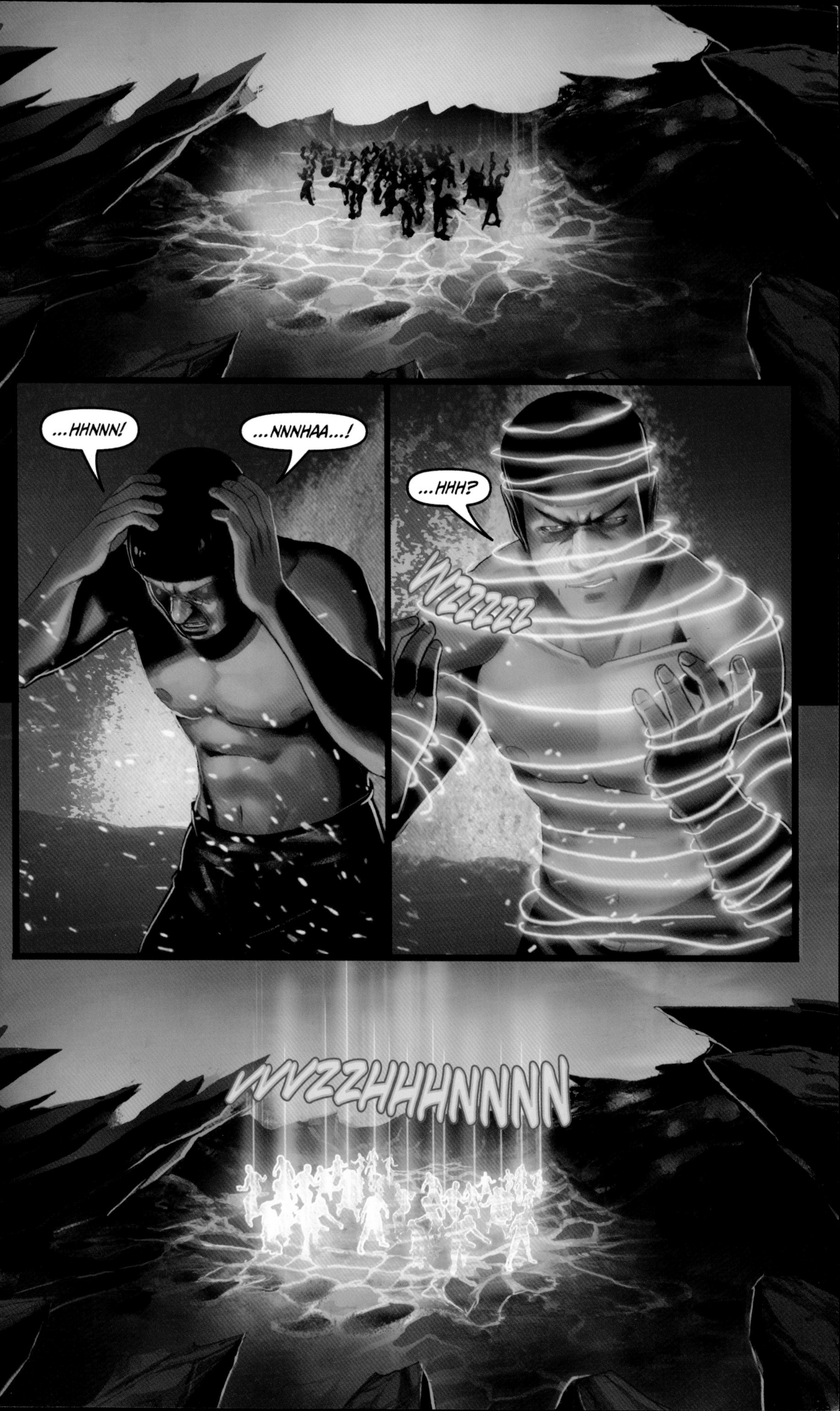
...HHNNN!
...NNNHAA...!
...HHH?
WZZZZZZ
VVVZZHHHNNNNN

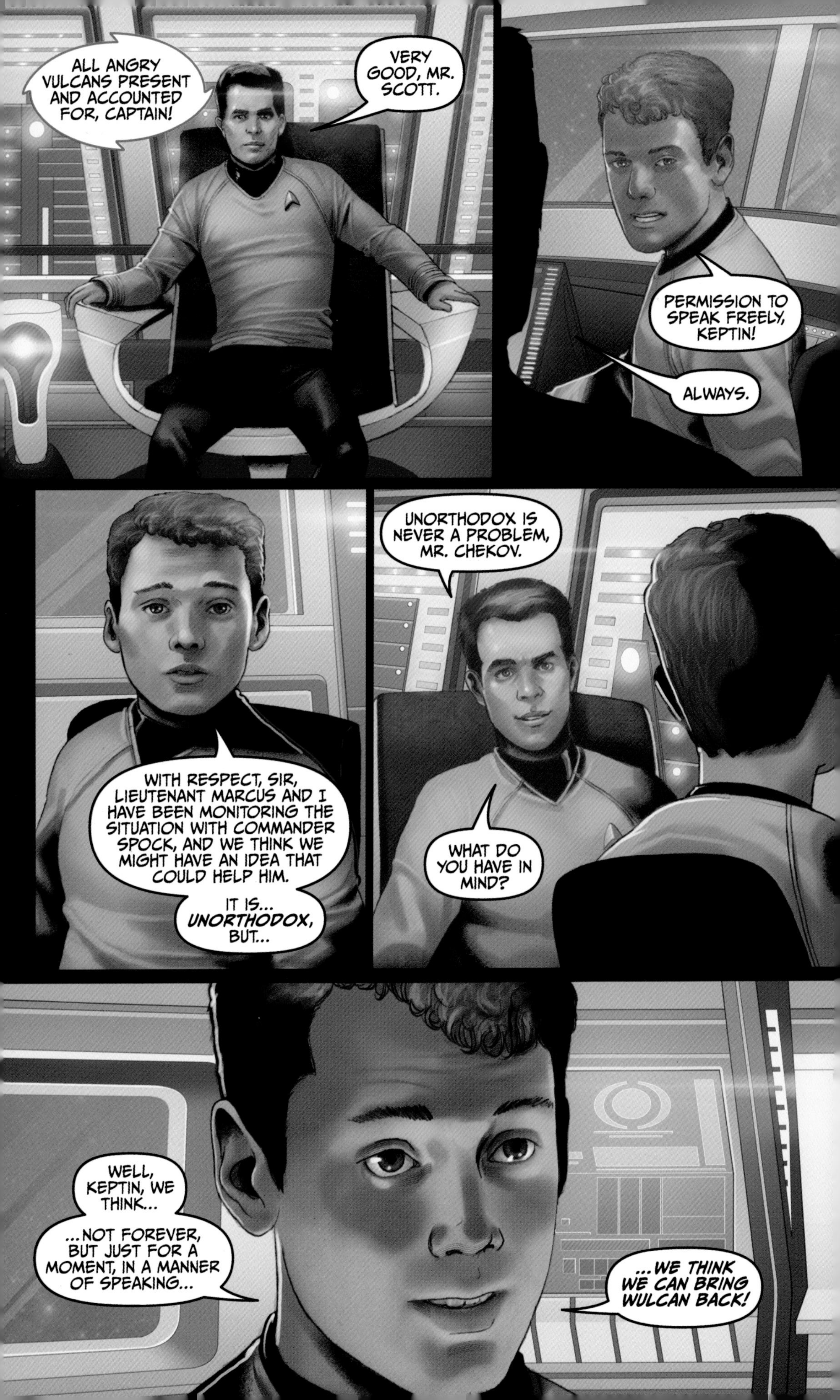
ALL ANGRY VULCANS PRESENT AND ACCOUNTED FOR, CAPTAIN!
VERY GOOD, MR. SCOTT.
PERMISSION TO SPEAK FREELY, KEPTIN!
ALWAYS.
WITH RESPECT, SIR, LIEUTENANT MARCUS AND I HAVE BEEN MONITORING THE SITUATION WITH COMMANDER SPOCK, AND WE THINK WE MIGHT HAVE AN IDEA THAT COULD HELP HIM.
IT IS... *UNORTHODOX*, BUT...
UNORTHODOX IS NEVER A PROBLEM, MR. CHEKOV.
WHAT DO YOU HAVE IN MIND?
WELL, KEPTIN, WE THINK...
...NOT FOREVER, BUT JUST FOR A MOMENT, IN A MANNER OF SPEAKING...
...WE THINK WE CAN BRING WULCAN BACK!

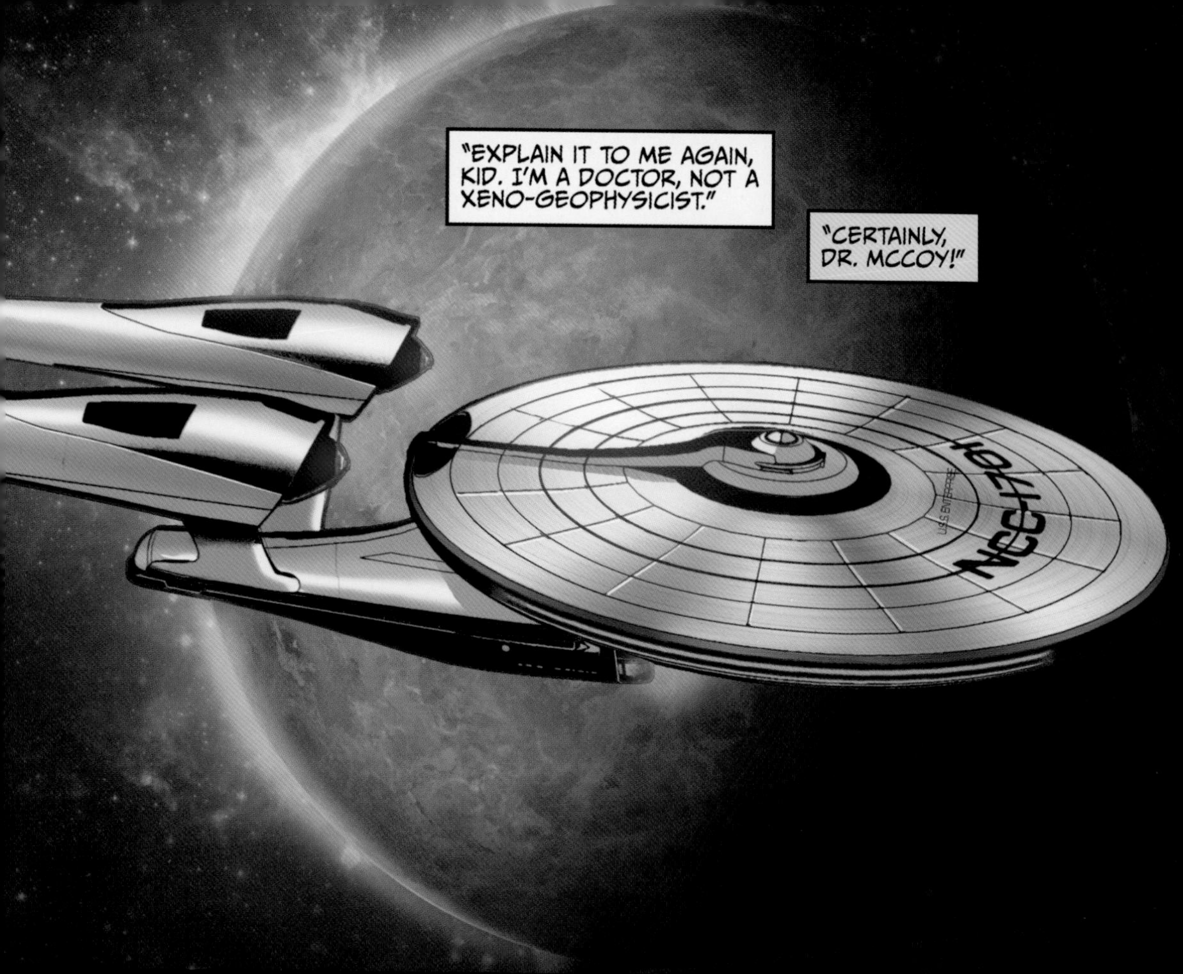
"EXPLAIN IT TO ME AGAIN, KID. I'M A DOCTOR, NOT A XENO-GEOPHYSICIST."
"CERTAINLY, DR. MCCOY!"
NCC-1701

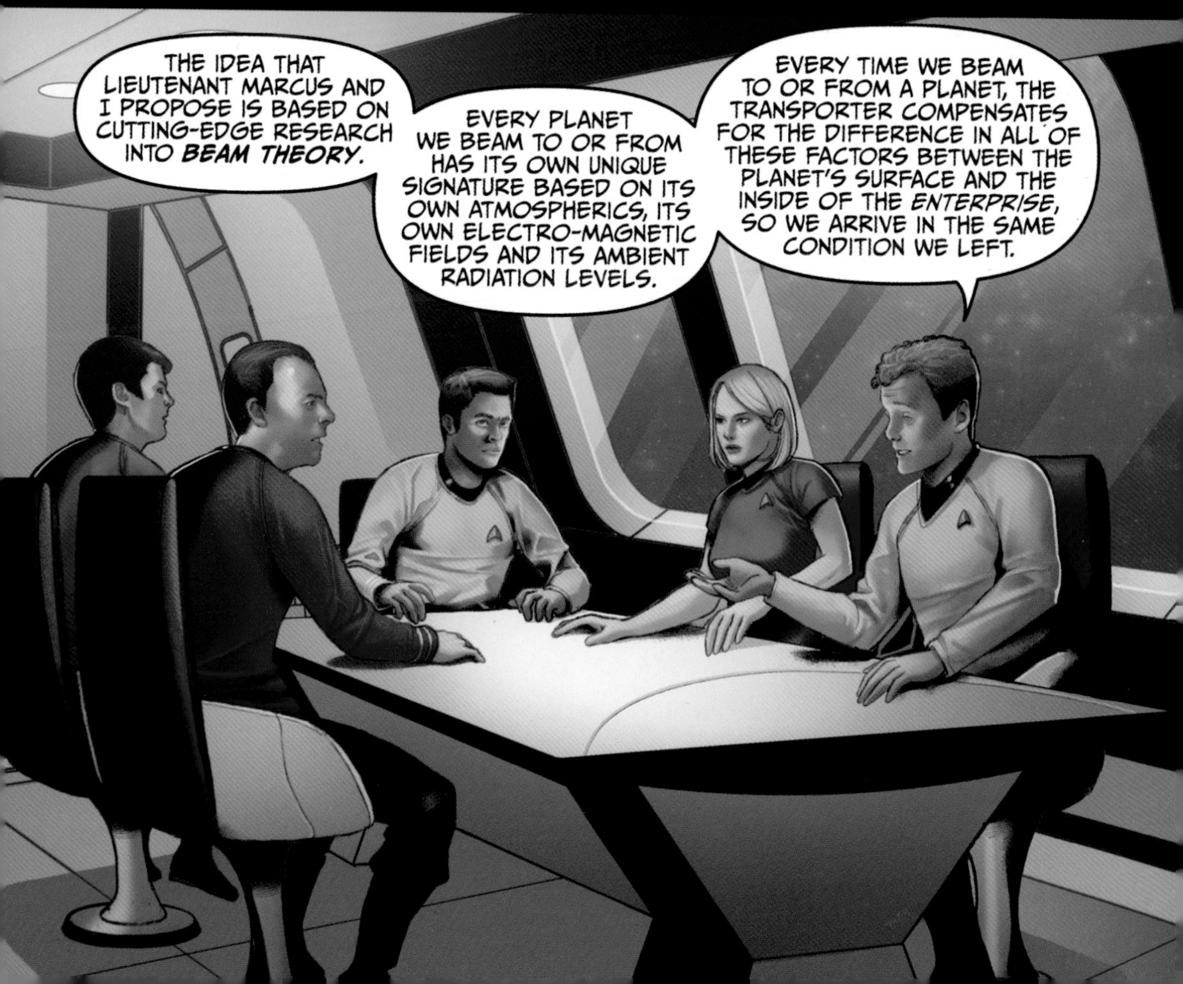
THE IDEA THAT LIEUTENANT MARCUS AND I PROPOSE IS BASED ON CUTTING-EDGE RESEARCH INTO *BEAM THEORY*.
EVERY PLANET WE BEAM TO OR FROM HAS ITS OWN UNIQUE SIGNATURE BASED ON ITS OWN ATMOSPHERICS, ITS OWN ELECTRO-MAGNETIC FIELDS AND ITS AMBIENT RADIATION LEVELS.
EVERY TIME WE BEAM TO OR FROM A PLANET, THE TRANSPORTER COMPENSATES FOR THE DIFFERENCE IN ALL OF THESE FACTORS BETWEEN THE PLANET'S SURFACE AND THE INSIDE OF THE *ENTERPRISE*, SO WE ARRIVE IN THE SAME CONDITION WE LEFT.

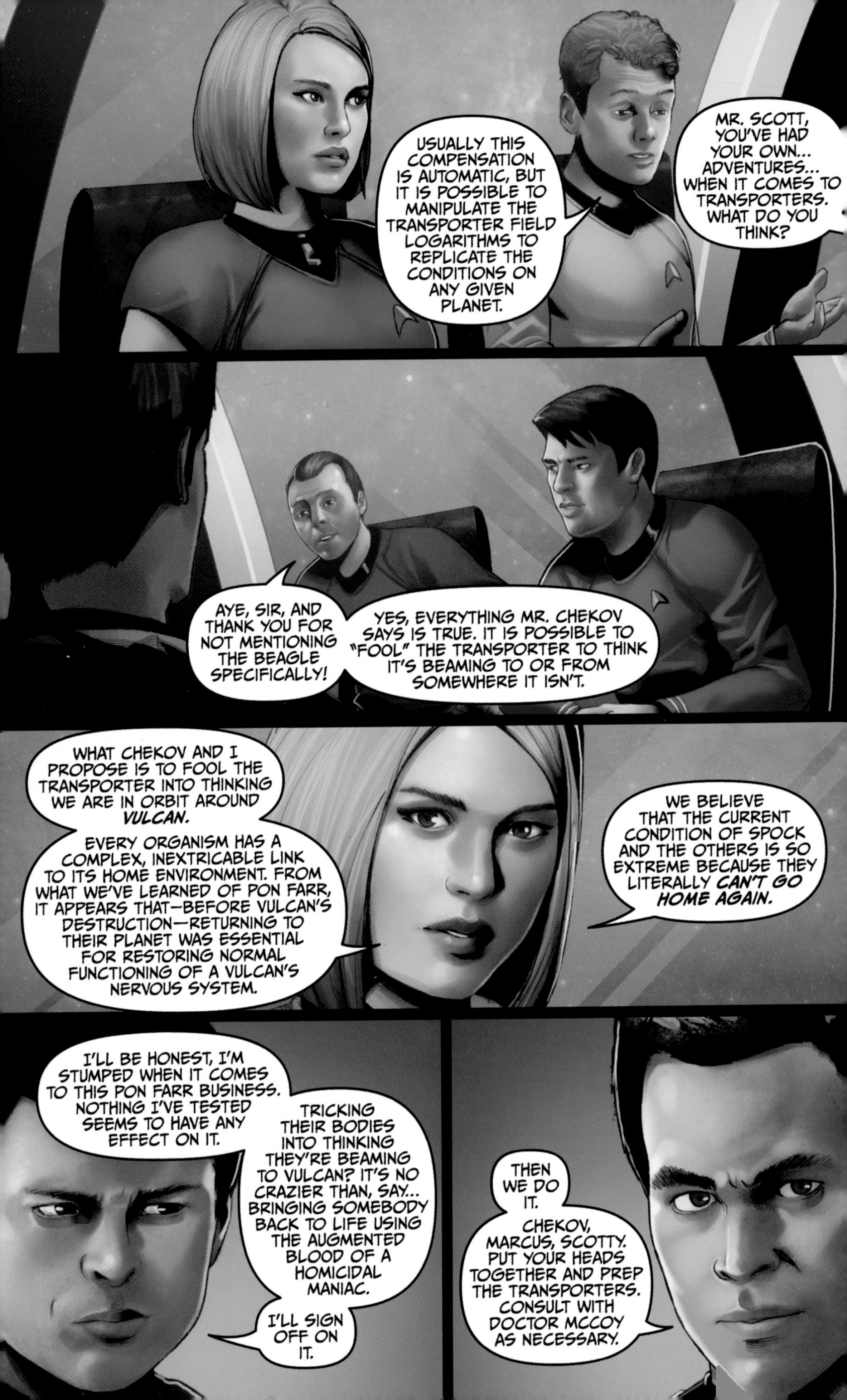
USUALLY THIS COMPENSATION IS AUTOMATIC, BUT IT IS POSSIBLE TO MANIPULATE THE TRANSPORTER FIELD LOGARITHMS TO REPLICATE THE CONDITIONS ON ANY GIVEN PLANET.
MR. SCOTT, YOU'VE HAD YOUR OWN... ADVENTURES... WHEN IT COMES TO TRANSPORTERS. WHAT DO YOU THINK?
AYE, SIR, AND THANK YOU FOR NOT MENTIONING THE BEAGLE SPECIFICALLY!
YES, EVERYTHING MR. CHEKOV SAYS IS TRUE. IT IS POSSIBLE TO "FOOL" THE TRANSPORTER TO THINK IT'S BEAMING TO OR FROM SOMEWHERE IT ISN'T.
WHAT CHEKOV AND I PROPOSE IS TO FOOL THE TRANSPORTER INTO THINKING WE ARE IN ORBIT AROUND ***VULCAN.***
EVERY ORGANISM HAS A COMPLEX, INEXTRICABLE LINK TO ITS HOME ENVIRONMENT. FROM WHAT WE'VE LEARNED OF PON FARR, IT APPEARS THAT—BEFORE VULCAN'S DESTRUCTION—RETURNING TO THEIR PLANET WAS ESSENTIAL FOR RESTORING NORMAL FUNCTIONING OF A VULCAN'S NERVOUS SYSTEM.
WE BELIEVE THAT THE CURRENT CONDITION OF SPOCK AND THE OTHERS IS SO EXTREME BECAUSE THEY LITERALLY ***CAN'T GO HOME AGAIN.***
I'LL BE HONEST, I'M STUMPED WHEN IT COMES TO THIS PON FARR BUSINESS. NOTHING I'VE TESTED SEEMS TO HAVE ANY EFFECT ON IT.
TRICKING THEIR BODIES INTO THINKING THEY'RE BEAMING TO VULCAN? IT'S NO CRAZIER THAN, SAY... BRINGING SOMEBODY BACK TO LIFE USING THE AUGMENTED BLOOD OF A HOMICIDAL MANIAC.
I'LL SIGN OFF ON IT.
THEN WE DO IT.
CHEKOV, MARCUS, SCOTTY. PUT YOUR HEADS TOGETHER AND PREP THE TRANSPORTERS. CONSULT WITH DOCTOR MCCOY AS NECESSARY.

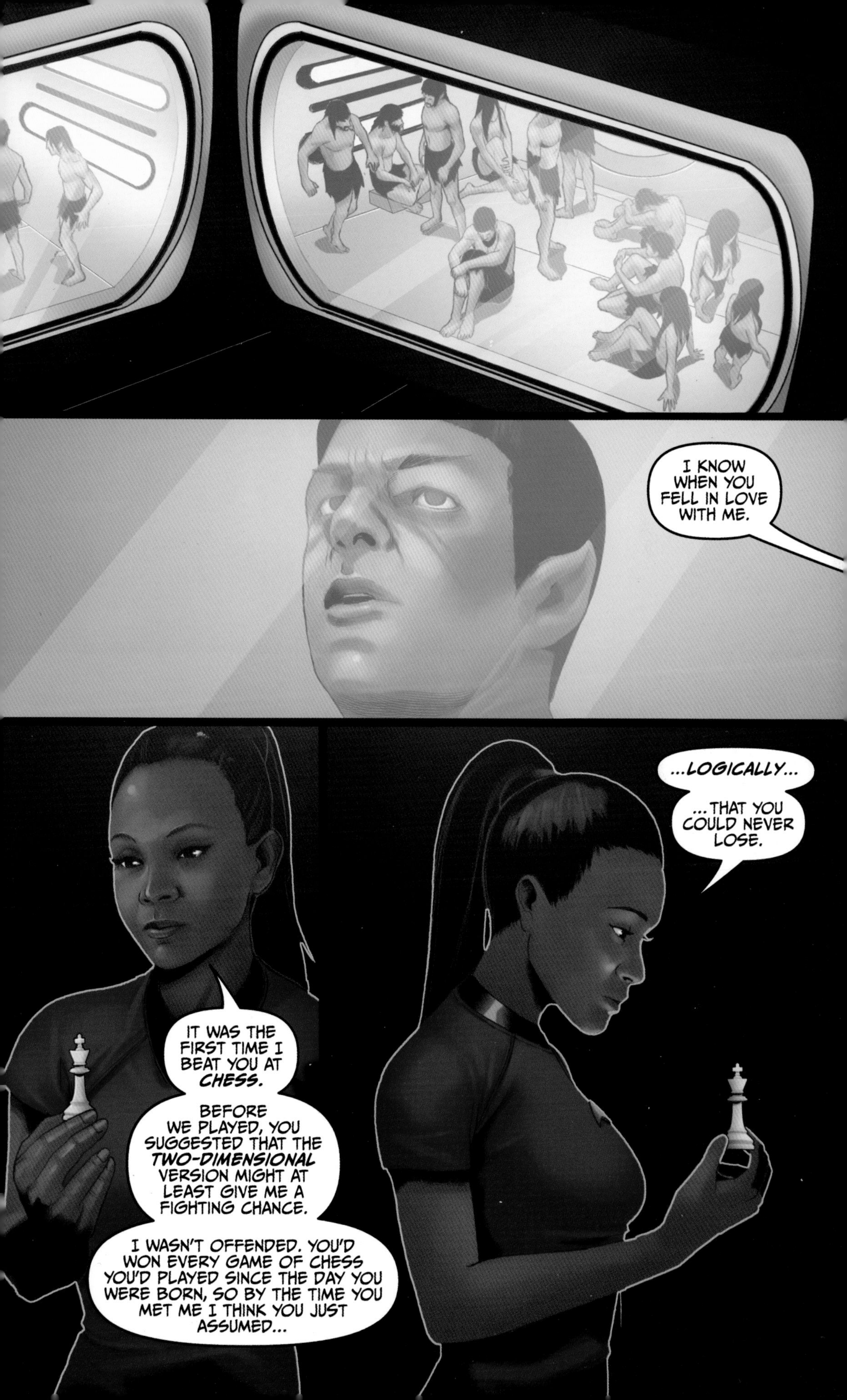
I KNOW WHEN YOU FELL IN LOVE WITH ME.
...LOGICALLY...
...THAT YOU COULD NEVER LOSE.
IT WAS THE FIRST TIME I BEAT YOU AT CHESS.
BEFORE WE PLAYED, YOU SUGGESTED THAT THE TWO-DIMENSIONAL VERSION MIGHT AT LEAST GIVE ME A FIGHTING CHANCE.
I WASN'T OFFENDED. YOU'D WON EVERY GAME OF CHESS YOU'D PLAYED SINCE THE DAY YOU WERE BORN, SO BY THE TIME YOU MET ME I THINK YOU JUST ASSUMED...

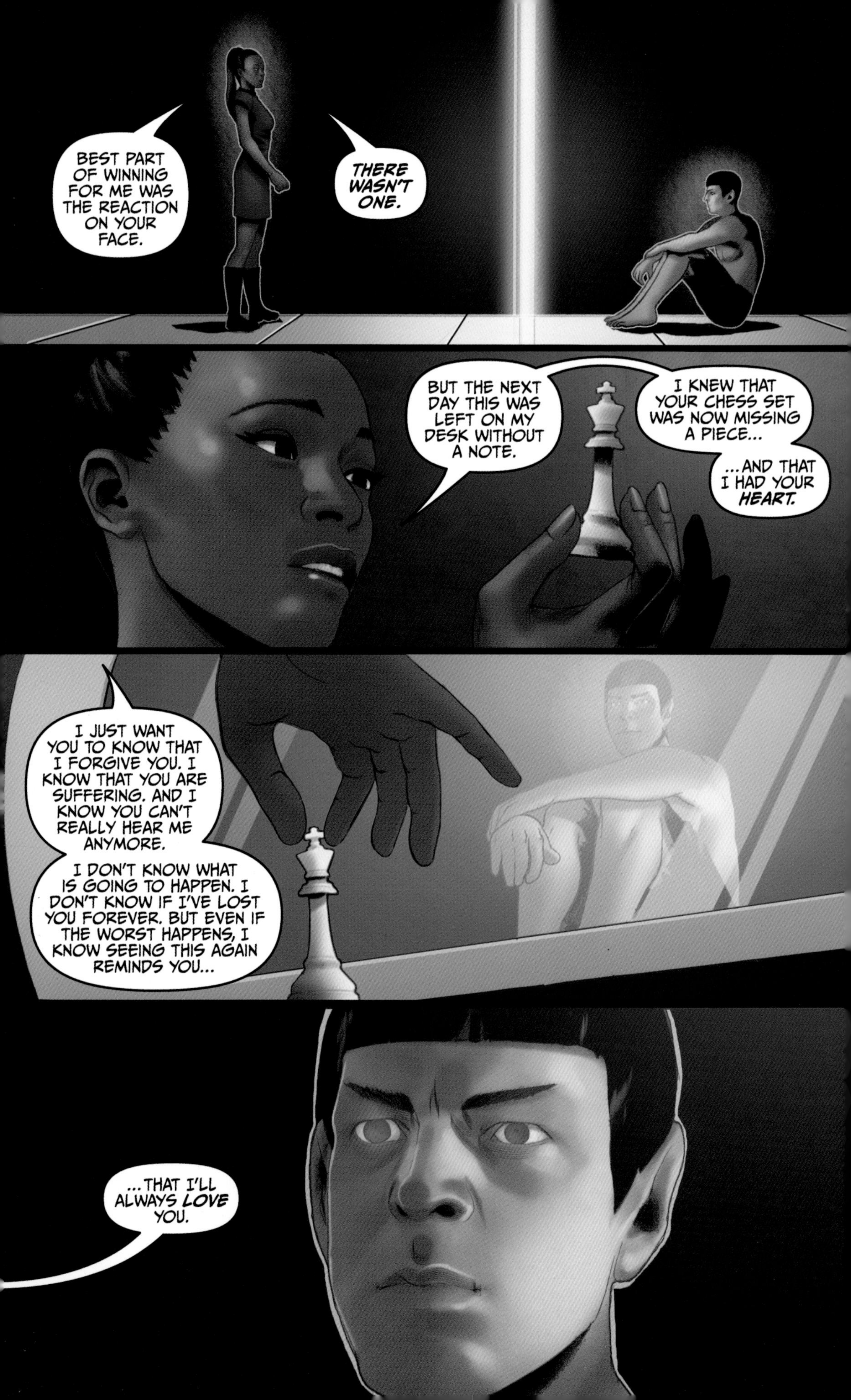
BEST PART OF WINNING FOR ME WAS THE REACTION ON YOUR FACE.
THERE WASN'T ONE.
BUT THE NEXT DAY THIS WAS LEFT ON MY DESK WITHOUT A NOTE.
I KNEW THAT YOUR CHESS SET WAS NOW MISSING A PIECE...
...AND THAT I HAD YOUR ***HEART.***
I JUST WANT YOU TO KNOW THAT I FORGIVE YOU. I KNOW THAT YOU ARE SUFFERING. AND I KNOW YOU CAN'T REALLY HEAR ME ANYMORE.
I DON'T KNOW WHAT IS GOING TO HAPPEN. I DON'T KNOW IF I'VE LOST YOU FOREVER. BUT EVEN IF THE WORST HAPPENS, I KNOW SEEING THIS AGAIN REMINDS YOU...
...THAT I'LL ALWAYS ***LOVE*** YOU.

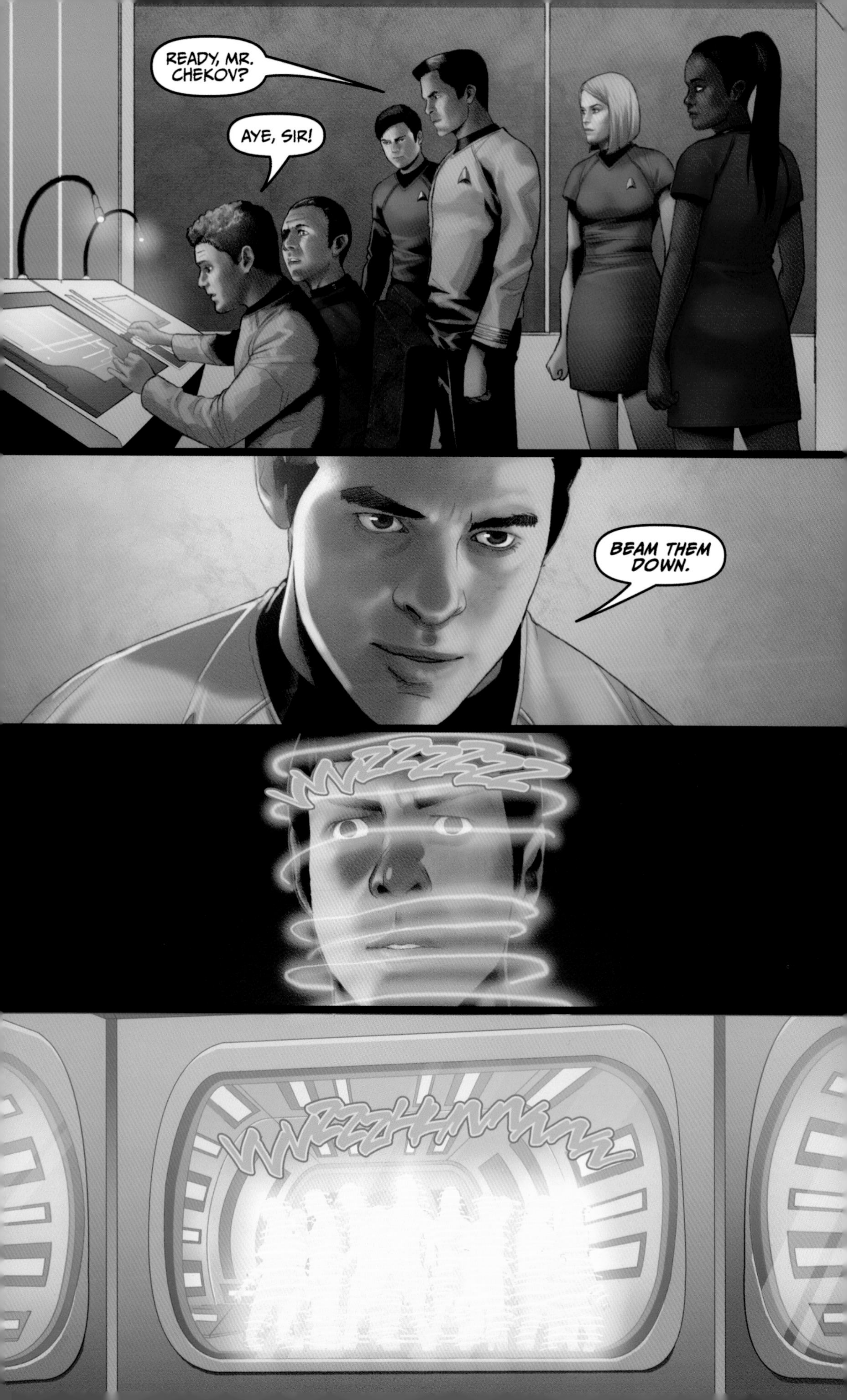
READY, MR. CHEKOV?
AYE, SIR!
BEAM THEM DOWN.

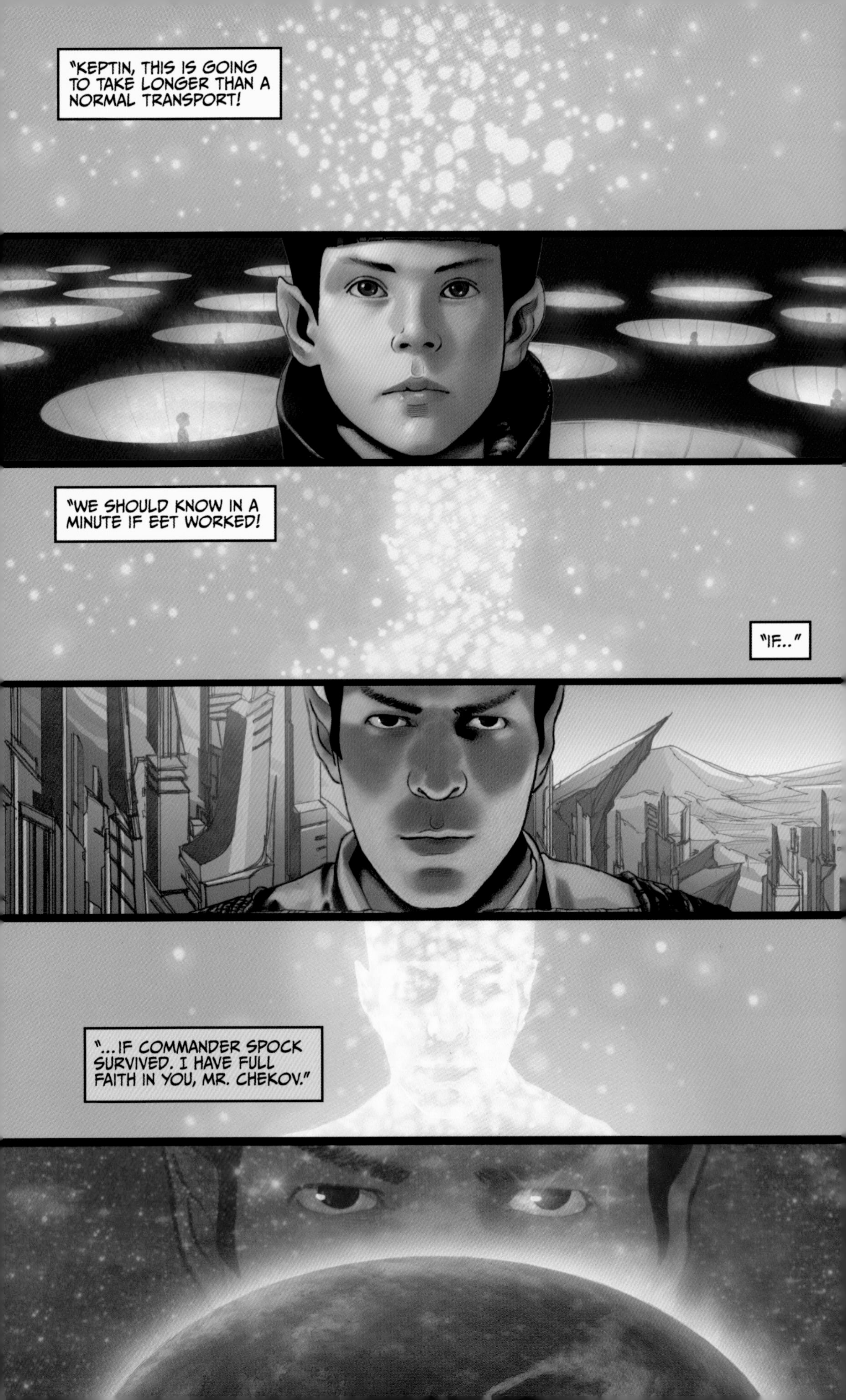
"KEPTIN, THIS IS GOING TO TAKE LONGER THAN A NORMAL TRANSPORT!
"WE SHOULD KNOW IN A MINUTE IF EET WORKED!
"IF..."
"...IF COMMANDER SPOCK SURVIVED. I HAVE FULL FAITH IN YOU, MR. CHEKOV."

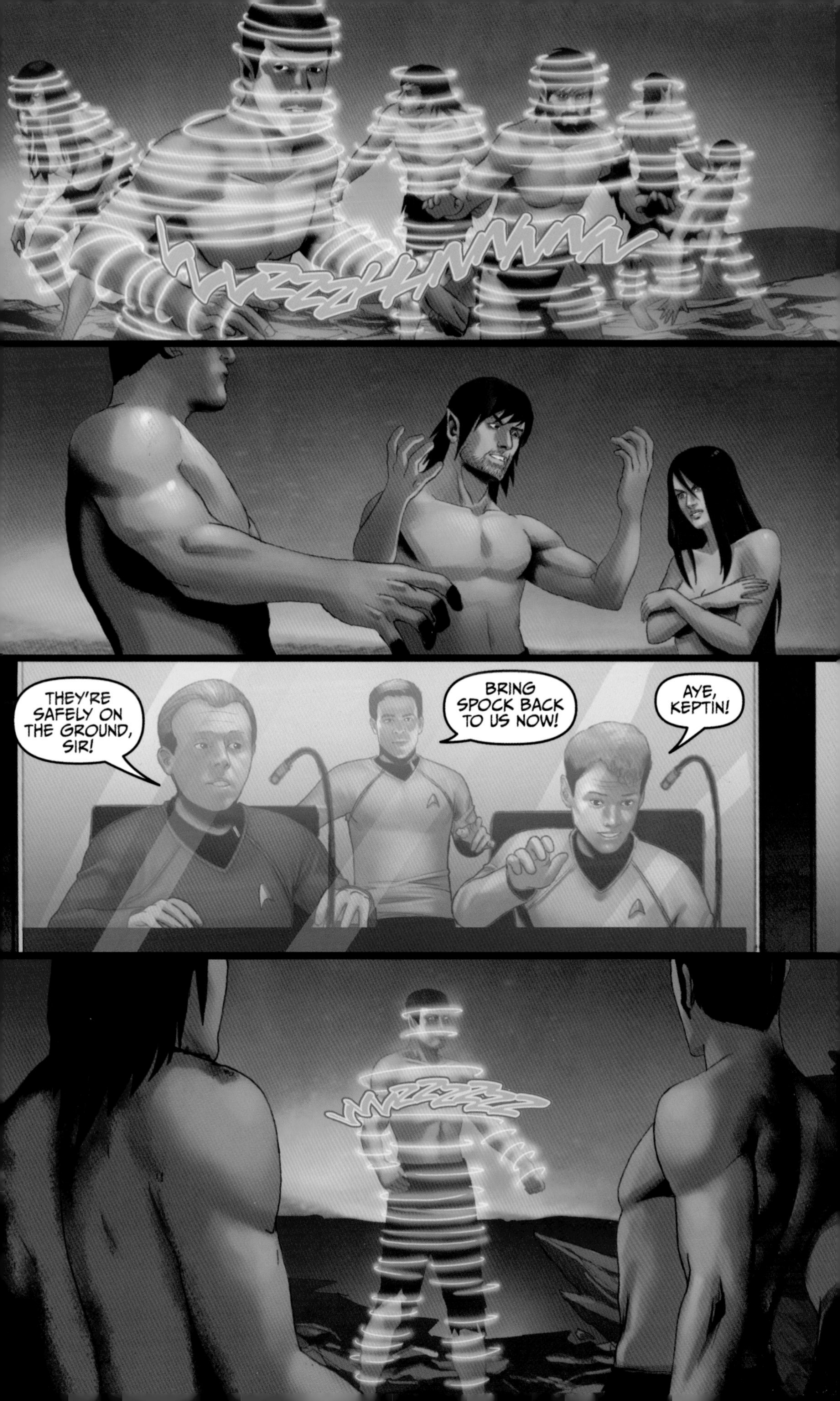
WWZZZHHNNNNNN
THEY'RE SAFELY ON THE GROUND, SIR!
BRING SPOCK BACK TO US NOW!
AYE, KEPTIN!
WWZZZZZZ

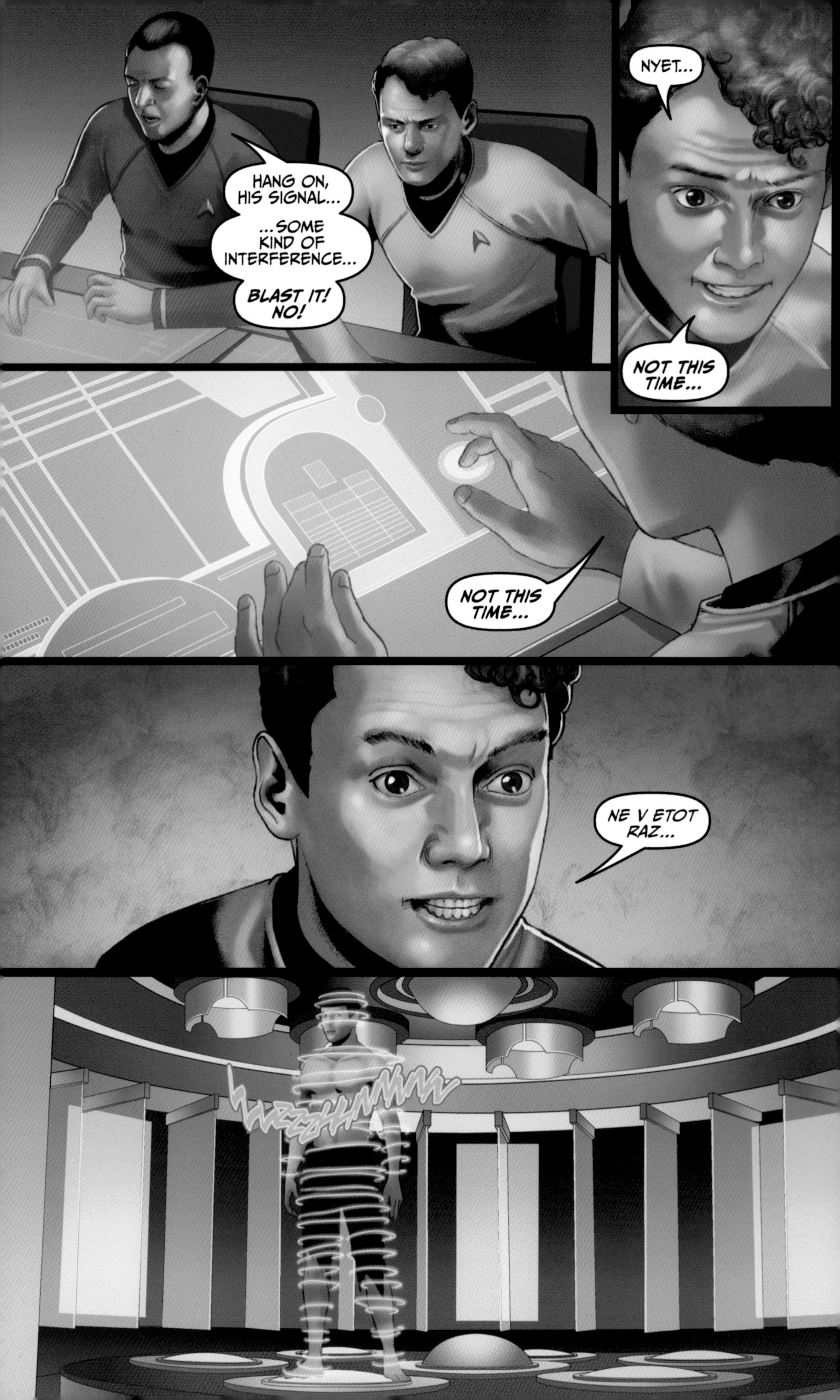
HANG ON, HIS SIGNAL...
...SOME KIND OF INTERFERENCE...
BLAST IT! NO!
NYET...
NOT THIS TIME...
NOT THIS TIME...
NE V ETOT RAZ...
HZZZHHMMMM

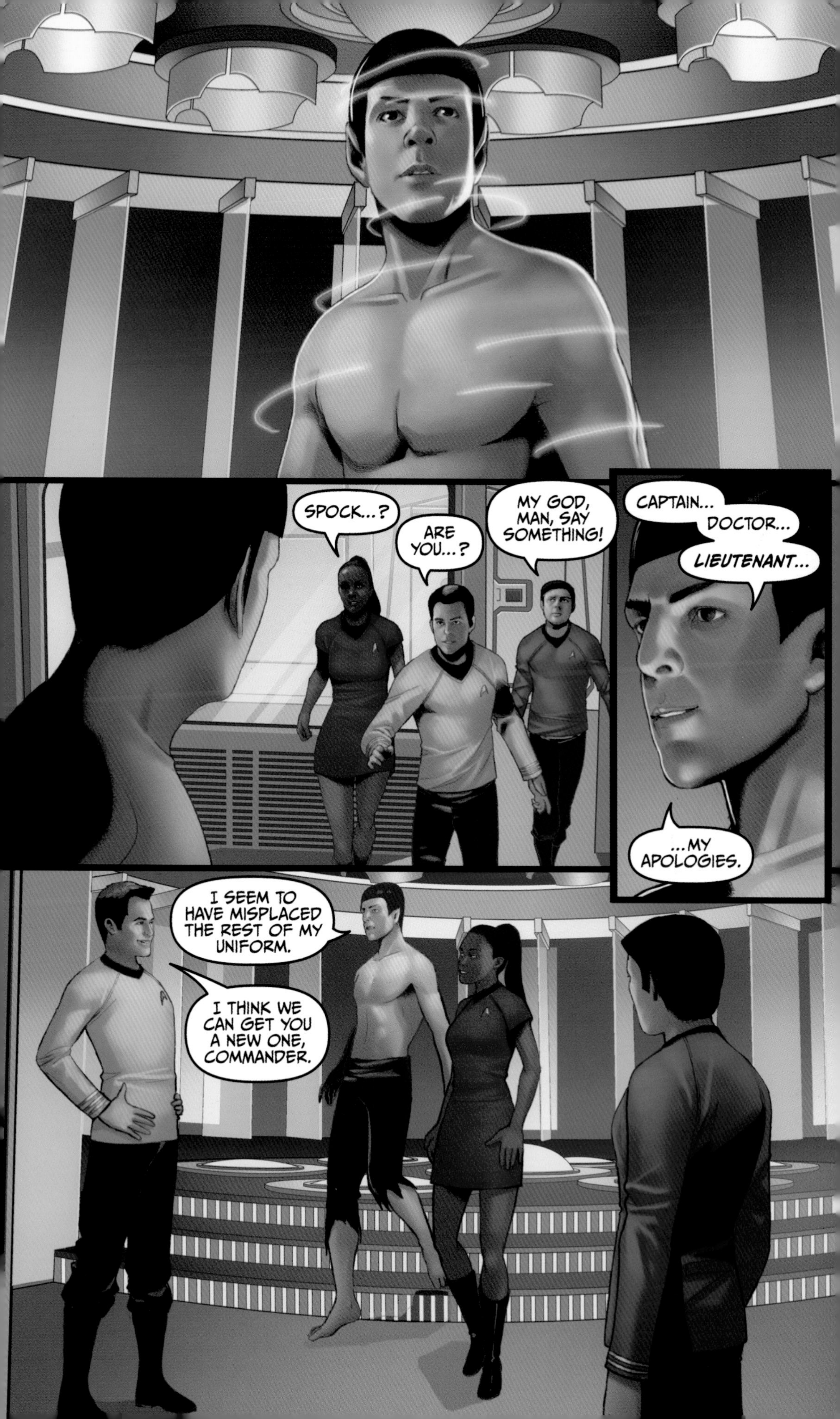
SPOCK...?
ARE YOU...?
MY GOD, MAN, SAY SOMETHING!
CAPTAIN...
DOCTOR...
LIEUTENANT...
...MY APOLOGIES.
I SEEM TO HAVE MISPLACED THE REST OF MY UNIFORM.
I THINK WE CAN GET YOU A NEW ONE, COMMANDER.

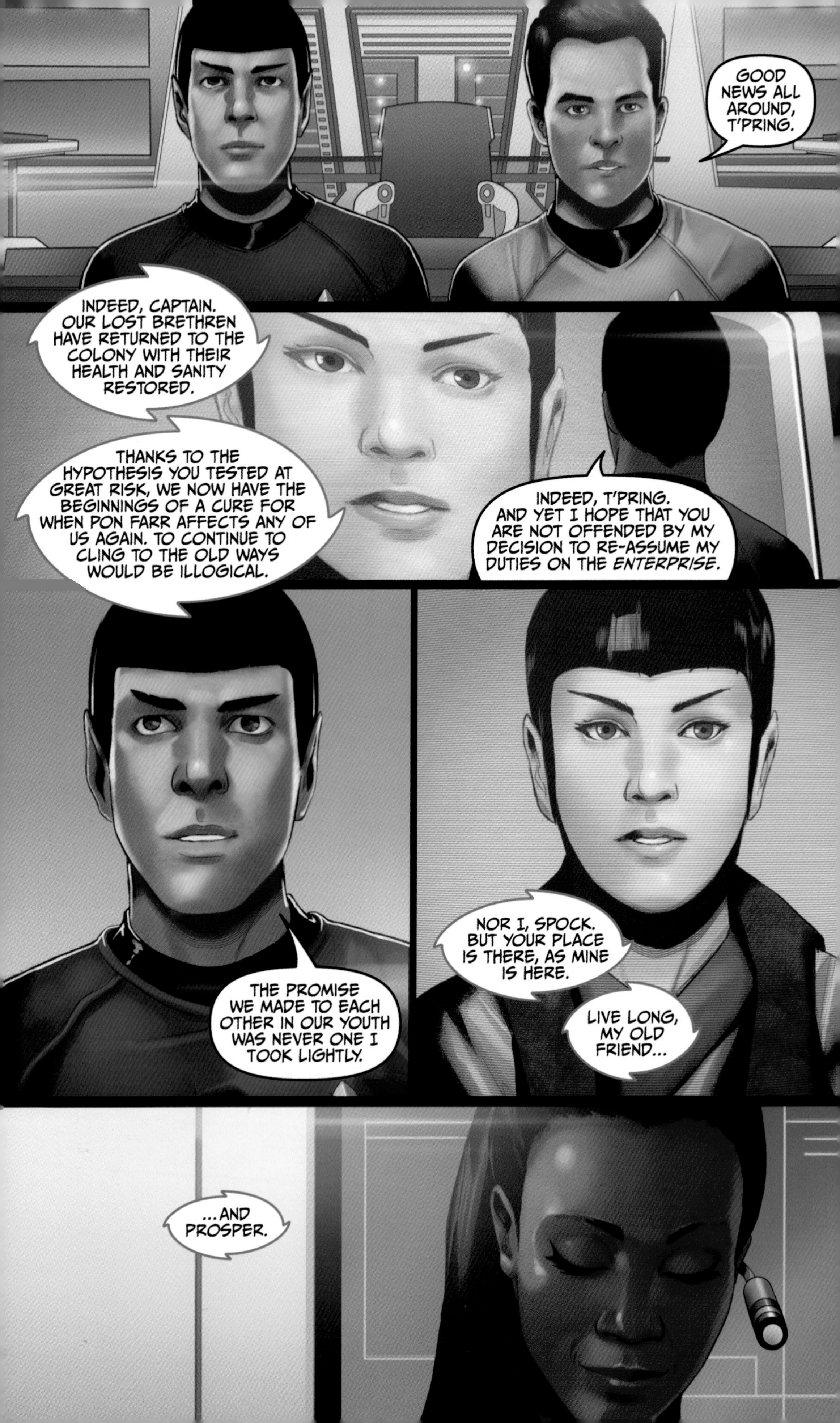
GOOD NEWS ALL AROUND, T'PRING.
INDEED, CAPTAIN. OUR LOST BRETHREN HAVE RETURNED TO THE COLONY WITH THEIR HEALTH AND SANITY RESTORED.
THANKS TO THE HYPOTHESIS YOU TESTED AT GREAT RISK, WE NOW HAVE THE BEGINNINGS OF A CURE FOR WHEN PON FARR AFFECTS ANY OF US AGAIN. TO CONTINUE TO CLING TO THE OLD WAYS WOULD BE ILLOGICAL.
INDEED, T'PRING. AND YET I HOPE THAT YOU ARE NOT OFFENDED BY MY DECISION TO RE-ASSUME MY DUTIES ON THE *ENTERPRISE*.
THE PROMISE WE MADE TO EACH OTHER IN OUR YOUTH WAS NEVER ONE I TOOK LIGHTLY.
NOR I, SPOCK. BUT YOUR PLACE IS THERE, AS MINE IS HERE.
LIVE LONG, MY OLD FRIEND...
...AND PROSPER.

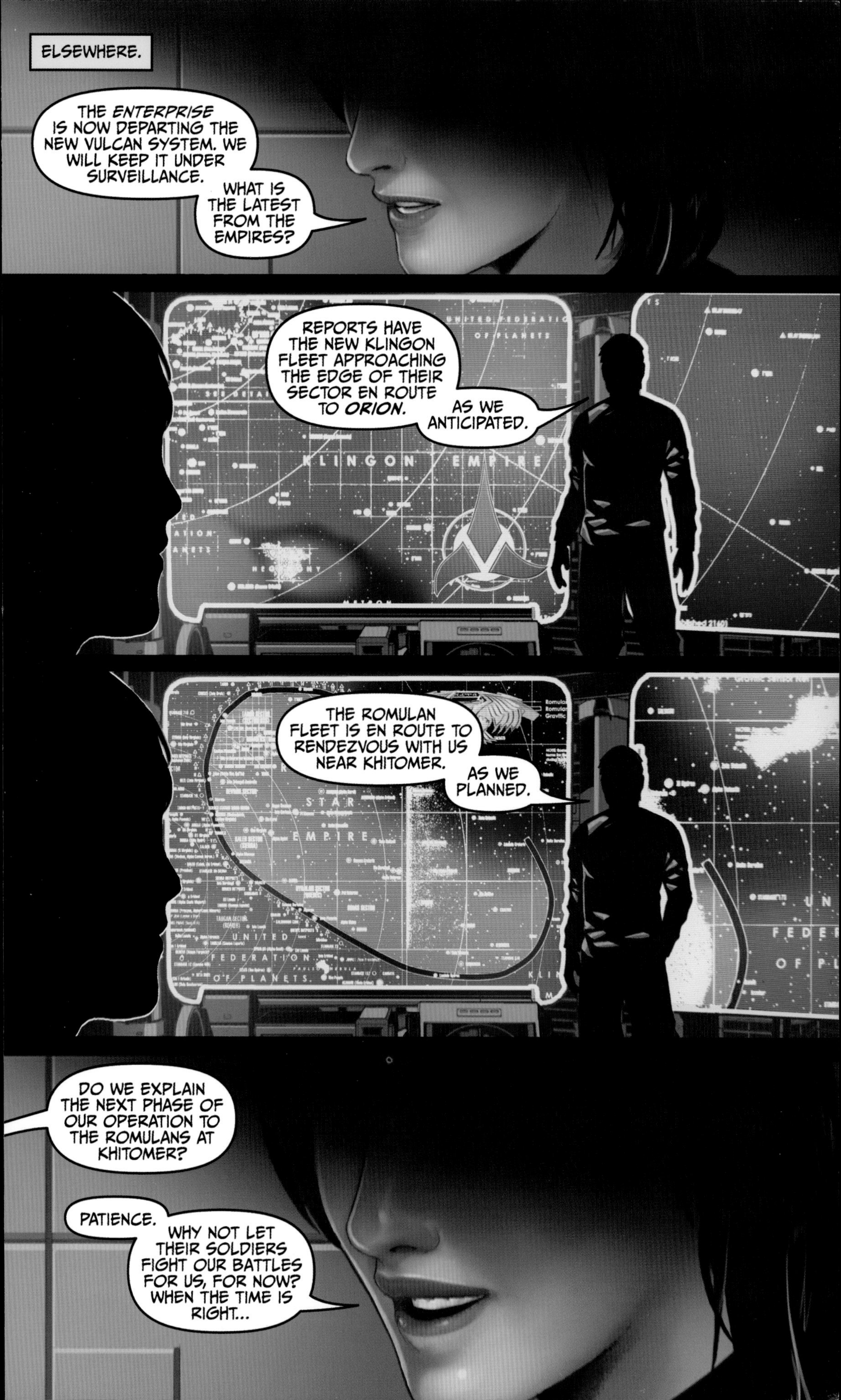
ELSEWHERE.
THE ENTERPRISE IS NOW DEPARTING THE NEW VULCAN SYSTEM. WE WILL KEEP IT UNDER SURVEILLANCE.
WHAT IS THE LATEST FROM THE EMPIRES?
REPORTS HAVE THE NEW KLINGON FLEET APPROACHING THE EDGE OF THEIR SECTOR EN ROUTE TO ORION.
AS WE ANTICIPATED.
KLINGON EMPIRE
THE ROMULAN FLEET IS EN ROUTE TO RENDEZVOUS WITH US NEAR KHITOMER.
AS WE PLANNED.
STAR EMPIRE
UNITED FEDERATION OF PLANETS
DO WE EXPLAIN THE NEXT PHASE OF OUR OPERATION TO THE ROMULANS AT KHITOMER?
PATIENCE.
WHY NOT LET THEIR SOLDIERS FIGHT OUR BATTLES FOR US, FOR NOW? WHEN THE TIME IS RIGHT...

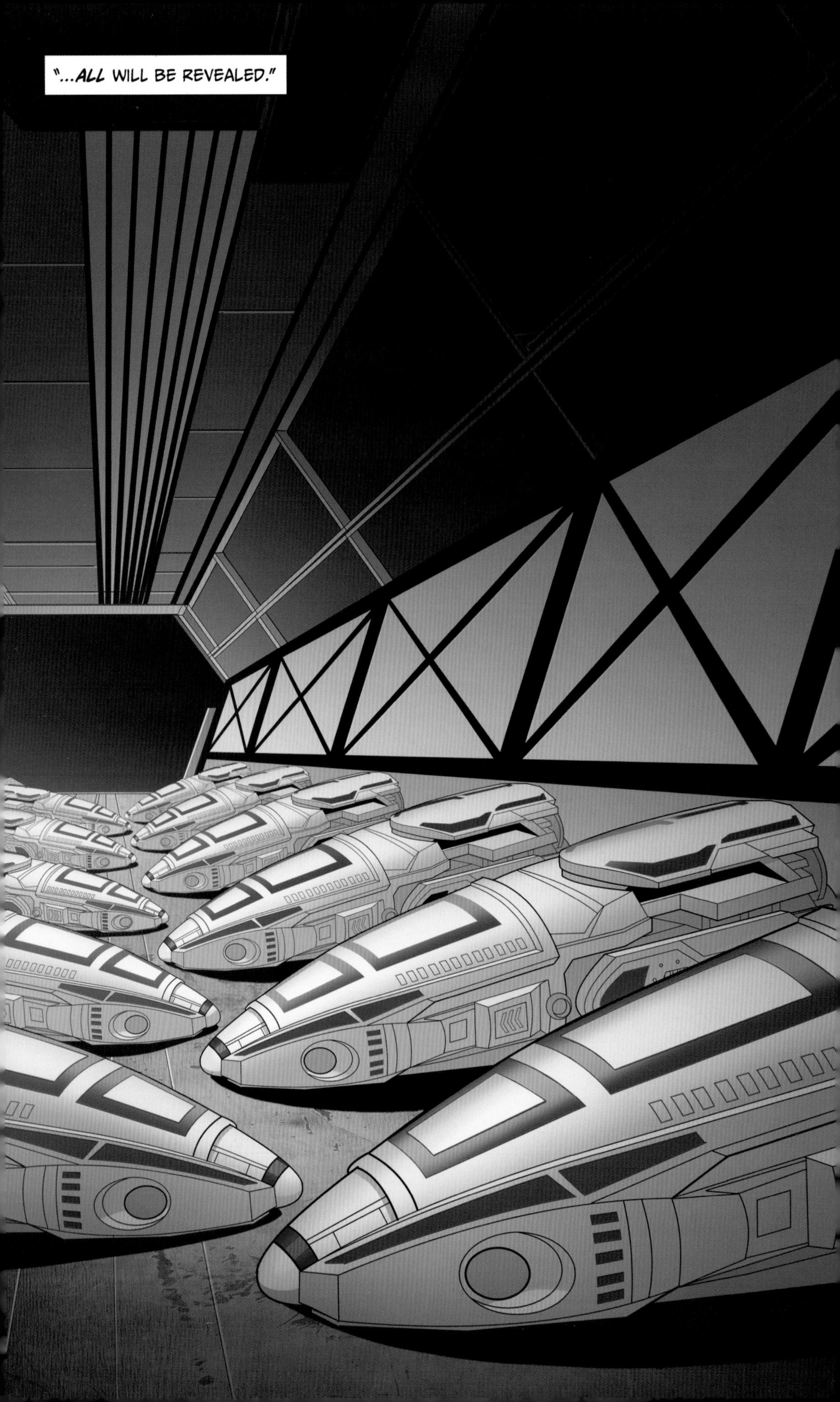
"...ALL WILL BE REVEALED."

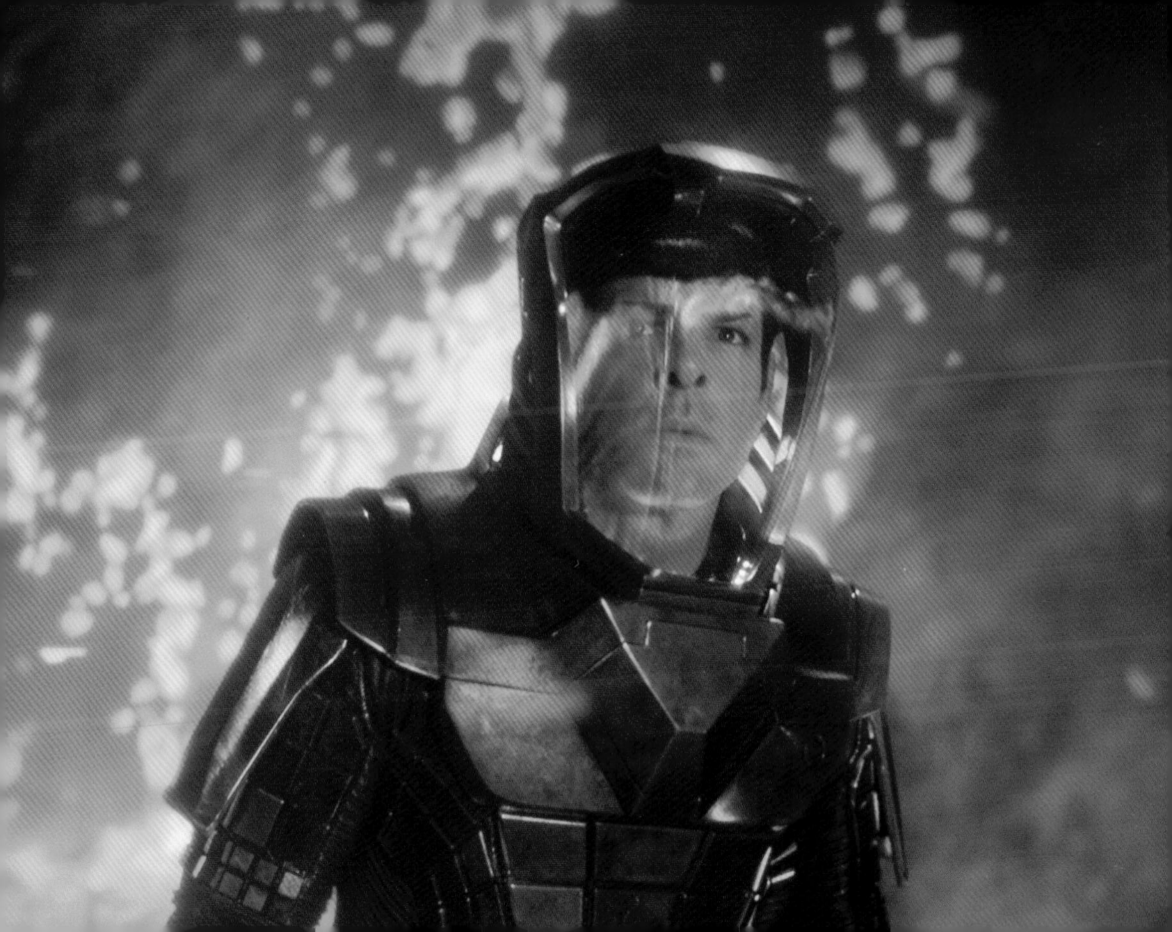

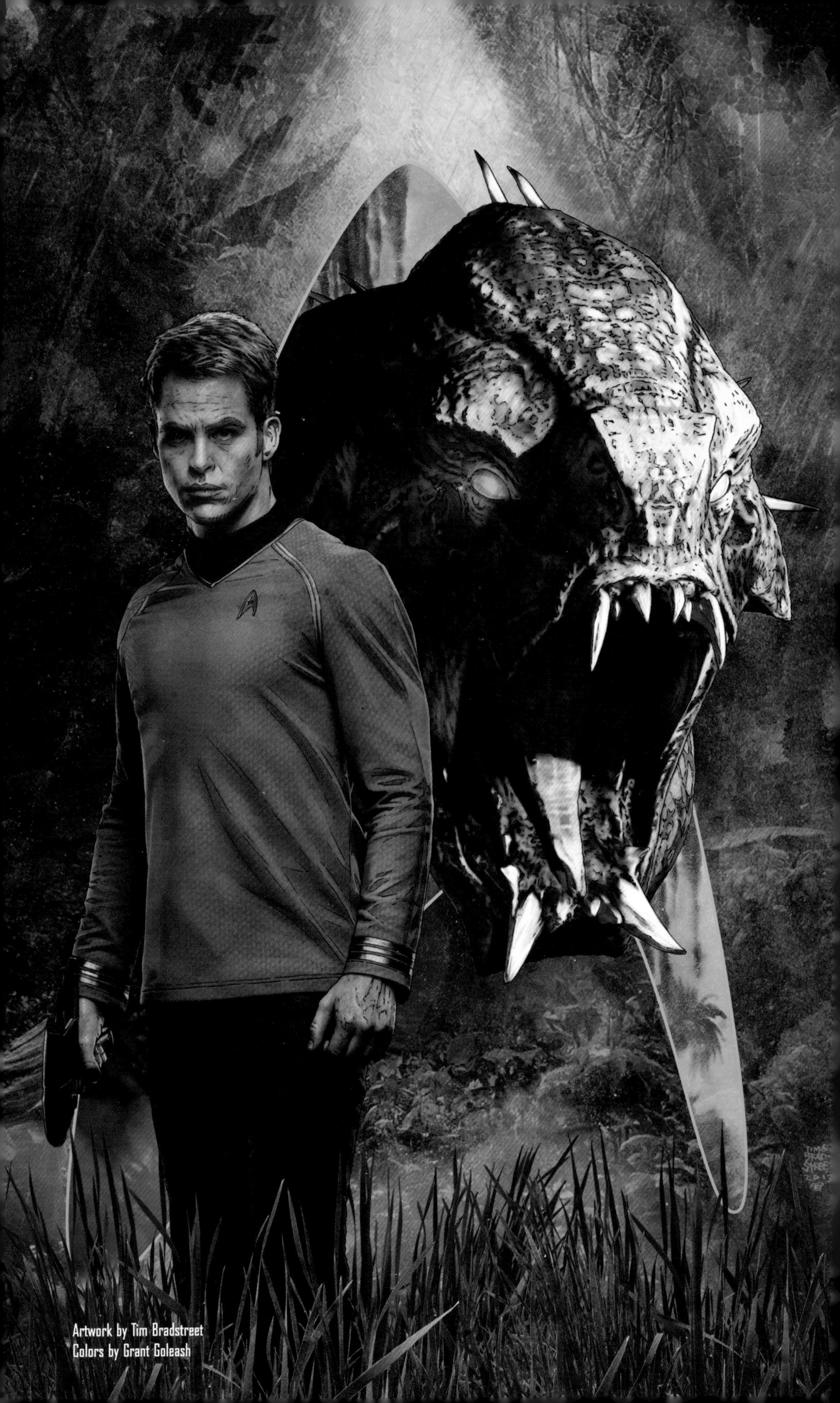

Artwork by Tim Bradstreet
Colors by Grant Goleash

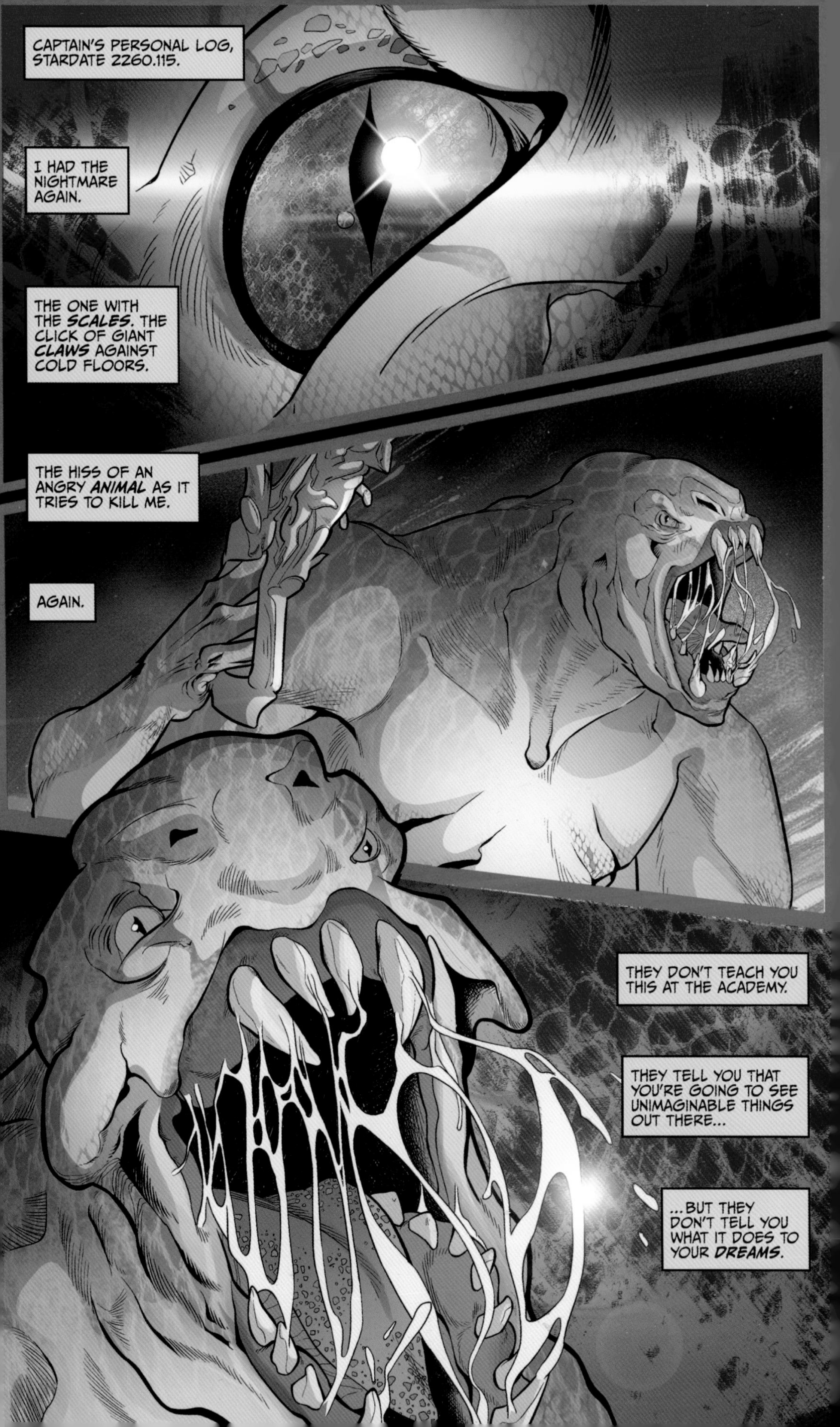
CAPTAIN'S PERSONAL LOG, STARDATE 2260.115.
I HAD THE NIGHTMARE AGAIN.
THE ONE WITH THE *SCALES*. THE CLICK OF GIANT *CLAWS* AGAINST COLD FLOORS.
THE HISS OF AN ANGRY *ANIMAL* AS IT TRIES TO KILL ME.
AGAIN.
THEY DON'T TEACH YOU THIS AT THE ACADEMY.
THEY TELL YOU THAT YOU'RE GOING TO SEE UNIMAGINABLE THINGS OUT THERE...
...BUT THEY DON'T TELL YOU WHAT IT DOES TO YOUR *DREAMS*.

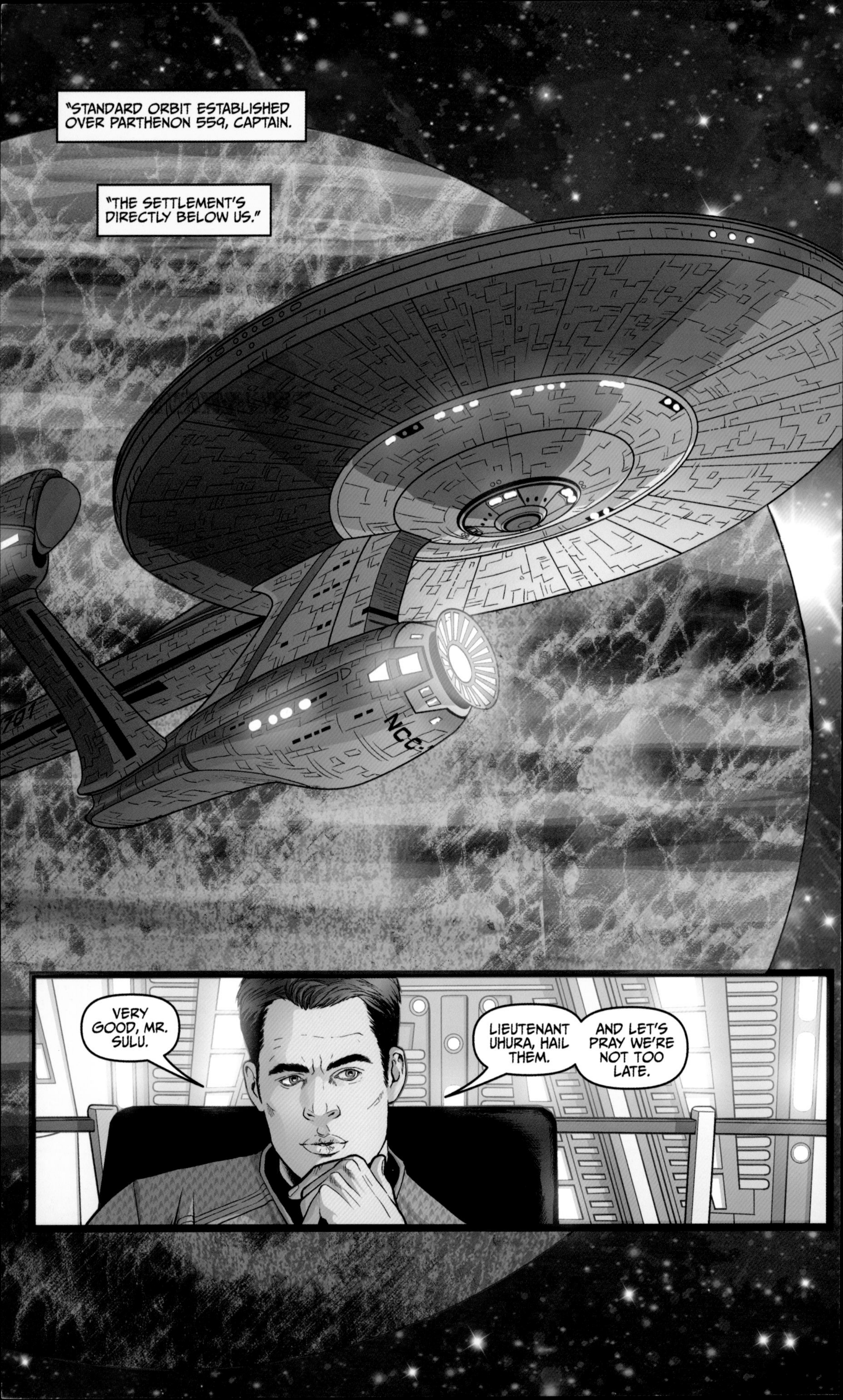
"STANDARD ORBIT ESTABLISHED OVER PARTHENON 559, CAPTAIN.
"THE SETTLEMENT'S DIRECTLY BELOW US."
VERY GOOD, MR. SULU.
LIEUTENANT UHURA, HAIL THEM.
AND LET'S PRAY WE'RE NOT TOO LATE.

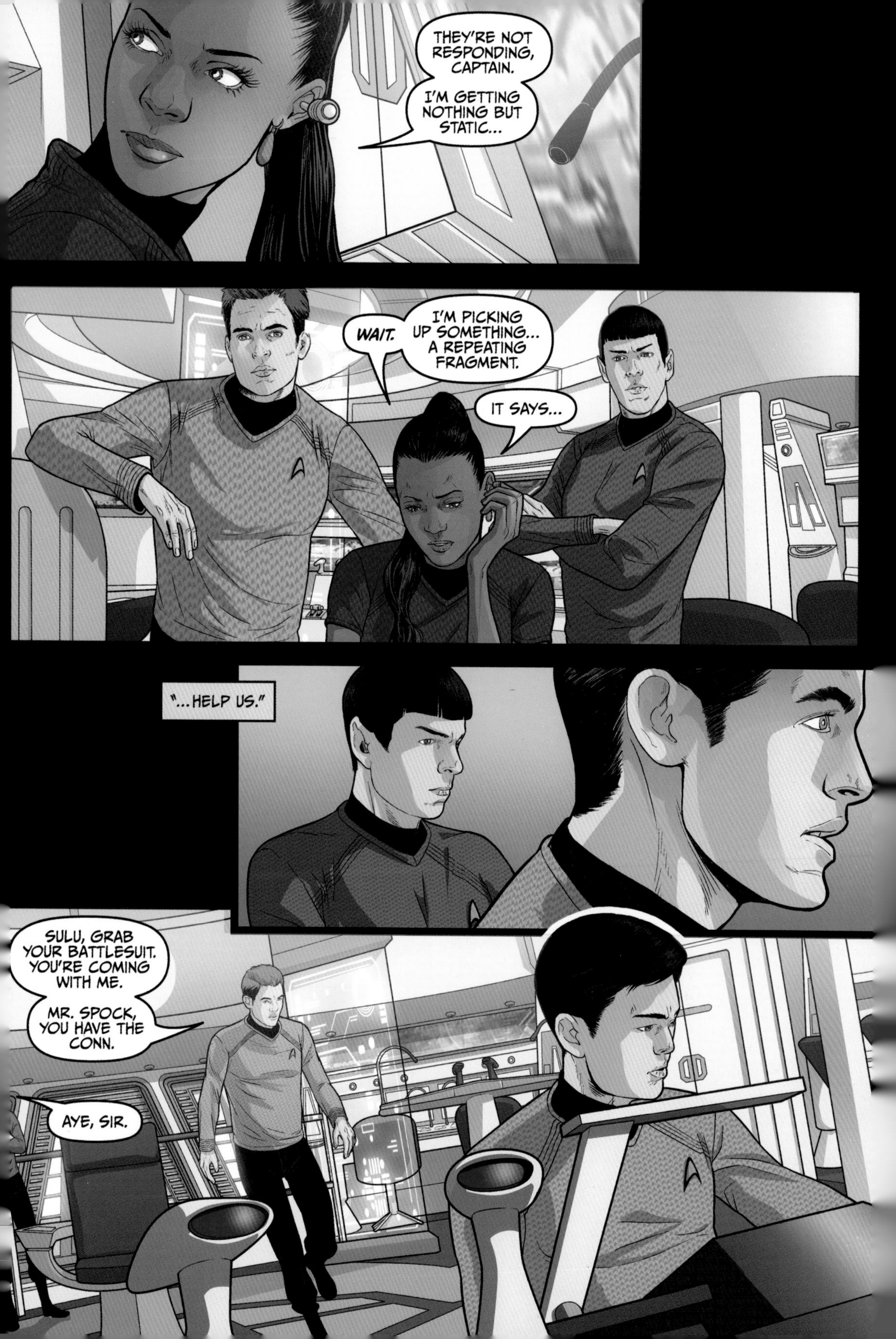
THEY'RE NOT RESPONDING, CAPTAIN.
I'M GETTING NOTHING BUT STATIC...
WAIT.
I'M PICKING UP SOMETHING... A REPEATING FRAGMENT.
IT SAYS...
"...HELP US."
SULU, GRAB YOUR BATTLESUIT. YOU'RE COMING WITH ME.
MR. SPOCK, YOU HAVE THE CONN.
AYE, SIR.

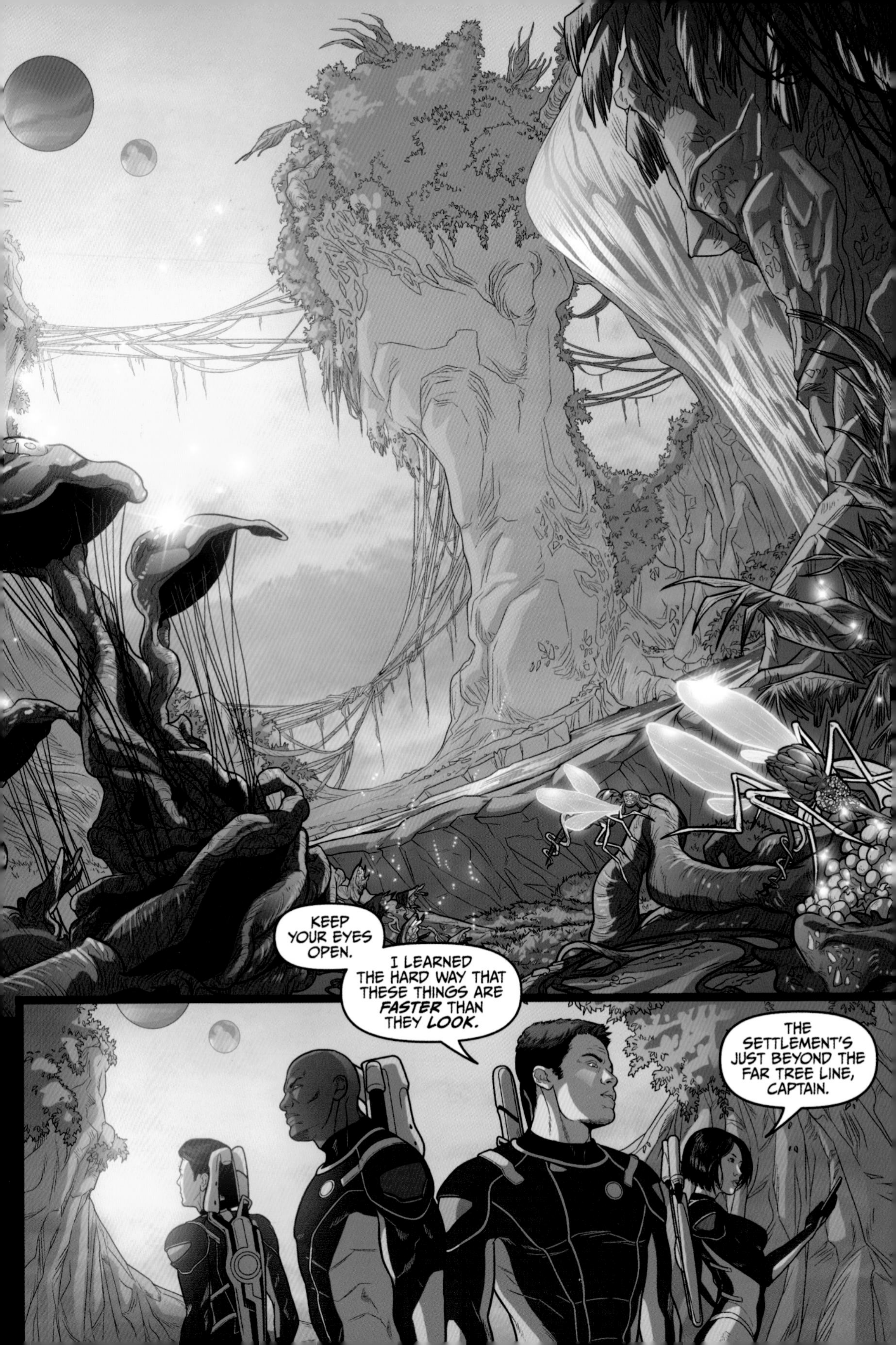
KEEP YOUR EYES OPEN.
I LEARNED THE HARD WAY THAT THESE THINGS ARE FASTER THAN THEY LOOK.
THE SETTLEMENT'S JUST BEYOND THE FAR TREE LINE, CAPTAIN.

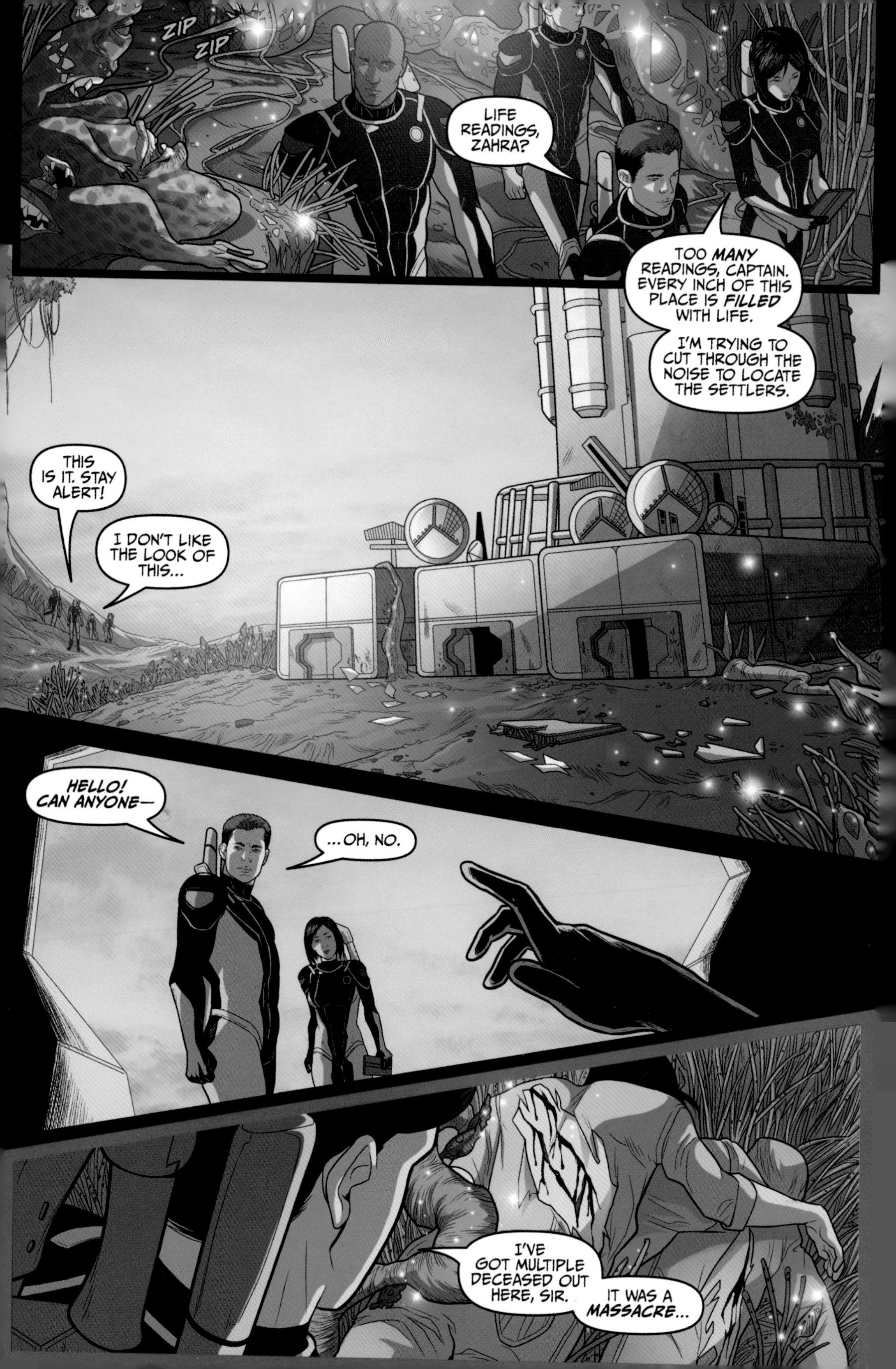
ZIP
ZIP
LIFE READINGS, ZAHRA?
TOO MANY READINGS, CAPTAIN. EVERY INCH OF THIS PLACE IS FILLED WITH LIFE.
I'M TRYING TO CUT THROUGH THE NOISE TO LOCATE THE SETTLERS.
THIS IS IT. STAY ALERT!
I DON'T LIKE THE LOOK OF THIS...
HELLO! CAN ANYONE—
...OH, NO.
I'VE GOT MULTIPLE DECEASED OUT HERE, SIR.
IT WAS A MASSACRE...

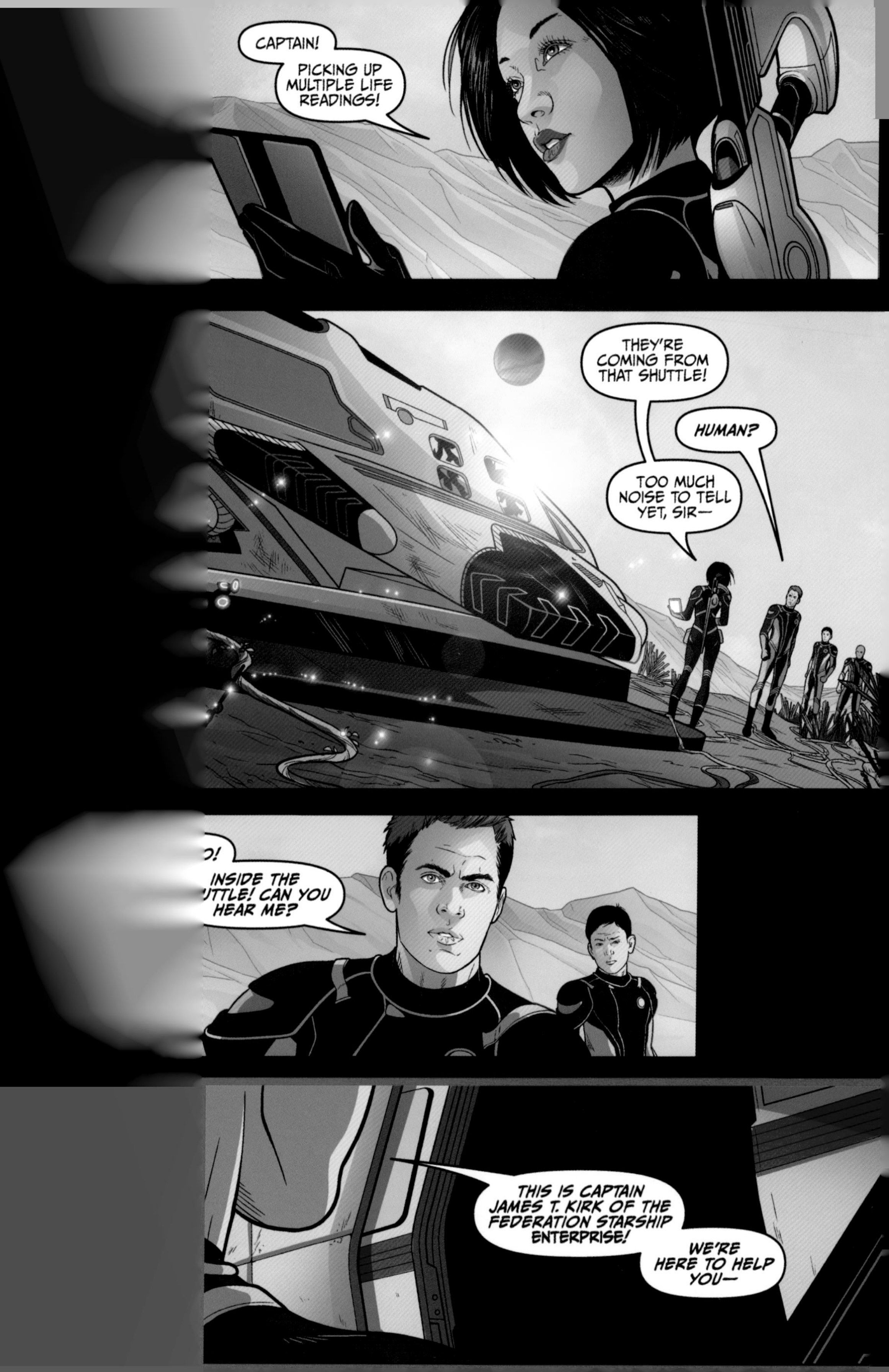
CAPTAIN!
PICKING UP MULTIPLE LIFE READINGS!
THEY'RE COMING FROM THAT SHUTTLE!
HUMAN?
TOO MUCH NOISE TO TELL YET, SIR—
O! INSIDE THE UTTLE! CAN YOU HEAR ME?
THIS IS CAPTAIN JAMES T. KIRK OF THE FEDERATION STARSHIP ENTERPRISE!
WE'RE HERE TO HELP YOU—

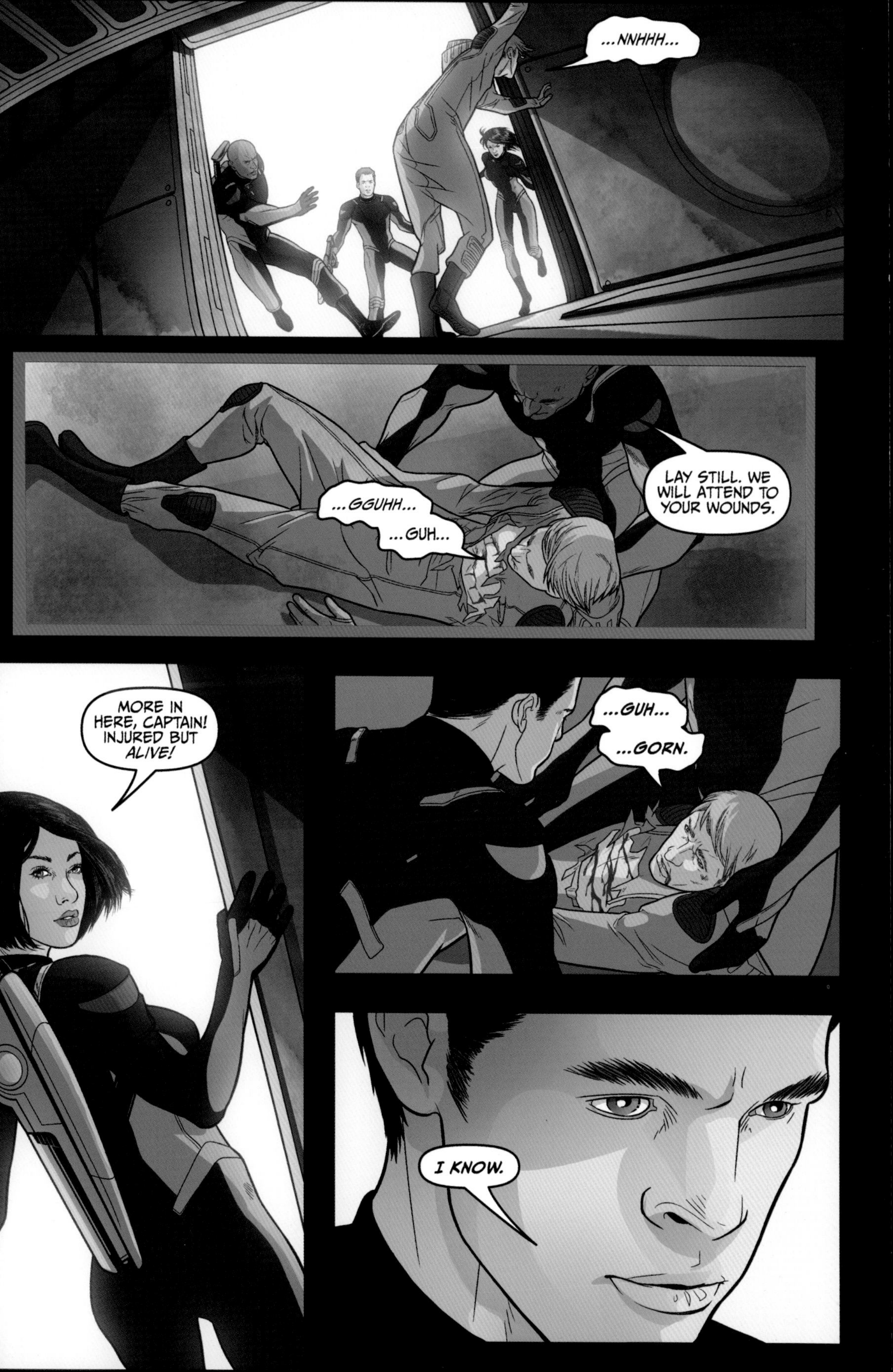
...NNHHH...
LAY STILL. WE WILL ATTEND TO YOUR WOUNDS.
...GGUHH...
...GUH...
MORE IN HERE, CAPTAIN! INJURED BUT ALIVE!
...GUH...
...GORN.
I KNOW.

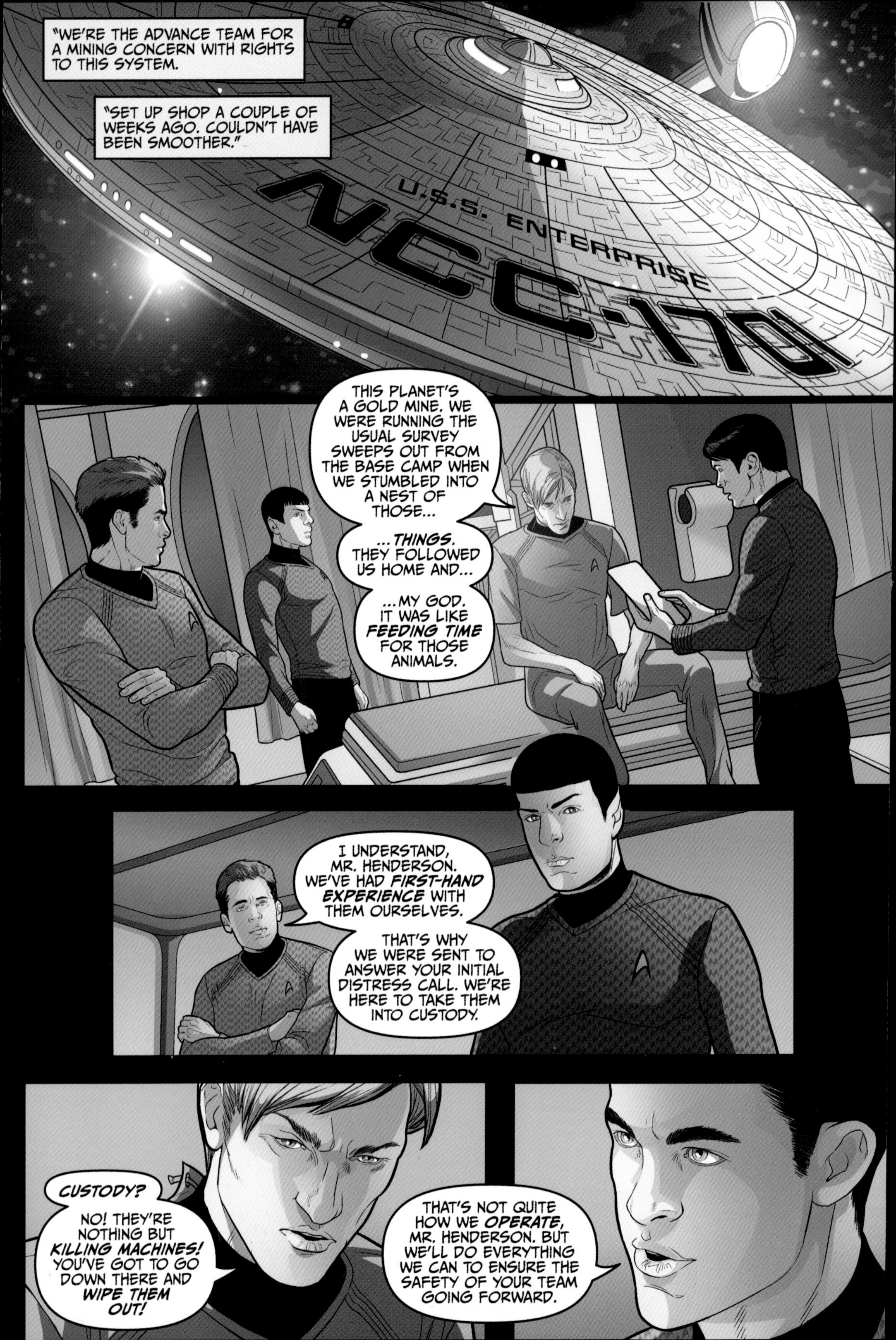
"WE'RE THE ADVANCE TEAM FOR A MINING CONCERN WITH RIGHTS TO THIS SYSTEM.
"SET UP SHOP A COUPLE OF WEEKS AGO. COULDN'T HAVE BEEN SMOOTHER."
U.S.S. ENTERPRISE
NCC-1701
THIS PLANET'S A GOLD MINE. WE WERE RUNNING THE USUAL SURVEY SWEEPS OUT FROM THE BASE CAMP WHEN WE STUMBLED INTO A NEST OF THOSE...
...THINGS. THEY FOLLOWED US HOME AND...
...MY GOD. IT WAS LIKE FEEDING TIME FOR THOSE ANIMALS.
I UNDERSTAND, MR. HENDERSON. WE'VE HAD FIRST-HAND EXPERIENCE WITH THEM OURSELVES.
THAT'S WHY WE WERE SENT TO ANSWER YOUR INITIAL DISTRESS CALL. WE'RE HERE TO TAKE THEM INTO CUSTODY.
CUSTODY?
NO! THEY'RE NOTHING BUT KILLING MACHINES! YOU'VE GOT TO GO DOWN THERE AND WIPE THEM OUT!
THAT'S NOT QUITE HOW WE OPERATE, MR. HENDERSON. BUT WE'LL DO EVERYTHING WE CAN TO ENSURE THE SAFETY OF YOUR TEAM GOING FORWARD.

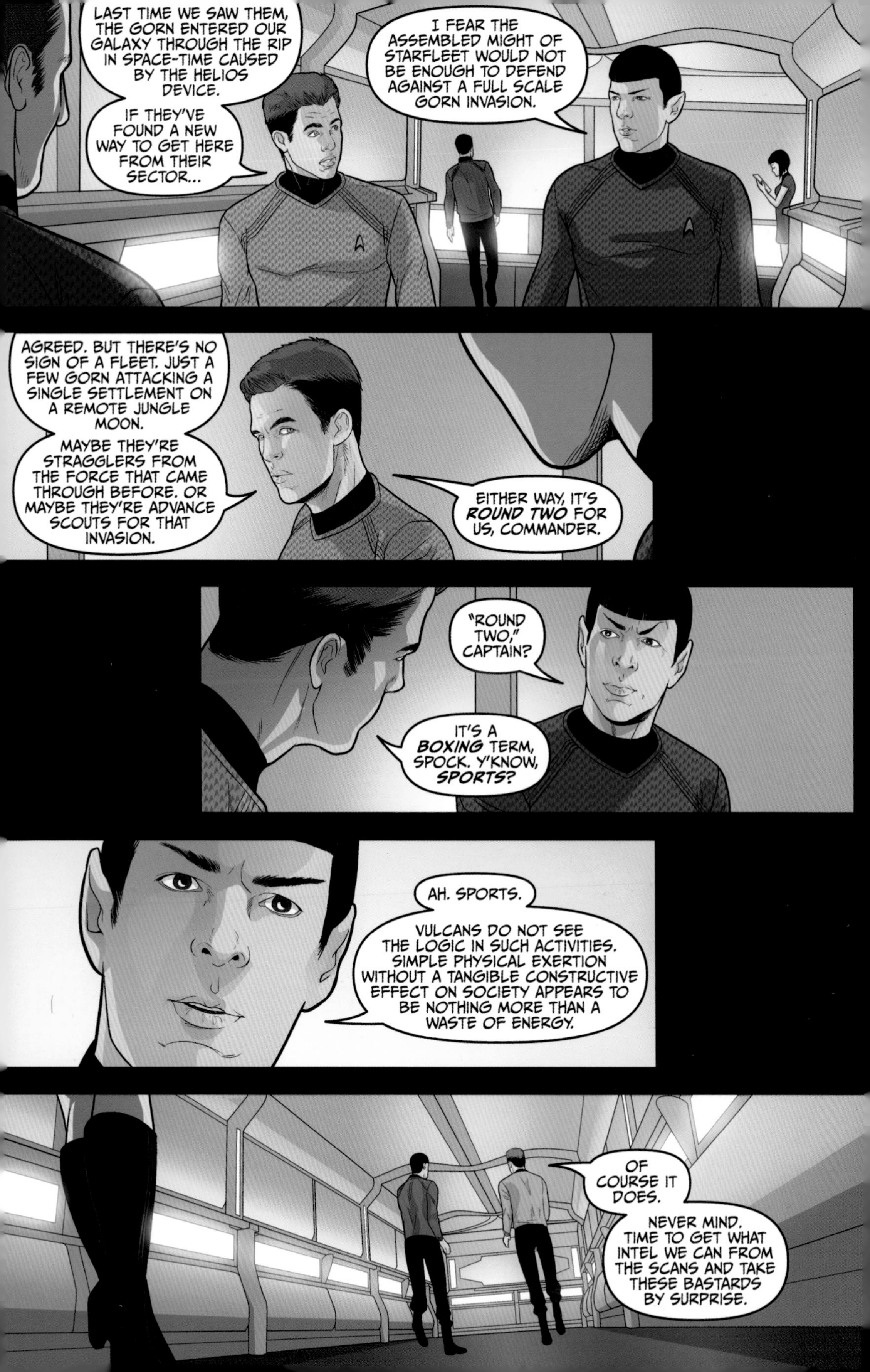
LAST TIME WE SAW THEM, THE GORN ENTERED OUR GALAXY THROUGH THE RIP IN SPACE-TIME CAUSED BY THE HELIOS DEVICE.
IF THEY'VE FOUND A NEW WAY TO GET HERE FROM THEIR SECTOR...
I FEAR THE ASSEMBLED MIGHT OF STARFLEET WOULD NOT BE ENOUGH TO DEFEND AGAINST A FULL SCALE GORN INVASION.
AGREED. BUT THERE'S NO SIGN OF A FLEET. JUST A FEW GORN ATTACKING A SINGLE SETTLEMENT ON A REMOTE JUNGLE MOON.
MAYBE THEY'RE STRAGGLERS FROM THE FORCE THAT CAME THROUGH BEFORE. OR MAYBE THEY'RE ADVANCE SCOUTS FOR THAT INVASION.
EITHER WAY, IT'S ***ROUND TWO*** FOR US, COMMANDER.
"ROUND TWO," CAPTAIN?
IT'S A ***BOXING*** TERM, SPOCK. Y'KNOW, ***SPORTS?***
AH. SPORTS.
VULCANS DO NOT SEE THE LOGIC IN SUCH ACTIVITIES. SIMPLE PHYSICAL EXERTION WITHOUT A TANGIBLE CONSTRUCTIVE EFFECT ON SOCIETY APPEARS TO BE NOTHING MORE THAN A WASTE OF ENERGY.
OF COURSE IT DOES.
NEVER MIND. TIME TO GET WHAT INTEL WE CAN FROM THE SCANS AND TAKE THESE BASTARDS BY SURPRISE.

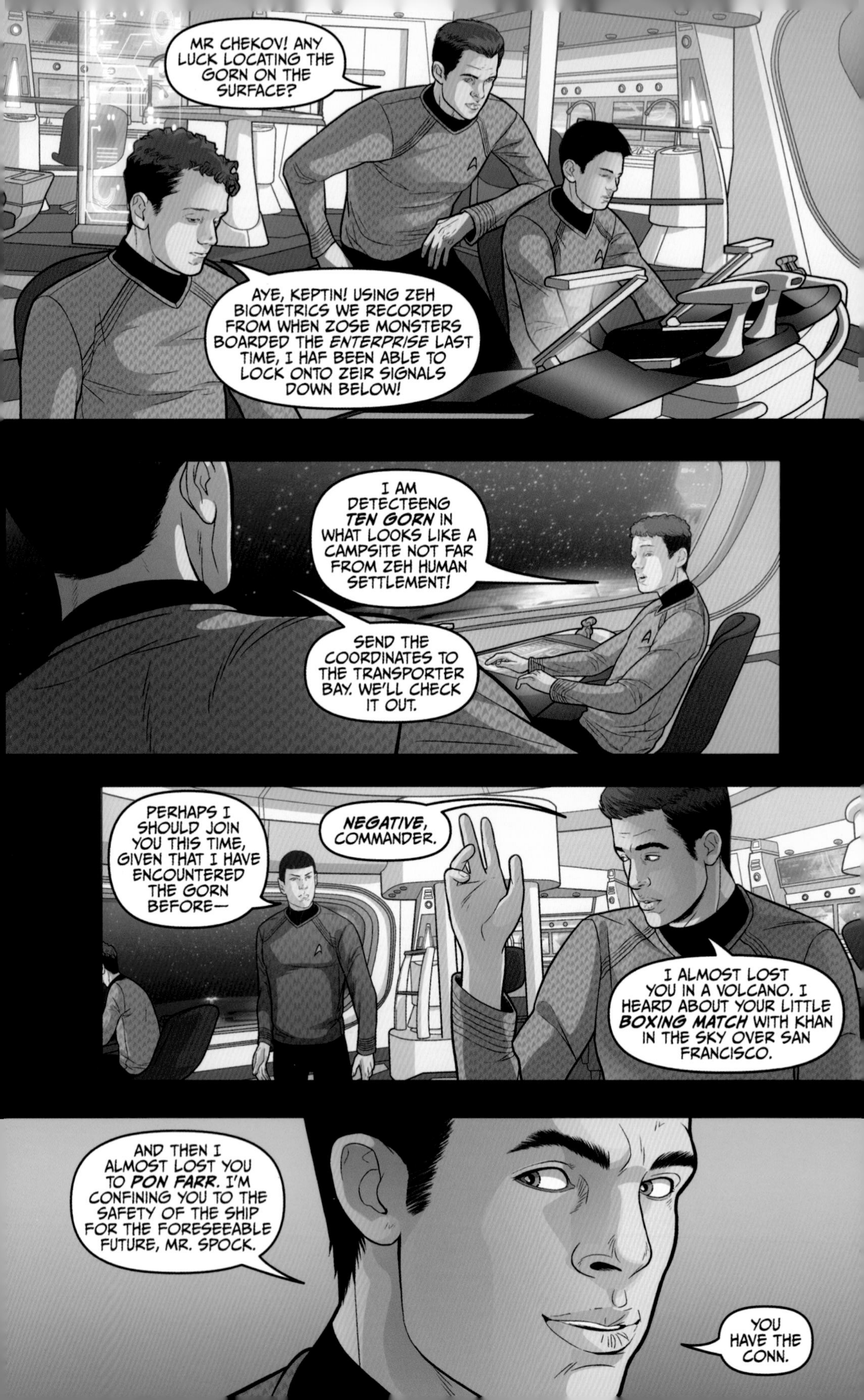
MR CHEKOV! ANY LUCK LOCATING THE GORN ON THE SURFACE?
AYE, KEPTIN! USING ZEH BIOMETRICS WE RECORDED FROM WHEN ZOSE MONSTERS BOARDED THE *ENTERPRISE* LAST TIME, I HAF BEEN ABLE TO LOCK ONTO ZEIR SIGNALS DOWN BELOW!
I AM DETECTEENG **TEN GORN** IN WHAT LOOKS LIKE A CAMPSITE NOT FAR FROM ZEH HUMAN SETTLEMENT!
SEND THE COORDINATES TO THE TRANSPORTER BAY. WE'LL CHECK IT OUT.
PERHAPS I SHOULD JOIN YOU THIS TIME, GIVEN THAT I HAVE ENCOUNTERED THE GORN BEFORE—
NEGATIVE, COMMANDER.
I ALMOST LOST YOU IN A VOLCANO. I HEARD ABOUT YOUR LITTLE ***BOXING MATCH*** WITH KHAN IN THE SKY OVER SAN FRANCISCO.
AND THEN I ALMOST LOST YOU TO ***PON FARR***. I'M CONFINING YOU TO THE SAFETY OF THE SHIP FOR THE FORESEEABLE FUTURE, MR. SPOCK.
YOU HAVE THE CONN.

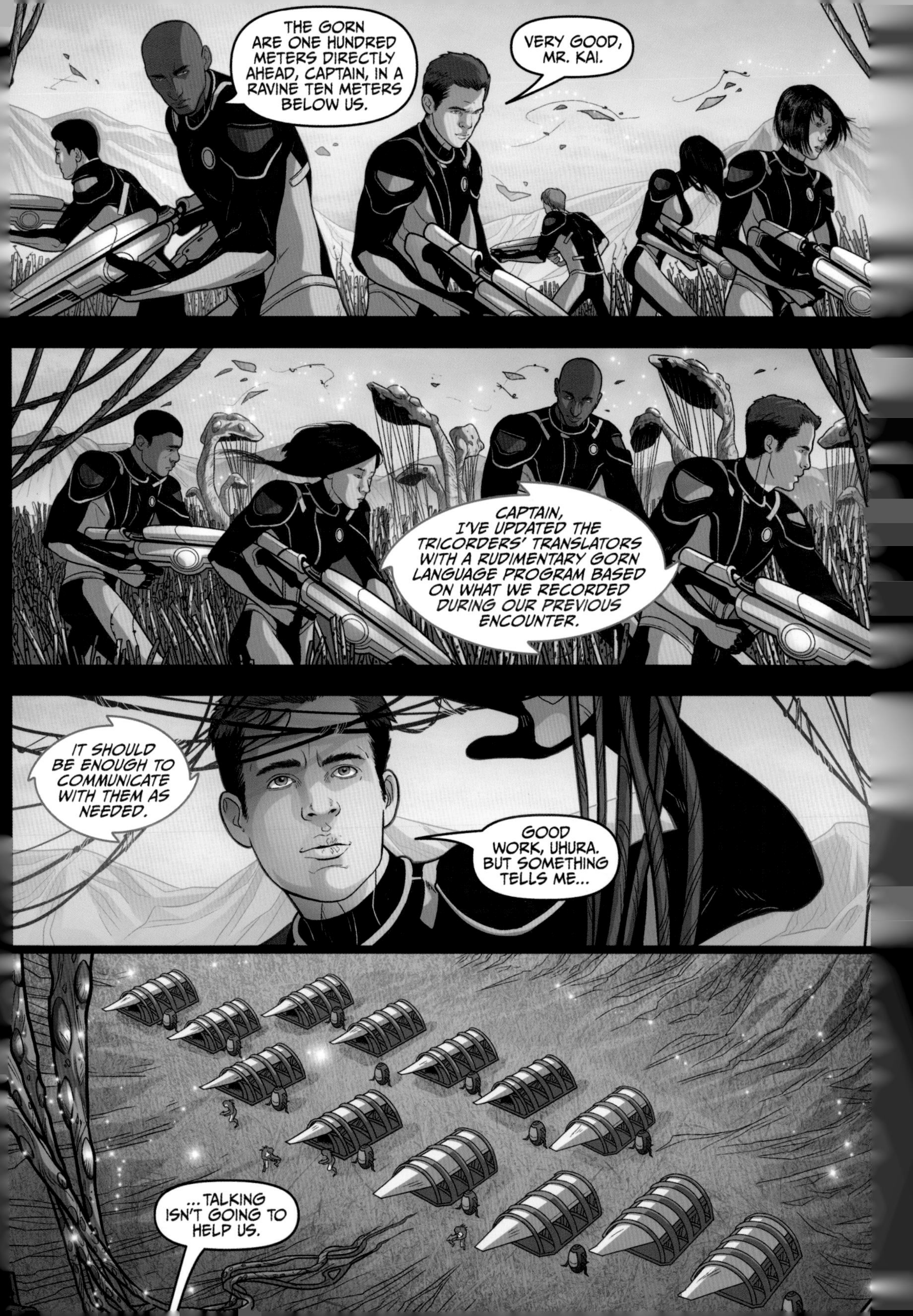
THE GORN ARE ONE HUNDRED METERS DIRECTLY AHEAD, CAPTAIN, IN A RAVINE TEN METERS BELOW US.
VERY GOOD, MR. KAI.
CAPTAIN, I'VE UPDATED THE TRICORDERS' TRANSLATORS WITH A RUDIMENTARY GORN LANGUAGE PROGRAM BASED ON WHAT WE RECORDED DURING OUR PREVIOUS ENCOUNTER.
IT SHOULD BE ENOUGH TO COMMUNICATE WITH THEM AS NEEDED.
GOOD WORK, UHURA. BUT SOMETHING TELLS ME...
...TALKING ISN'T GOING TO HELP US.

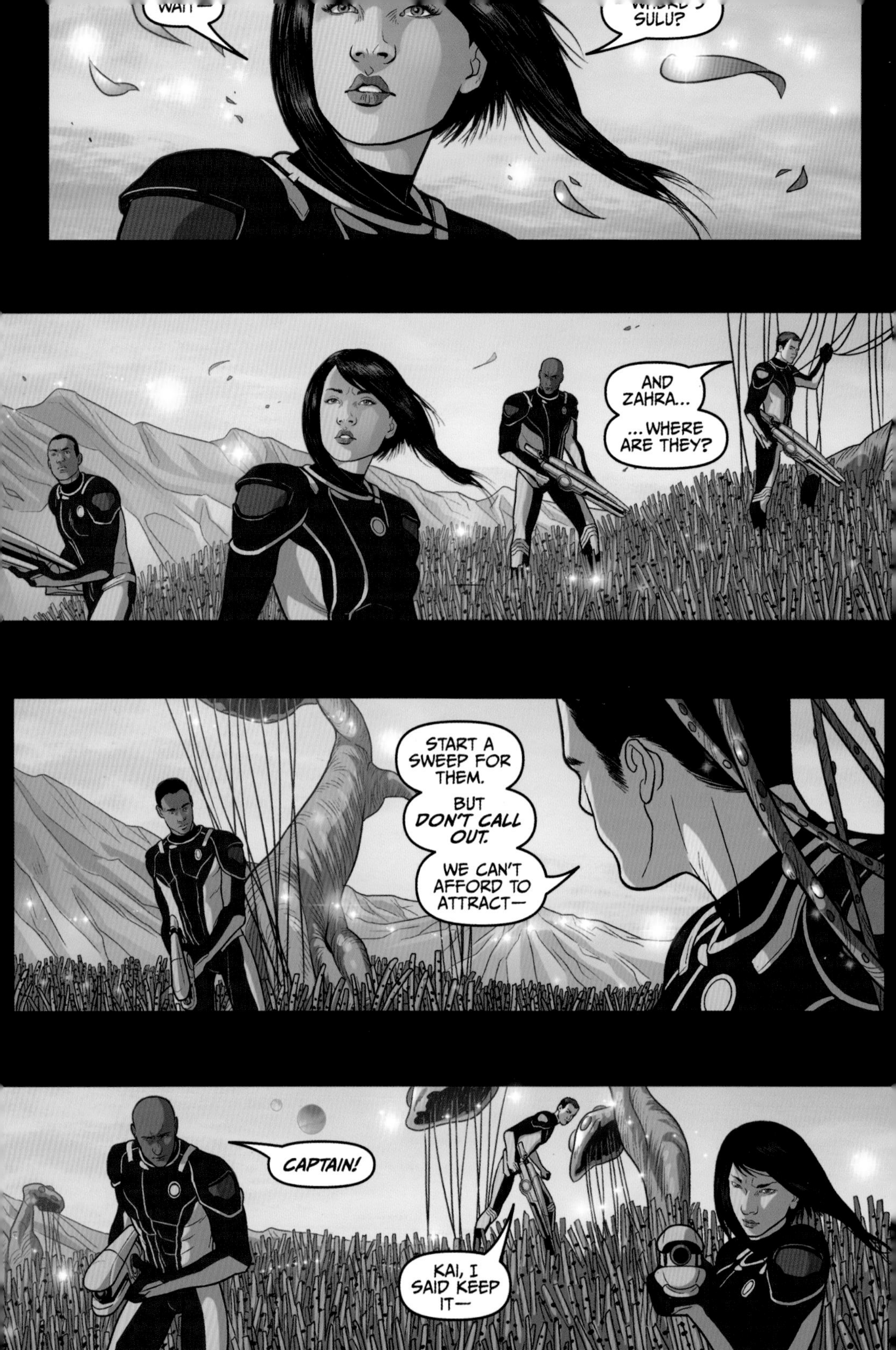
SULU?
AND ZAHRA... ...WHERE ARE THEY?
START A SWEEP FOR THEM.
BUT *DON'T CALL OUT.*
WE CAN'T AFFORD TO ATTRACT—
CAPTAIN!
KAI, I SAID KEEP IT—

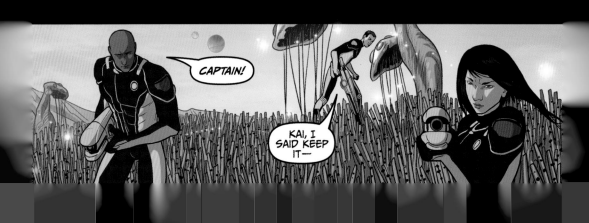

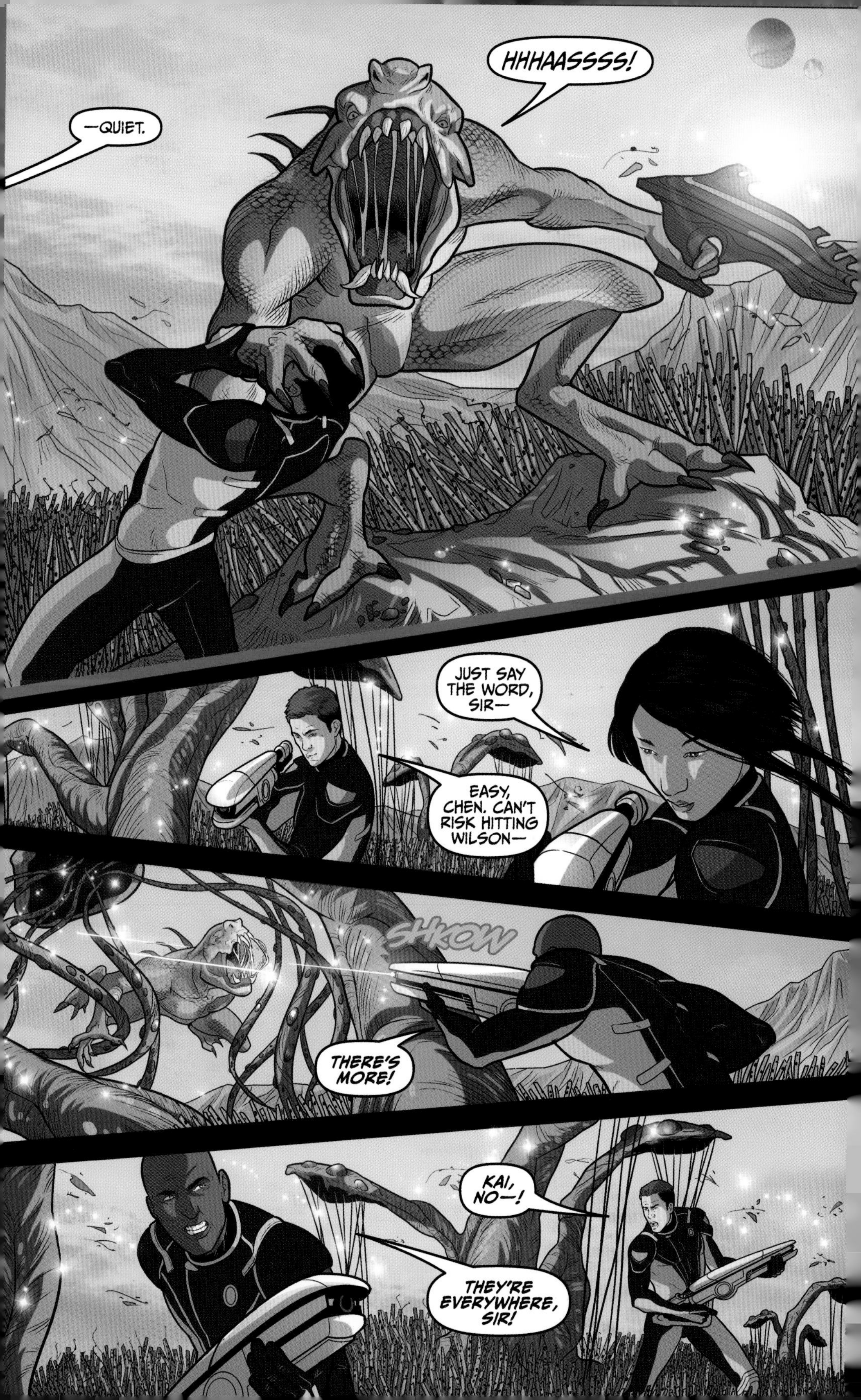
—QUIET.
HHHAASSSS!
JUST SAY THE WORD, SIR—
EASY, CHEN. CAN'T RISK HITTING WILSON—
SHKOW
THERE'S MORE!
KAI, NO—!
THEY'RE EVERYWHERE, SIR!

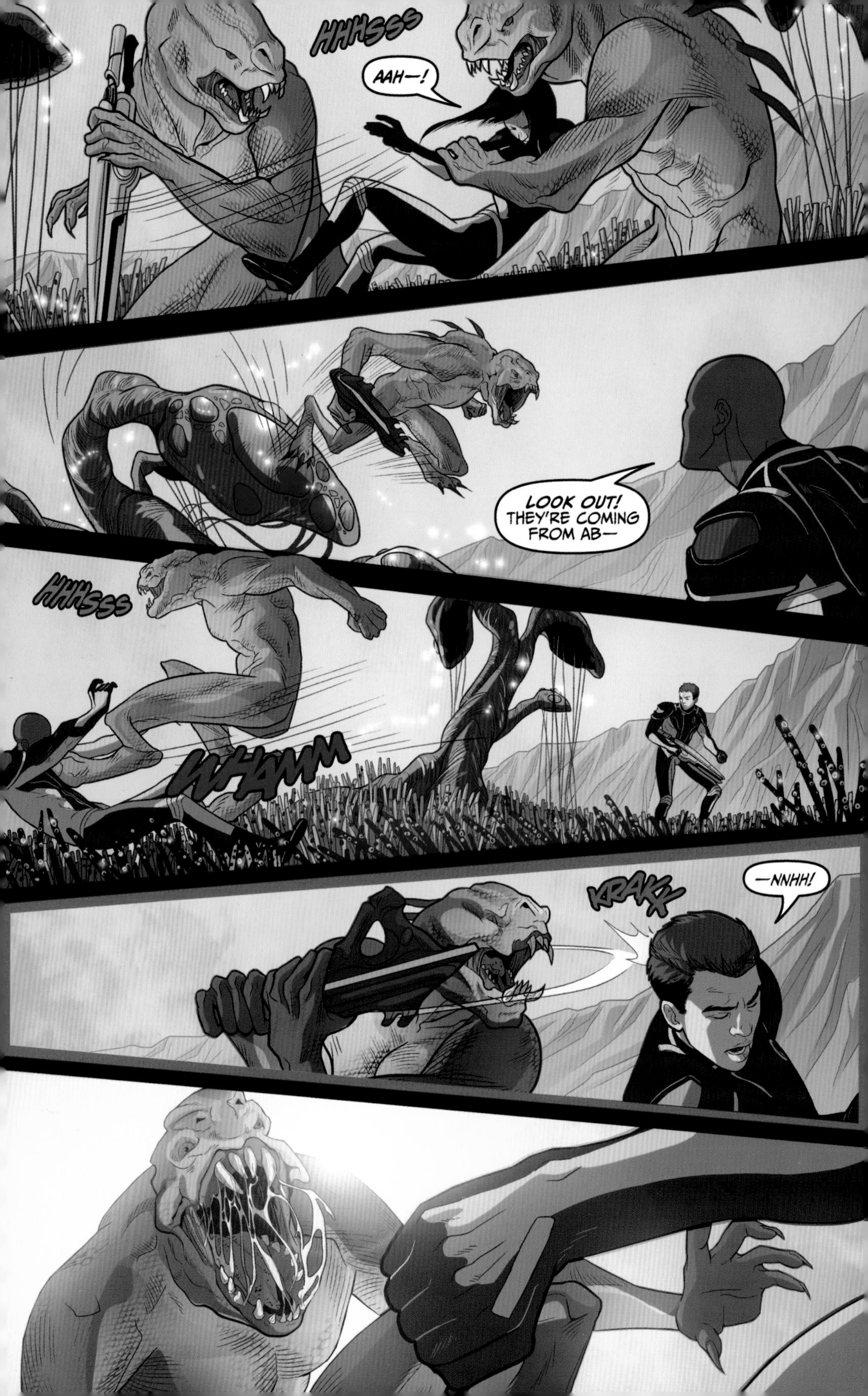
HHHSSS
AAH—!
LOOK OUT! THEY'RE COMING FROM AB—
HHHSSS
WHAMM
KRAKK
—NNHH!

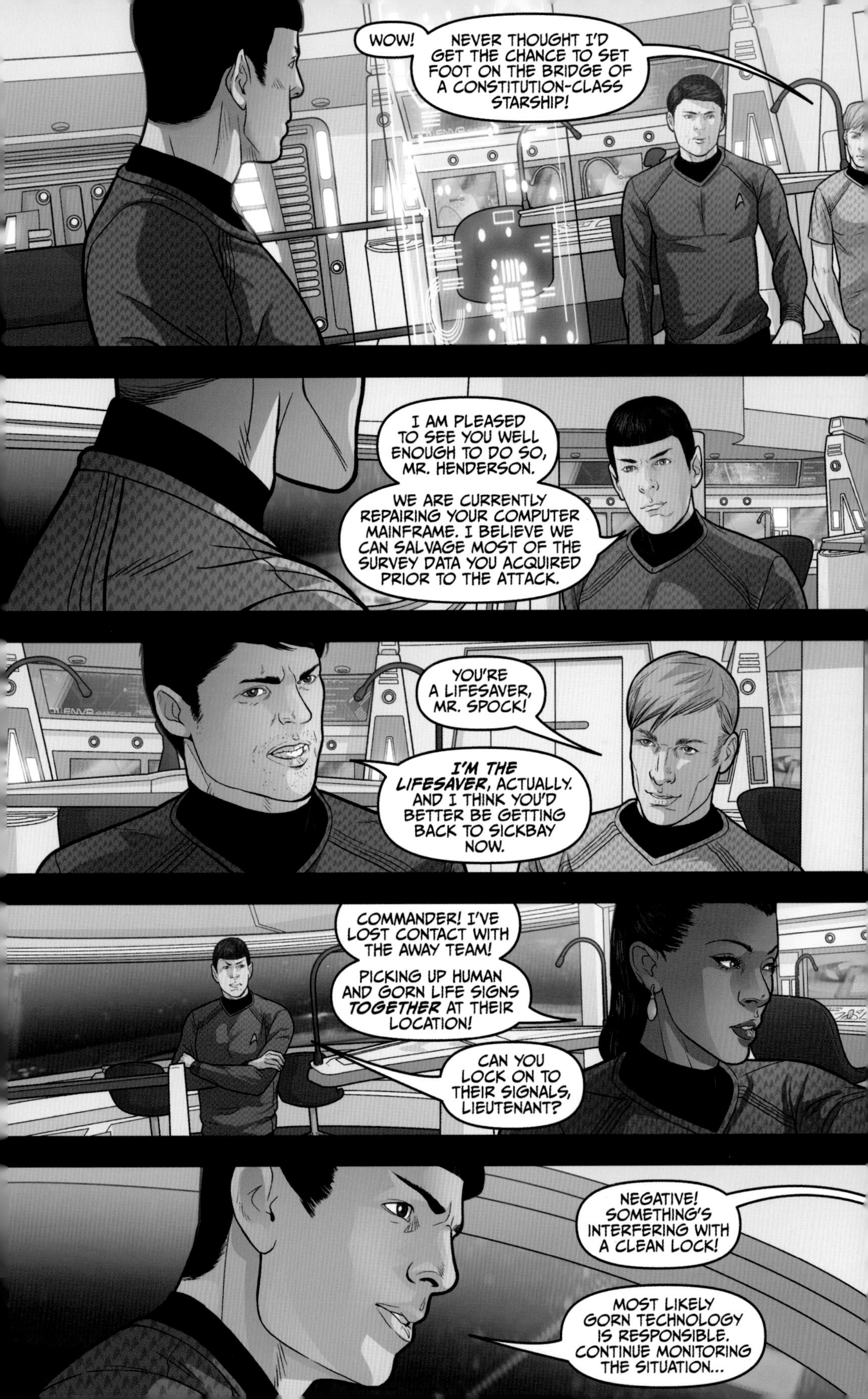
WOW!
NEVER THOUGHT I'D GET THE CHANCE TO SET FOOT ON THE BRIDGE OF A CONSTITUTION-CLASS STARSHIP!
I AM PLEASED TO SEE YOU WELL ENOUGH TO DO SO, MR. HENDERSON.
WE ARE CURRENTLY REPAIRING YOUR COMPUTER MAINFRAME. I BELIEVE WE CAN SALVAGE MOST OF THE SURVEY DATA YOU ACQUIRED PRIOR TO THE ATTACK.
YOU'RE A LIFESAVER, MR. SPOCK!
I'M THE LIFESAVER, ACTUALLY. AND I THINK YOU'D BETTER BE GETTING BACK TO SICKBAY NOW.
COMMANDER! I'VE LOST CONTACT WITH THE AWAY TEAM!
PICKING UP HUMAN AND GORN LIFE SIGNS *TOGETHER* AT THEIR LOCATION!
CAN YOU LOCK ON TO THEIR SIGNALS, LIEUTENANT?
NEGATIVE! SOMETHING'S INTERFERING WITH A CLEAN LOCK!
MOST LIKELY GORN TECHNOLOGY IS RESPONSIBLE. CONTINUE MONITORING THE SITUATION...

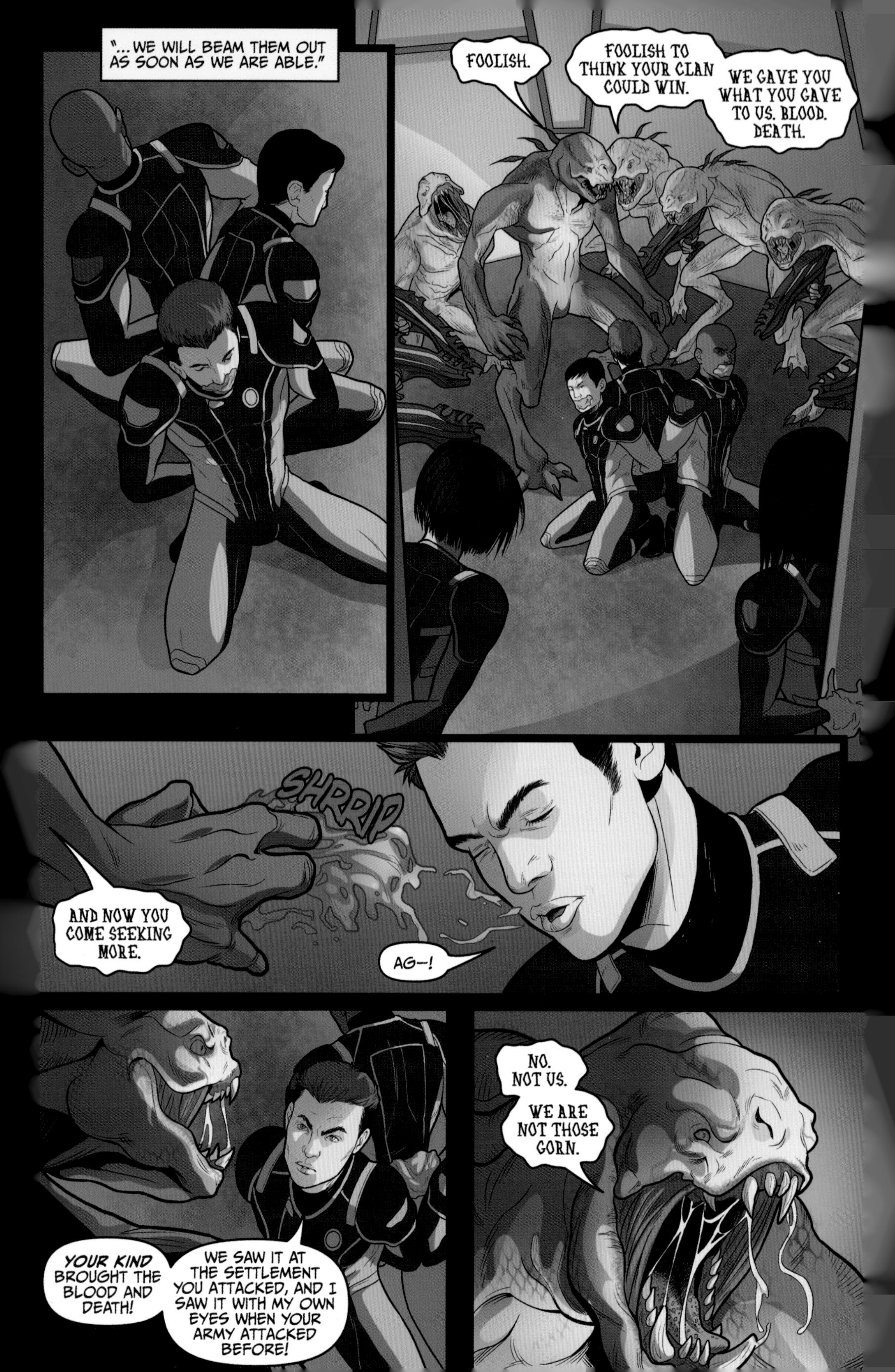
"...WE WILL BEAM THEM OUT AS SOON AS WE ARE ABLE."
FOOLISH.
FOOLISH TO THINK YOUR CLAN COULD WIN.
WE GAVE YOU WHAT YOU GAVE TO US. BLOOD. DEATH.
SHRRIP
AND NOW YOU COME SEEKING MORE.
AG--!
YOUR KIND BROUGHT THE BLOOD AND DEATH!
WE SAW IT AT THE SETTLEMENT YOU ATTACKED, AND I SAW IT WITH MY OWN EYES WHEN YOUR ARMY ATTACKED BEFORE!
NO. NOT US.
WE ARE NOT THOSE GORN.

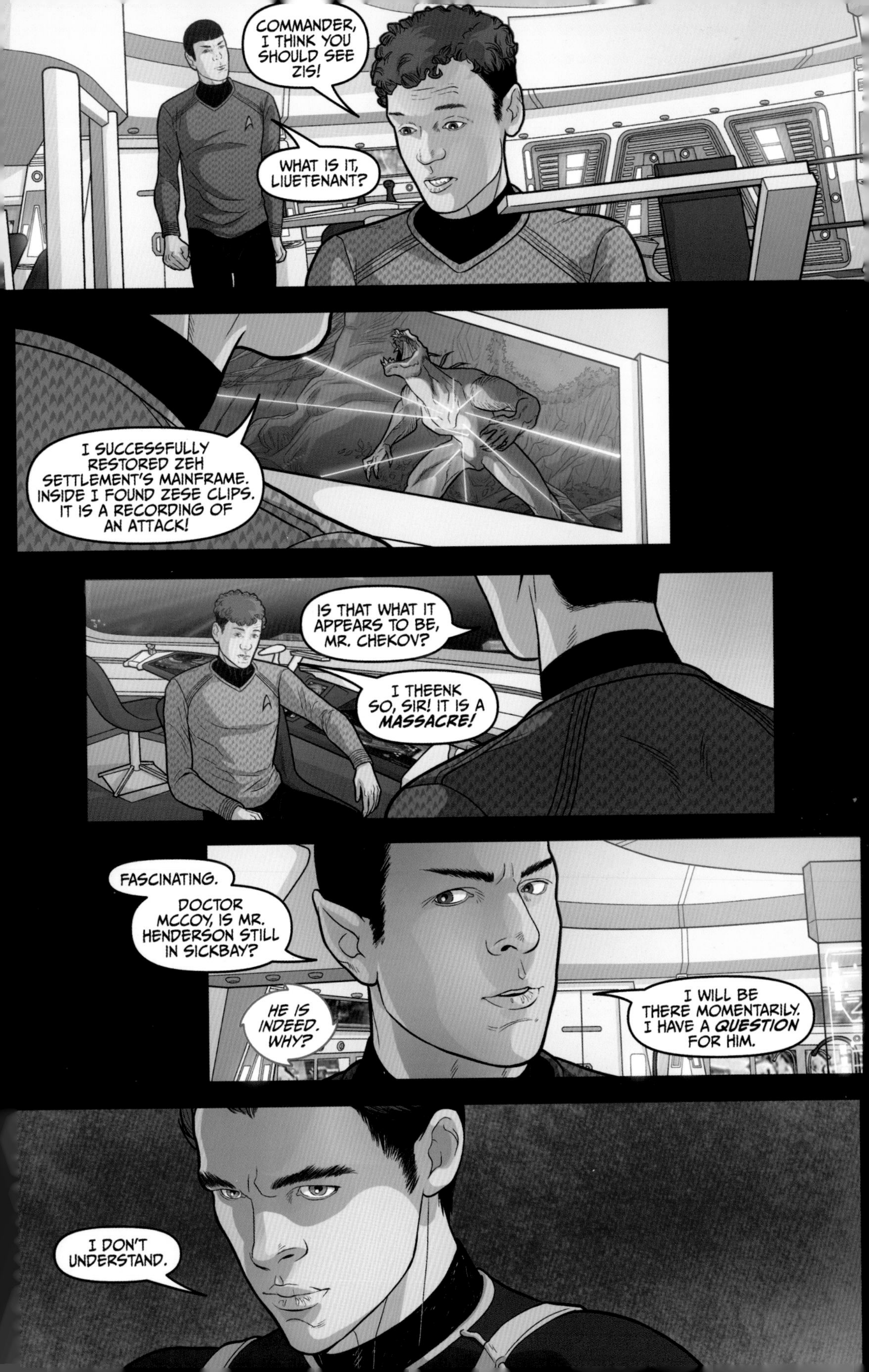
COMMANDER, I THINK YOU SHOULD SEE ZIS!
WHAT IS IT, LIUETENANT?
I SUCCESSFULLY RESTORED ZEH SETTLEMENT'S MAINFRAME. INSIDE I FOUND ZESE CLIPS. IT IS A RECORDING OF AN ATTACK!
IS THAT WHAT IT APPEARS TO BE, MR. CHEKOV?
I THEENK SO, SIR! IT IS A *MASSACRE!*
FASCINATING.
DOCTOR MCCOY, IS MR. HENDERSON STILL IN SICKBAY?
HE IS INDEED. WHY?
I WILL BE THERE MOMENTARILY. I HAVE A *QUESTION* FOR HIM.
I DON'T UNDERSTAND.

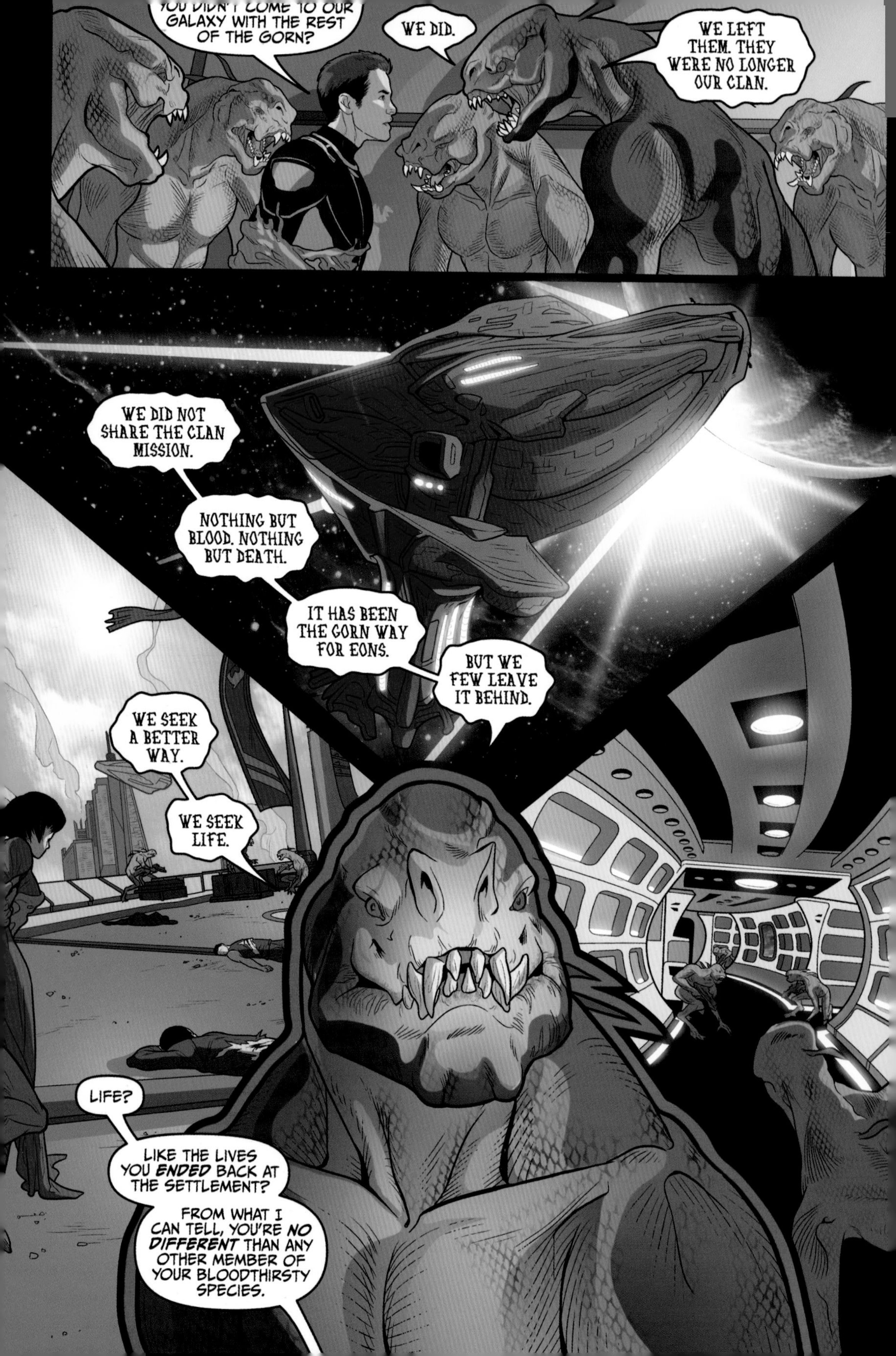
YOU DIDN'T COME TO OUR GALAXY WITH THE REST OF THE GORN?
WE DID.
WE LEFT THEM. THEY WERE NO LONGER OUR CLAN.
WE DID NOT SHARE THE CLAN MISSION.
NOTHING BUT BLOOD. NOTHING BUT DEATH.
IT HAS BEEN THE GORN WAY FOR EONS.
BUT WE FEW LEAVE IT BEHIND.
WE SEEK A BETTER WAY.
WE SEEK LIFE.
LIFE?
LIKE THE LIVES YOU *ENDED* BACK AT THE SETTLEMENT?
FROM WHAT I CAN TELL, YOU'RE *NO DIFFERENT* THAN ANY OTHER MEMBER OF YOUR BLOODTHIRSTY SPECIES.

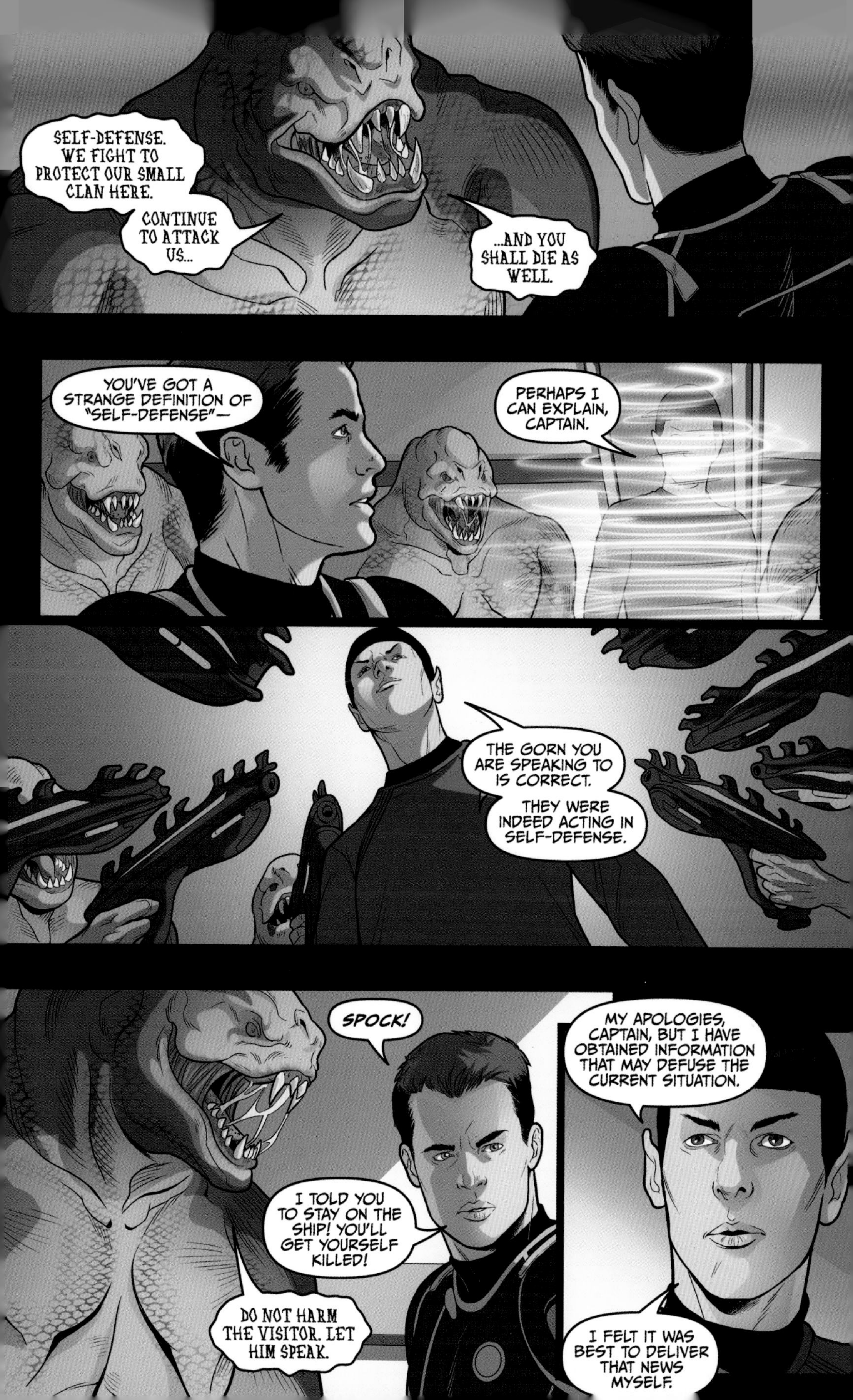

SELF-DEFENSE. WE FIGHT TO PROTECT OUR SMALL CLAN HERE.
CONTINUE TO ATTACK US...
...AND YOU SHALL DIE AS WELL.
YOU'VE GOT A STRANGE DEFINITION OF "SELF-DEFENSE"—
PERHAPS I CAN EXPLAIN, CAPTAIN.
THE GORN YOU ARE SPEAKING TO IS CORRECT.
THEY WERE INDEED ACTING IN SELF-DEFENSE.
SPOCK!
I TOLD YOU TO STAY ON THE SHIP! YOU'LL GET YOURSELF KILLED!
DO NOT HARM THE VISITOR. LET HIM SPEAK.
MY APOLOGIES, CAPTAIN, BUT I HAVE OBTAINED INFORMATION THAT MAY DEFUSE THE CURRENT SITUATION.
I FELT IT WAS BEST TO DELIVER THAT NEWS MYSELF.

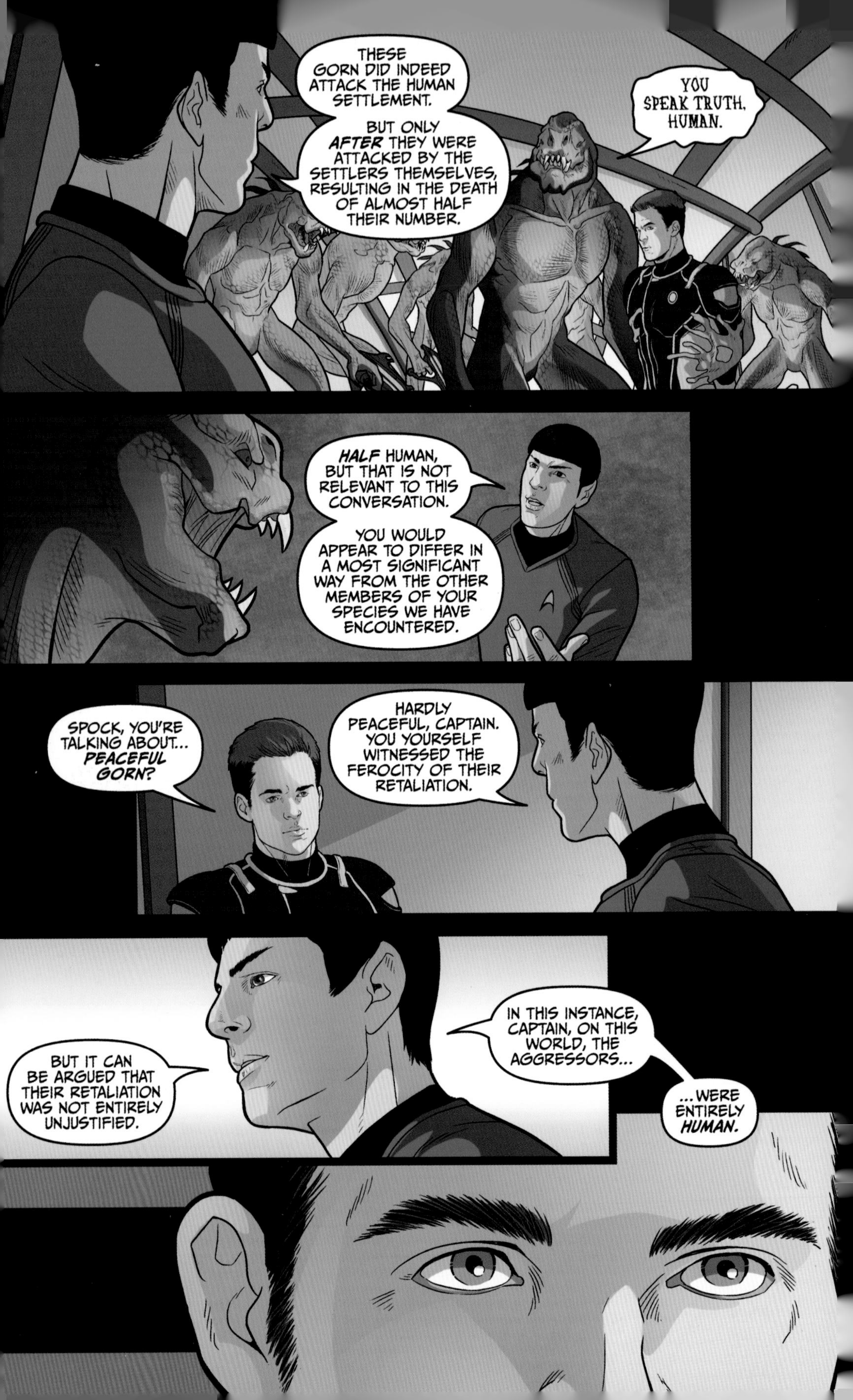
THESE GORN DID INDEED ATTACK THE HUMAN SETTLEMENT.
BUT ONLY *AFTER* THEY WERE ATTACKED BY THE SETTLERS THEMSELVES, RESULTING IN THE DEATH OF ALMOST HALF THEIR NUMBER.
YOU SPEAK TRUTH, HUMAN.
HALF HUMAN, BUT THAT IS NOT RELEVANT TO THIS CONVERSATION.
YOU WOULD APPEAR TO DIFFER IN A MOST SIGNIFICANT WAY FROM THE OTHER MEMBERS OF YOUR SPECIES WE HAVE ENCOUNTERED.
SPOCK, YOU'RE TALKING ABOUT... *PEACEFUL GORN?*
HARDLY PEACEFUL, CAPTAIN. YOU YOURSELF WITNESSED THE FEROCITY OF THEIR RETALIATION.
BUT IT CAN BE ARGUED THAT THEIR RETALIATION WAS NOT ENTIRELY UNJUSTIFIED.
IN THIS INSTANCE, CAPTAIN, ON THIS WORLD, THE AGGRESSORS...
...WERE ENTIRELY *HUMAN.*

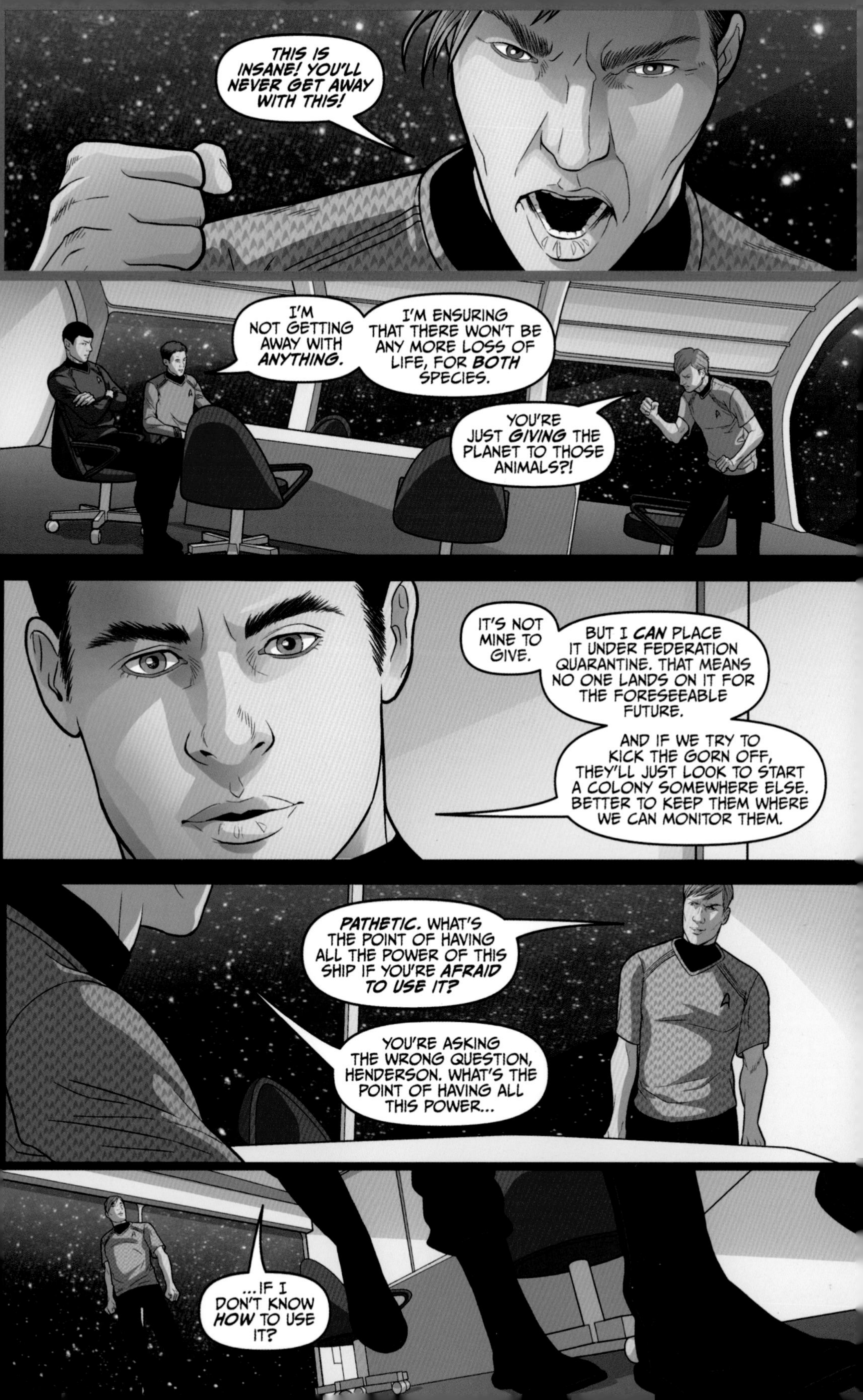
THIS IS INSANE! YOU'LL NEVER GET AWAY WITH THIS!
I'M NOT GETTING AWAY WITH ANYTHING.
I'M ENSURING THAT THERE WON'T BE ANY MORE LOSS OF LIFE, FOR BOTH SPECIES.
YOU'RE JUST GIVING THE PLANET TO THOSE ANIMALS?!
IT'S NOT MINE TO GIVE.
BUT I CAN PLACE IT UNDER FEDERATION QUARANTINE. THAT MEANS NO ONE LANDS ON IT FOR THE FORESEEABLE FUTURE.
AND IF WE TRY TO KICK THE GORN OFF, THEY'LL JUST LOOK TO START A COLONY SOMEWHERE ELSE. BETTER TO KEEP THEM WHERE WE CAN MONITOR THEM.
PATHETIC. WHAT'S THE POINT OF HAVING ALL THE POWER OF THIS SHIP IF YOU'RE AFRAID TO USE IT?
YOU'RE ASKING THE WRONG QUESTION, HENDERSON. WHAT'S THE POINT OF HAVING ALL THIS POWER...
...IF I DON'T KNOW HOW TO USE IT?

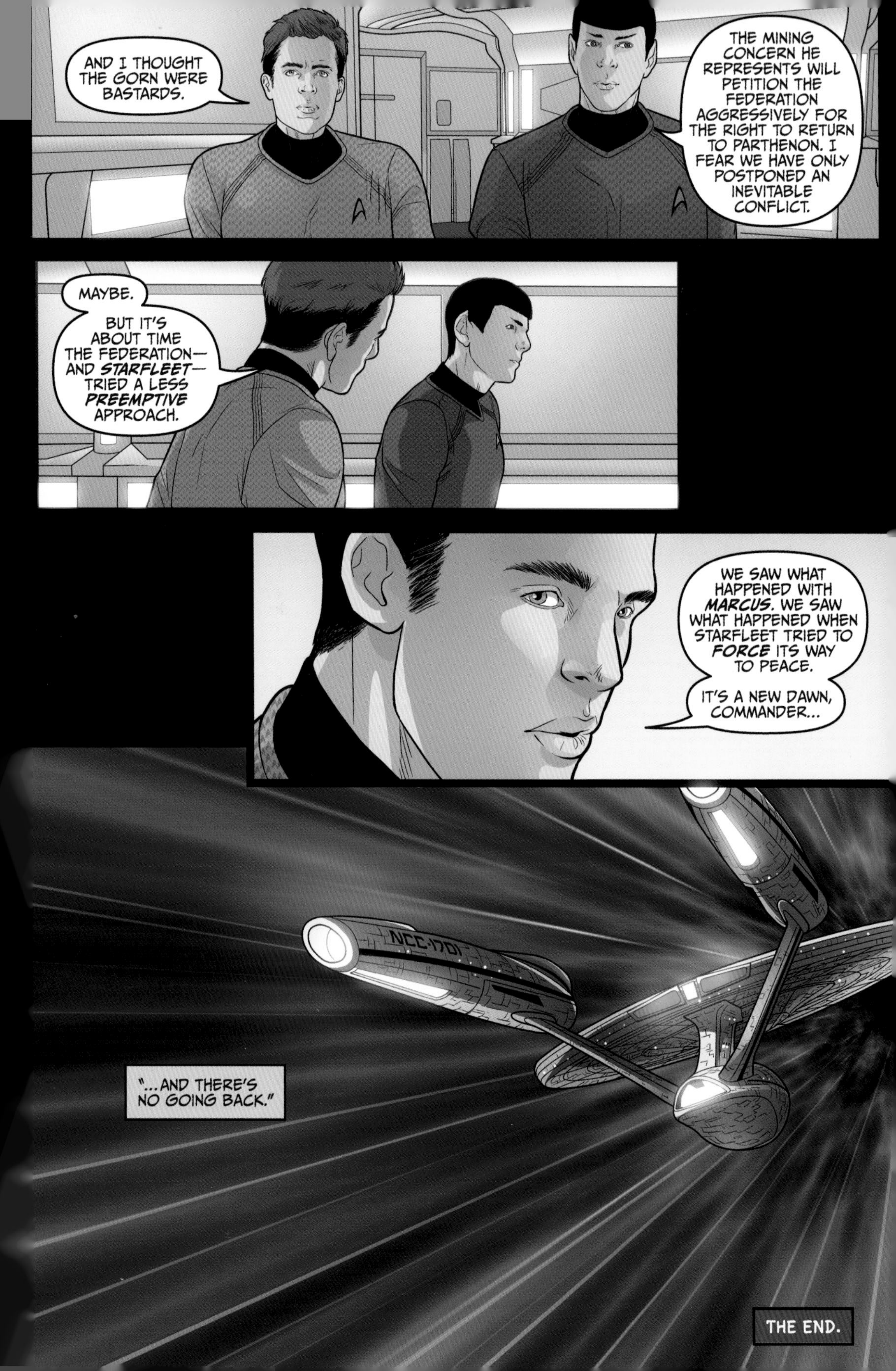
AND I THOUGHT THE GORN WERE BASTARDS.
THE MINING CONCERN HE REPRESENTS WILL PETITION THE FEDERATION AGGRESSIVELY FOR THE RIGHT TO RETURN TO PARTHENON. I FEAR WE HAVE ONLY POSTPONED AN INEVITABLE CONFLICT.
MAYBE.
BUT IT'S ABOUT TIME THE FEDERATION—AND *STARFLEET*—TRIED A LESS *PREEMPTIVE* APPROACH.
WE SAW WHAT HAPPENED WITH *MARCUS*. WE SAW WHAT HAPPENED WHEN STARFLEET TRIED TO *FORCE* ITS WAY TO PEACE.
IT'S A NEW DAWN, COMMANDER...
NCC-1701
"...AND THERE'S NO GOING BACK."
THE END.

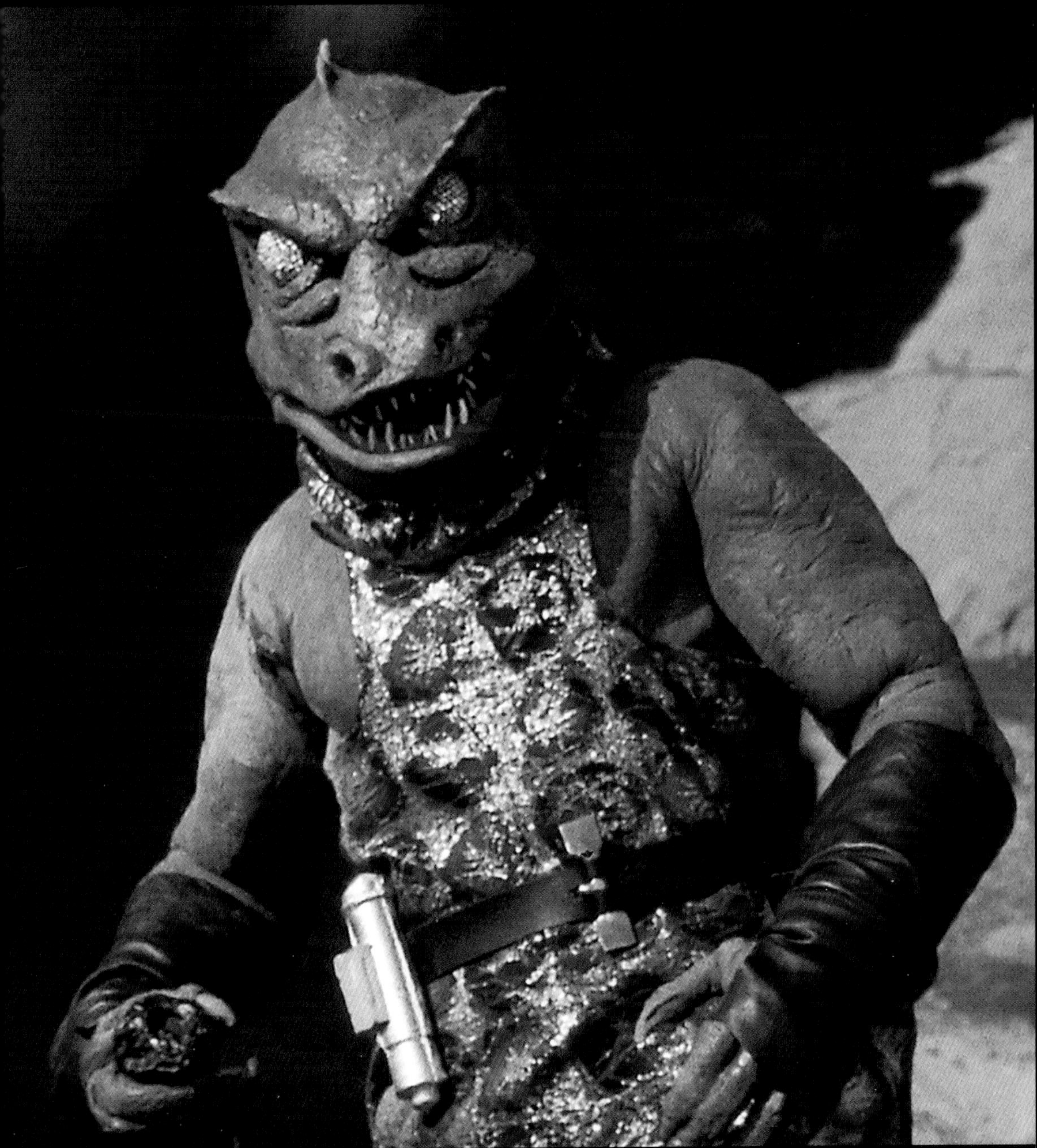

Artwork by
Tim Bradstreet

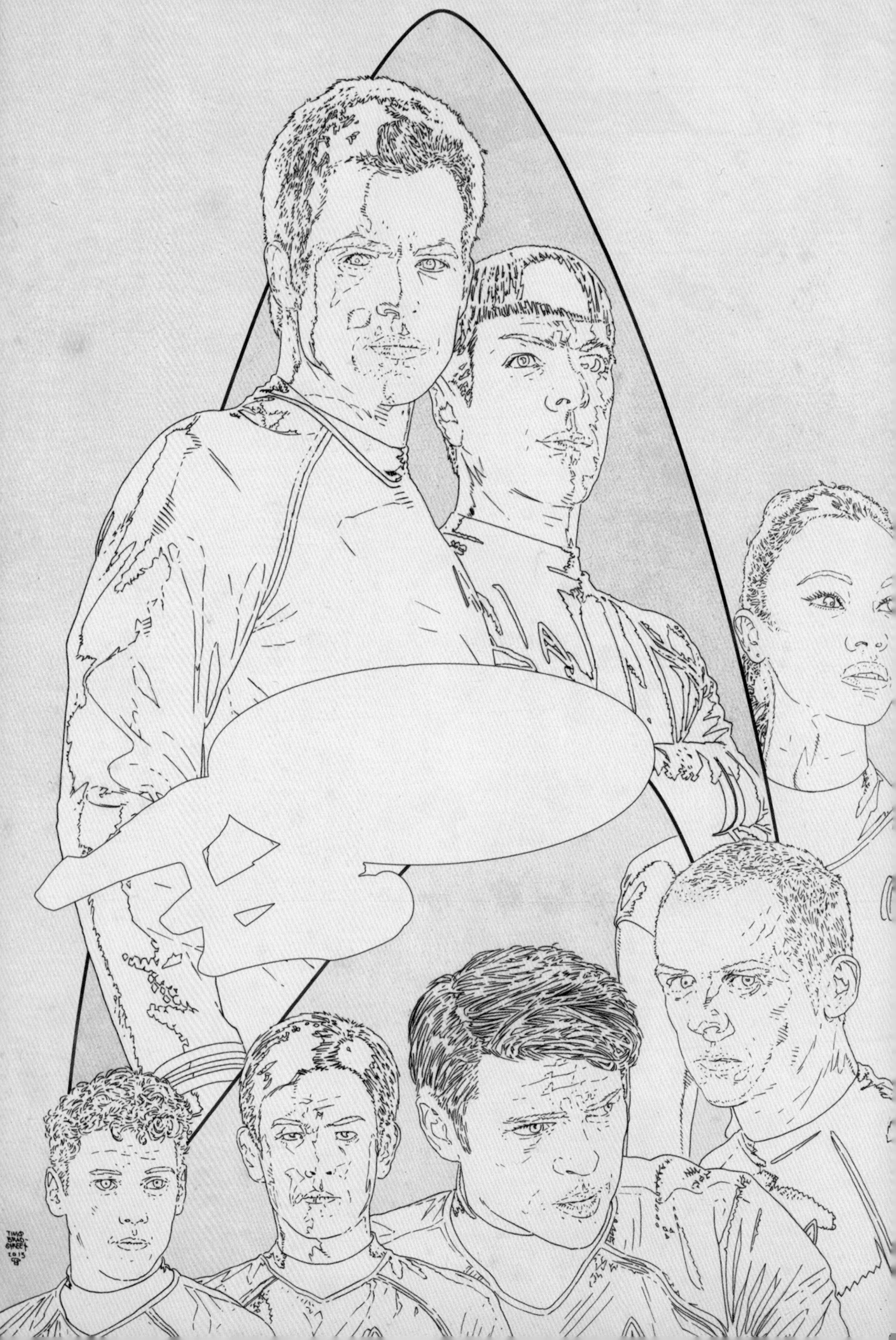

Artwork by
Tim Bradstreet

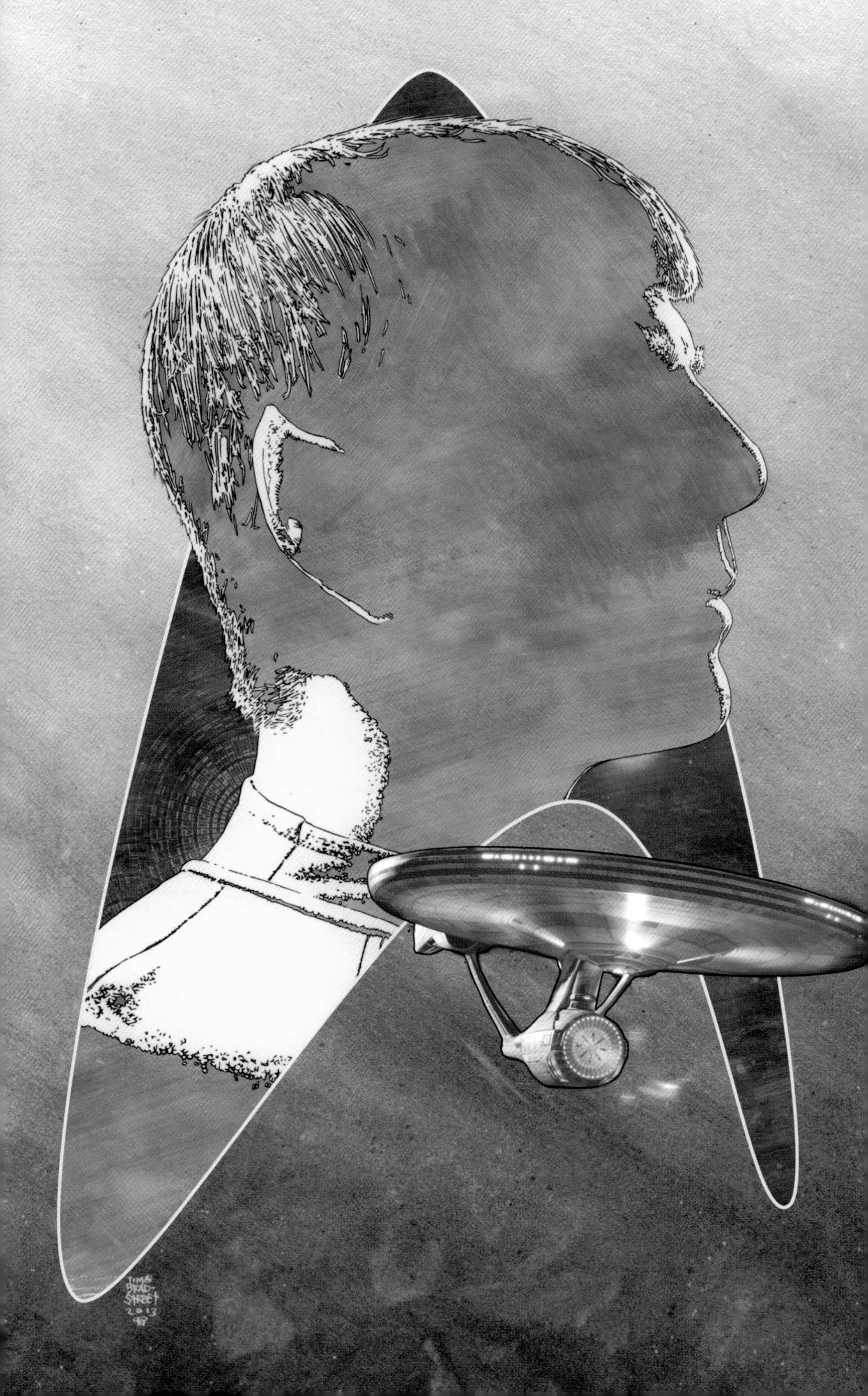

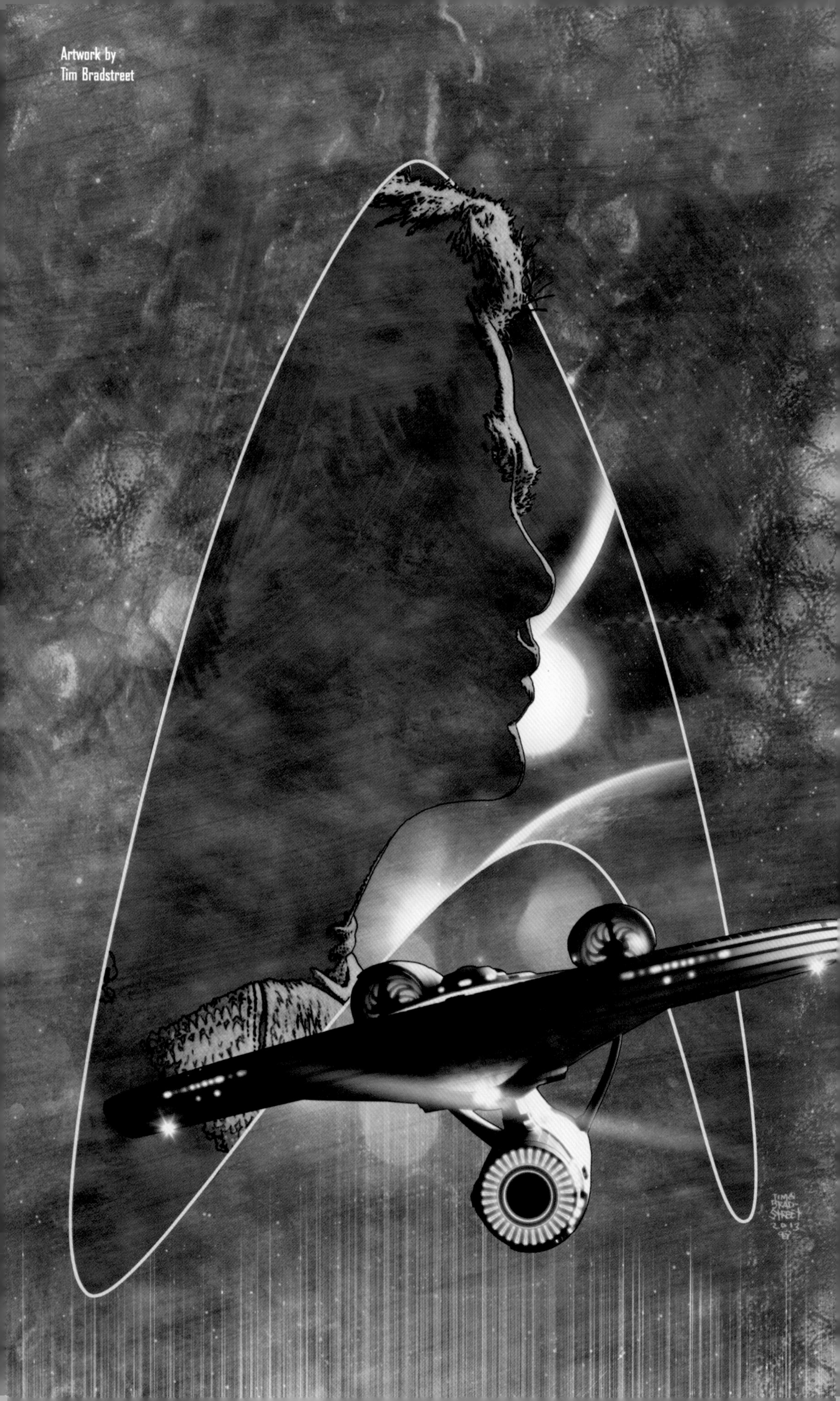
TIM BRAD-STREET 2013
Artwork by
Tim Bradstreet

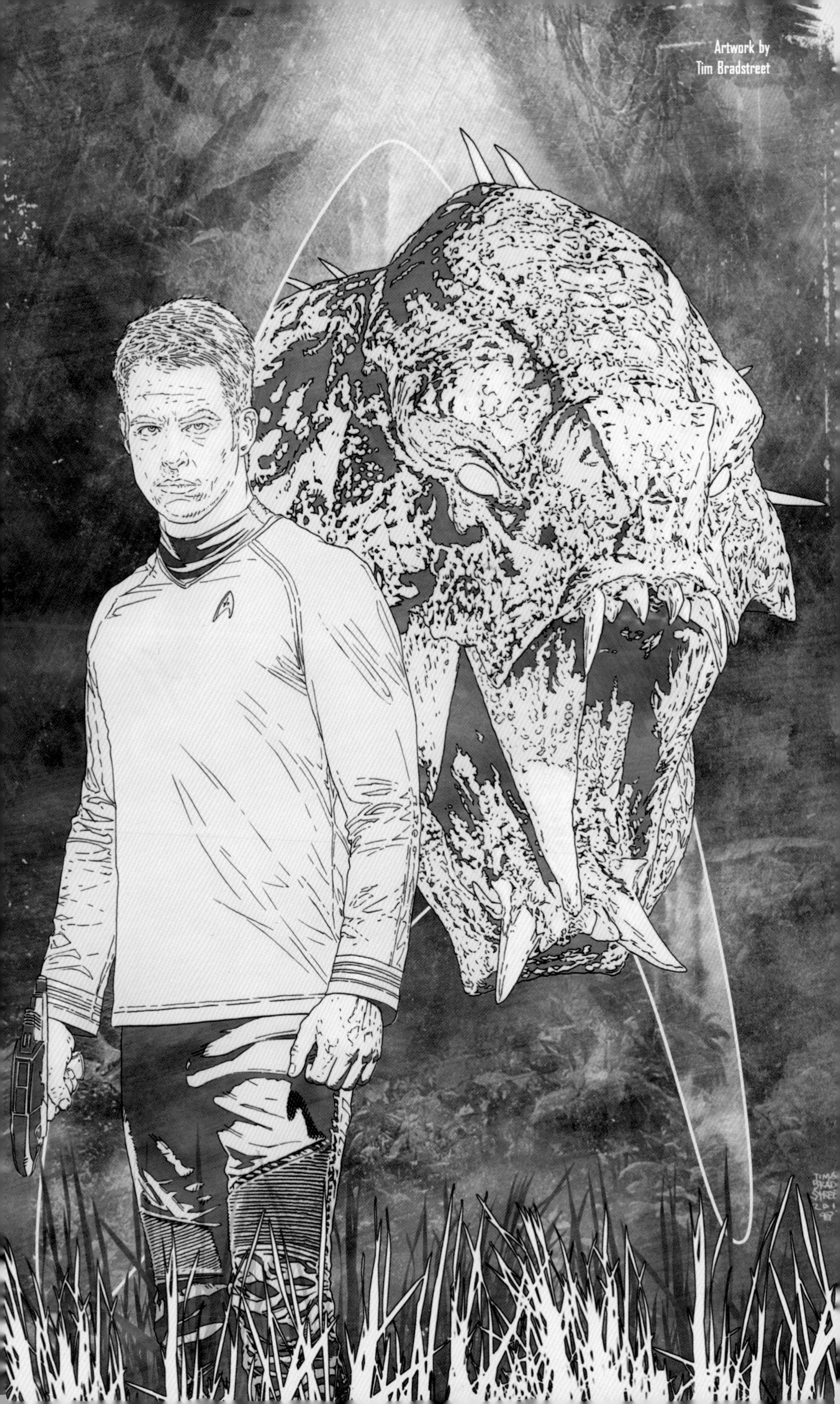

Artwork by
Tim Bradstreet

Artwork by Garrie Gastonny
Colors by Ifansyah Noor

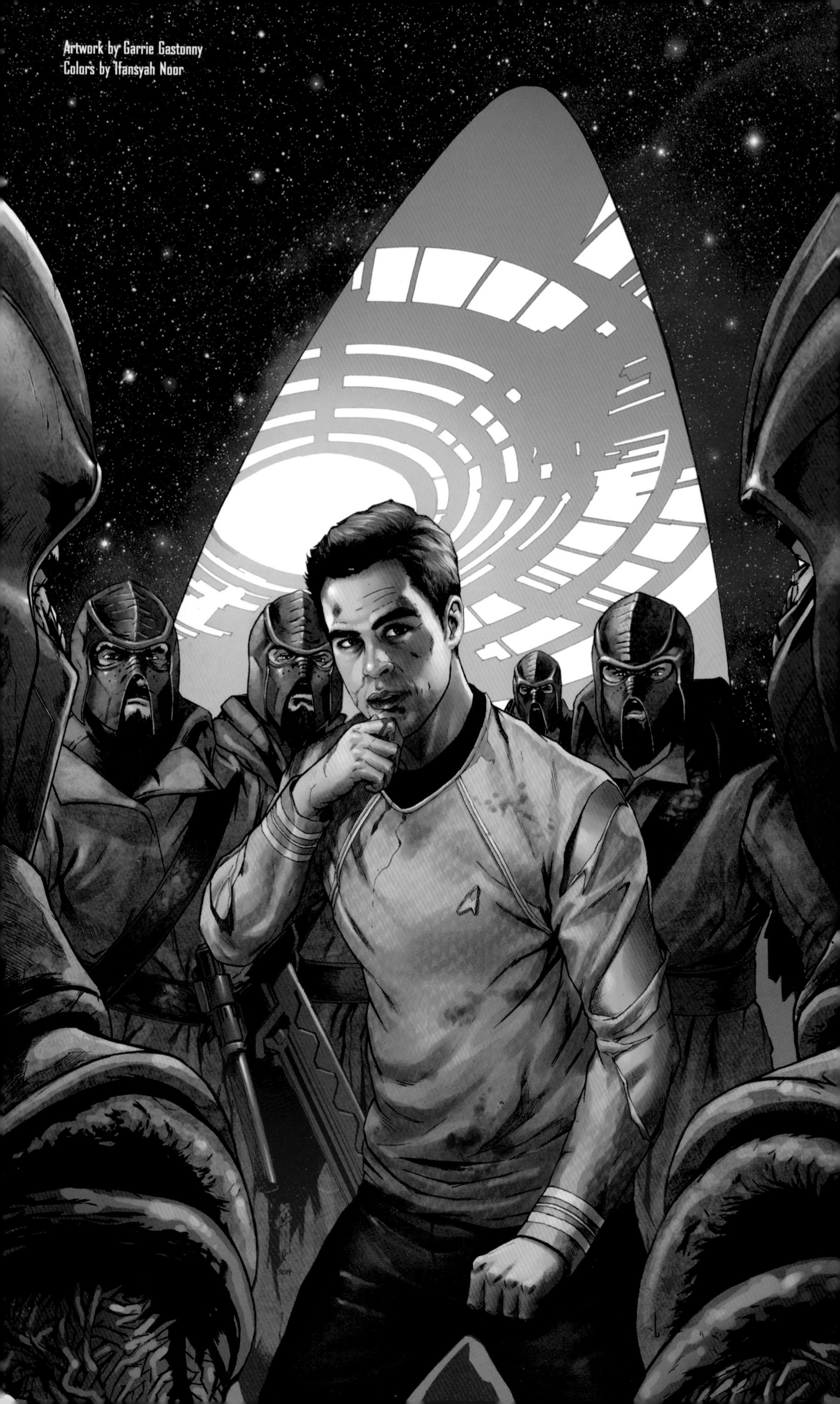